ANYBODY CAN DO ANYTHING

Books by Betty MacDonald

The Egg and I

The Plague and I

Anybody Can Do Anything

Onions in the Stew

Who, Me? The Autobiography of Betty MacDonald

Hello, Mrs. Piggle-Wiggle

Mrs. Piggle-Wiggle

Mrs. Piggle-Wiggle's Farm

Mrs. Piggle-Wiggle's Magic

Nancy and Plum

Betty
MacDonald

ANYBODY
Can Do
ANYTHING

UNIVERSITY OF WASHINGTON PRESS
Seattle and London

2016 paperback edition published by the University of Washington Press
Printed and bound in the United States of America
Design by Thomas Eykemans
Composed in Charter, typeface designed by Matthew Carter
20   19   18   17   5   4   3   2

UNIVERSITY OF WASHINGTON PRESS
www.washington.edu/uwpress

LIBRARY OF CONGRESS CATALOGING-IN-PUBLICATION DATA
Names: MacDonald, Betty Bard, author.
Title: Anybody can do anything / Betty MacDonald.
Description: Paperback edition. | Seattle : University of Washington Press, [2016]
Identifiers: LCCN 2016008390 | ISBN 9780295999791 (softcover : acid-free paper)
Classification: LCC PS3525.A1946 Z46 2016 | DDC 813/.54 [B] —dc23
LC record available at https://lccn.loc.gov/2016008390

"Pale Hands I Love (Kashmiri Song)" by Lawrence Hope. By permission of William Heinemann & Company, London, England.

"At Dawning" by Charles Wakefield Cadman. From the song "At Dawning" published and copyright (1906) by Oliver Ditson Company. Words reprinted by permission.

"Less Than the Dust" by Lawrence Hope.

By permission of William Heinemann & Company, London, England.

"The Congo" by Nicholas Vachel Lindsay. From *The Congo and Other Poems,* copyright 1914, 1942 by The Macmillan Company and used with their permission.

"Judy" by Hoagy Carmichael. Used by permission, Southern Music Publishing Co., Inc.

The paper used in this publication is acid-free and meets the minimum requirements
of American National Standard for Information Sciences—Permanence of Paper for
Printed Library Materials, ANSI Z39.48–1984. ∞

CONTENTS

ANYBODY CAN DO ANYTHING

1

"Anybody Can Do Anything Especially Betty"

THE BEST THING ABOUT THE DEPRESSION WAS THE WAY IT RE-
united our family and gave my sister Mary a real opportunity to
prove that anybody can do anything, especially Betty.

Mary's belief that accomplishment is merely a matter of application, was inherited from both Mother and Daddy. Mother,
who has become, through the years and her own efforts, a clever
artist, inspired cook, excellent gardener, qualified midwife, skillful
seamstress, reliable encyclopedia of general information, book-a-
day reader, good practical nurse, dependable veterinary, tireless
listener, fine equestrienne, strong swimmer, adequate carpenter,
experienced farmer, competent dog trainer, and splendid stone
mason, was working for a dress designer in Boston when she met
my father, an ambitious young mining engineer who, though row-
ing on the crew, working all night in the Observatory, and tutoring
rich boys during the day, graduated from Harvard with honors in
three years. The union of these two spirited people produced five
children, four girls and one boy, all born in different parts of the
United States, all tall and redheaded except my sister Dede, who
is small and hardheaded.

Mary, the oldest of the children, was born in Butte, Montana,
and indicated at a very early age that she had lots of ideas and
tremendous enthusiasm, especially for her own ideas. I, Betty, the
next child, emerged in Boulder, Colorado, and from the very first

leaned toward Mary's ideas like a divining rod toward water.

When I was but a few months old, Gammy, my father's mother who always lived with us, sent Mary to the kitchen to ask the cook for a drink of water for me. Mary returned in a matter of seconds with the bathroom glass half-filled with water. Gammy, suspicious, asked Mary where she had gotten the water. Mary said, "Out of the toilet." Gammy said, "Mary Bard, you're a naughty little girl." Mary pointed at me smiling and reaching for the cup and said, "No, I'm not, Gammy. See, she wants it. We always give it to her."

The rest of the family proved to be a little firmer textured, not so eager to be Mary's guinea pigs, so she has always generously allowed them to choose between their own little old wizened-up ideas and the great big juicy ripe tempting ones she offered.

My first memories of being the Trilby for Mary's Svengali go back to that winter in Butte, Montana, when each morning Mary marched importantly off to the second grade at McKinley School, while my brother Cleve and I, who could already read and write, shuffled despondently off to Miss Crispin's kindergarten, a gloomy institution where all the crayons were broken and had the peelings off.

The contrast between Miss Crispin's and real school, in fact between Miss Crispin's and anything but a mortuary, was heartbreakingly obvious even to four and five year olds, but the contrast between Miss Crispin's and the remarkable school that Mary attended and described so vividly to us, was unbearable. Nothing ever happened at Miss Crispin's except that some days it was gloomier and darker than on others and we had to bend so close to our coloring work to tell blue from purple or brown from black that our noses ran on the pictures; some days Miss Crispin, who was very nervous, yelled at us to be quiet, got purple blotches, and pulled and kneaded the skin on her neck like dough; and on Fridays to the halting accompaniment of her sight-reading at the piano, we skipped around the room and sang. Miss Crispin taught us all the verses of "Dixie," "Swanee River," "My Country 'Tis of Thee," and "Old Black Joe," and for the bottom rung on the ladder to enjoyment, I nominate skipping around the room dodging little kindergarten chairs and singing "Old Black Joe."

Compare this then to the big brick school that Mary attended where everyday occurrences (according to Mary and Joe Doner, a boy at school called on so often to prove incredible stories that "If you don't believe me, just ask Joe Doner" has become a family tag for all obvious untruths) were the beating of small children with spiked clubs, the whipping of older boys with a cat-o'-nine-tails in front of the whole school, the forcing of the first graders to drink ink and eat apple cores, the locking in the basement of anyone tardy, and the terribly cruel practice of never allowing anyone to go to the bathroom so that all screamed in pain and many wet their panties.

Naturally Cleve and I believed everything Mary told us, but also naturally, after a while, we grew blasé about the continual beatings, killings, and panty wettings that went on in the second grade at real school, so Mary, noting our waning interest, started the business about the "sausage book" and for months kept us feverish with curiosity and acid with envy.

One snowy winter afternoon she came bursting in from school, glazed with learning, but instead of her usual burden of horror stories, she was carrying a big notebook with a shiny, dark red, mottled cover, like salami. "Look at this," she announced to Gammy and Mother. "I call it my 'sausage book' and I put everything I learn in it. See!" Carefully she brushed the snow off her mittens, turned back the shiny cover and with great pride pointed to the first page. "That's what we did in school today, all by ourselves, without any help," she said.

"Why, that's beautiful, dear," Mother said. "Just beautiful!" Gammy echoed and Cleve and I crowded close to see what was beautiful. Immediately Mary grabbed the book, snapped it shut, and put it behind her back. "Hey, we want to see in your sausage book," Cleve and I said. Mary, in a maddeningly sweet, sad way, said, "I'd like to show it to you, Cleve and Betsy, I really would, but Miss O'Toole won't let me. She said it's all right to show our sausage books to our mothers and fathers but never ever to our little brothers and sisters." Mother and Gammy laughed and said, "Nonsense," so Mary stamped her foot and said, "If you don't believe me, just ask Joe Doner."

Day by day Mary built up the importance of the sausage book until I got so I dreamed about it at night and thought that I opened it and found it full of paper dolls and colored pencils. But no spy was ever more careful of his secret formula than Mary with that darned old notebook. Sometimes she did homework in it but she guarded it with her arms and leaned so far forward that she was drawing or writing under her stomach; she slept with it under her pillow, she even took it coasting and to dancing school. She never was cross or mean about not letting Cleve and me see inside it, but persisted in the attitude that she was only obeying her teacher and trying to protect us, because she realized, even if Mother and Gammy didn't, that seeing into her sausage book might lift the veil of our ignorance too quickly and send our feeble minds off balance. Our only recourse was not to show her the pictures we made at Miss Crispin's, which she didn't want to see anyway.

Then one day Miss Crispin ordered her kindergarteners to draw an apple tree and as not one of us little Butte children had ever seen an apple tree, she told us each to find a picture of one and bring it the next day. We told Mother and Gammy about our kindergarten assignment and Mother found us a very nice colored picture of an apple tree in our *Three Little Pigs* book. Mary looked at it critically for a minute then said, "I'll show you a much better one," and to Cleve's and my absolute joy opened up her sausage book, flipped over some pages and showed us a large drawing of what looked like a Kelly-green Brussels sprout covered with red dots and with a long spindly brown stem. "This," said Mary, "is the way they draw apple trees in real school. Here," she said, generously tearing out the page, "take this to Miss Crispin and just see what she says." We did and Miss Crispin looked at it a long time, pulled at her doughy neck and said, "Mmmmmmm."

The next winter, when we were six and eight, I started to real school and because of a shyness so terrible that I was unable to speak above a faint whisper, it took them several months to discover that I could read and write and really belonged in the second grade.

When the terrible ordeal of reading, in my faint whisper, before the principal and writing my name and several sentences on the blackboard in front of the whole giggling class, had been completed and I had been told that I was in the second grade, my first exultant thought was "Now I'll get my sausage book." But the whole morning went by and I didn't. I peered from under my eyelids at the other children and they didn't seem to have them either. Finally in desperation I raised my hand to ask the teacher and she, misinterpreting my wants, said, in a loud voice, "Number one or number two, Elizabeth." I said, "When do we get our sausage books?" She said, "Your what?" I repeated a little louder, "Our sausage books." She said, "I don't know what you're talking about, now open your reading books to page three."

I got up and went home. I didn't even stop for my coat or rubbers but ran sobbing through the streets and burst in on Mother and Gammy who were having a cup of coffee. "We don't get them," I shrieked. "Don't get what?" Mother said. "Sausage books," I said. "I'm in the second grade and I asked the teacher and she said she didn't know what I was talking about."

Mother explained that I had a different teacher from Mary's and that she probably didn't use sausage books. I refused to be comforted. School had come to mean but one thing to me. A sausage book of my very own filled with secret things that I'd let Cleve but not Mary see. I bawled all afternoon and finally Mother, in desperation, went downtown and bought me a new Lightning Glider sled.

When Mary came home from school, I was out in the back yard, a steep slope about a hundred feet long, reaching from a woodshed and toolhouse at the very back of the lot down to a small level place behind the house, still red-eyed and snuffling, coasting down our little hill on my new sled. When I told Mary about my second grade teacher not giving us sausage books, Mary was so outraged she was going right back to school and mark on the desks and put paste in the inkwells, but to her relief I pled with her and finally talked her out of this dangerous act of loyalty. So as a reward she tried to invent perpetual motion and knocked out all my front teeth.

The back yard was a dandy place to slide and for a while, until Mary had her inspiration, we happily climbed up the little hill and coasted down again, climbed up and coasted down, on the big new shiny sled. Then suddenly at the bottom of the hill, Mary jumped off the sled, dashed into the cellar and came out brandishing the clothes pole.

"Betsy," she said. "I have a wonderful idea. We'll both get on the sled at the top of the hill, I'll hold this pole out in front of us [the pole was about eight feet long] and when we slide down the pole will hit the house and push us back up the hill again. Then down we'll go, then up, then down, then up and we'll never have to climb the hill."

It sounded like a terribly good idea to me so when we had pulled the sled back up the hill to the woodshed, I climbed on the front and put my feet up on the steering bar and Mary got on the back and we both held the pole out in front of us in a direct line with my mouth. Mary gave us a big shove to send us off and whee! how we flew down the little hill. Then everything went black and I began spitting blood and teeth onto the white hard-packed snow, for the pole, when it hit the house, had been forced well back into my mouth. "Oh, Betsy," Mary said, her face so pale her freckles looked like brown moles, "I didn't mean to hurt you. I'm so sorry," and I knew she was because she gave me her old sausage book. Anyway they were only first teeth.

The next victim of Mary's ideas was my brother Cleve, then a sturdy little boy of five, with red hair and a deep mistrust of his sister Mary and her red-haired friend Marjorie.

It was a Saturday afternoon in the spring and we were playing circus, or rather Mary and Marjorie were directing a circus which had all the neighborhood children as paid admissions and Cleve

ANYBODY CAN DO ANYTHING

and me and Snooper, our dog, as the reluctant performers. Mother and Gammy had gone to a tea and left Sarah, our maid, to "keep an eye on us," but Sarah, who loathed children, especially red-haired children, was in the kitchen ironing, with her back to the window and the back door locked. As it would have been her great pleasure to see one or all of our lifeless bodies laid out ready to be carted away, she paid absolutely no attention to the bloodcurdling yells and piercing screams which arose from our back yard, as Cleve and I, for the benefit of the assembled neighborhood and after a great deal of persuasion, performed whatever daring feats Mary and Marjorie thought up.

We had already jumped off the woodshed into the sandpile backward, put lighted matches in our mouths, drunk castor oil and heart medicine (bitter cascara), and ridden around the yard on Snooper, but the biggest act was yet to come. Cleve was going to walk the two-by-four which supported our cellar doors. The two-by-four was only about six feet long but the cellar stairs were dark and steep and there wasn't anything to hold on to. It was a daring and dangerous feat and one which Cleve was not anxious to perform.

"I don' wanna," he kept saying stubbornly. "Now, Cleve," Mary and Marjorie said, "don't you want to be known as the bravest child in this whole neighborhood?" "No," Cleve said, patting Snooper. "Look, Cleve," Mary said, "I'll walk it first," and she did with light dancing steps, back and forth, back and forth. It didn't look too hard. "Why don't you do it for the circus?" Cleve asked. Mary said, "Because I'm the announcer. That's why." Cleve said, "Why doesn't Marjorie do it then?" "Because Marjorie's the ticket taker," Mary said. "You and Betty are the performers. Now come on." Cleve said, "I don' wanna." Then Mary and Marjorie said they would give him twenty-five cents of the gate receipts and that clinched things. Twenty-five cents would buy thirty pieces of "pick" candy (penny candy), six picks for a nickel, and we'd do anything for it.

"Ladees and Gentlemen!" Mary announced in a loud voice. "Come and watch this brave little child walk the tightrope across a deep black hole full of live snakes." She pointed dramatically to Cleve, who had crawled up and was standing on one of the folded-back cellar doors, clutching the twenty-five cents and looking suspiciously first at Mary and then at the narrow two-by-four. Mary's sudden inspiration about the black hole full of live snakes hadn't helped his courage any. All eyes were upon him but Cleve, suddenly deciding that he wasn't going to walk Mary's tightrope, sat down and started to slide down the cellar door.

Mary said, "Look, ladees and gentlemen, see how brave he is. That little tiny child has turned around so he won't have to look at those wreathy writhy snakes. But he is the most famous tightrope walker in the whole world and he is going to walk that dangerous tightrope, or you won't get your twenty-five cents," she hissed sotto voce at Cleve. Cleve looked at the twenty-five cents and then at the two-by-four and finally stood up and started across. His fat little legs wobbled and when he tried to get his balance, his arms went around like windmills and at the exact center, and just as Mother came home, he fell and landed on his back on the cellar stairs.

Mother carried him into the house and put him in a tub of hot water and when the doctor came he tested his reflexes and said Cleve wasn't hurt at all, but it was a long time before he would take an active part in any of Mary's and Marjorie's schemes, particularly when he learned that he had dropped his twenty-five cents when he fell and some little ghoul had stolen it.

As I look back on it, I couldn't have been too bright, because only one year later when I was seven, Mary and Marjorie got me to jump from the loft of a neighbor's stable on to a very small armful of straw, which they had carelessly thrown on top of an upturned rake.

We were playing vaudeville this time, because Mary and Marjorie had recently been taken to their first vaudeville, whose wonders, substantiated by Joe Doner, had included a human bird and a man who balanced steel balls on his ears. I couldn't balance steel balls on my ears but I could be Betty, the Human Bird, the Greatest

ANYBODY CAN DO ANYTHING

Jumper of All Times, which was why on that bright summer morning I was standing shivering in the little doorway of the unused loft. It was only about a ten- or twelve-foot jump but I'll never forget how high up I felt.

Big Butte, an extinct volcano which had always seemed to us to be the highest mountain in the world, was right in front of me. The big M-1915, painted in white on its black rock side by the daring School of Mines boys, was now at eye level. I could see the School of Mines where Daddy taught. I could see Mary the Cook hanging out washing in our back yard. I could see hundreds of great big blue mountains. I could see Mary marching around the yard with a stick pointing at me and shouting, "Ladees and Gentlemen! Look up at her, Betty, the Human Bird, the bravest child in the whole world. Just a little girl of seven who will jump from that terribly high building down onto this little pile of straw!"

I looked down at the pile of straw and it certainly was little. "That's not enough straw," I said, backing away from the edge of the doorway. "Sure it is," Mary said. "Anyway that's all Mr. Murphy would let us have. Hurry up, Betsy, it'll be fun," she called running a few wisps of straw through her fingers to prove it.

My stomach felt ice cold and my heart seemed to have moved up into my head. "Thump, thump, thump," it was hammering just behind my eyes. Mary had promised me on her word of honor that if I jumped off high enough things often enough, I would be able to fly like the man in the vaudeville show. She had started me jumping off fences, the woodshed roof, and our high front porch and as I jumped more and more I was less scared but I hadn't noticed that I landed any more gently.

Mary had said that some day when I jumped from a high enough place it would suddenly be just like a dream and I would float to earth. This was to be the big test, and if this dream came true and I floated, then there was a good chance that my dreams of having jet black curls down to my ankles and an entire Irish lace dress over a bright pink satin petticoat like the night watchman's little girl, might come true. Anyway it had been Mary's best selling point.

"Come on, Betsy, dear," she was calling. "I'll count for you and when I get to ten you jump." I looked down at the upturned admiring faces of the neighborhood children as Mary began counting in loud ominous tones. "Oneh, two-ah, three-ah." I took a deep breath, closed my eyes and jumped when she got to ten-ah. I did not fly. I landed hard on the pile of straw and two tines of the hidden rake went through my foot. Mary and Marjorie, truly appalled by their carelessness, carried me all the way home. At least Mary carried me and Marjorie held up the handle of the rake.

When we got home Mother called the doctor and while we waited for him I soaked my foot in a basin of hot Epsom salts and water and Gammy comforted me by saying, "Cheeldrun are nothing but savages. It won't surprise me at all if they have to cut off Betsy's legs."

"Not both legs," Mary said. "Only one." I had been very brave up to this point but now I began to bawl. "I don't want to have my leg cut off and only wear one roller skate," I sobbed.

Mary said, "Never mind, Betsy, dear, we'll make a little tiny roller skate for your crutch and in winter I'll pull you to school on the sled." Which, to her dismay, only made me bawl louder.

Then the doctor arrived, examined my foot and gave me a tetanus shot; Daddy came home, examined my foot, and gave Mary a spanking with the bristle side of the brush; Mother wiped away my tears, said of course my legs weren't going to be cut off, and called Gammy an old pessimist, which immediately cheered Mary and me because we thought pessimist was a bad word like bastard.

My next memory of being Mary's test pilot was the following summer, while visiting friends who lived in a small town in the mountains near an abandoned mine. "Don't ever go near the mine," we were cautioned. "There is no place as dangerous for children as a mine. Any mine. Particularly an old one with deep, dark, rotten shafts and rusty unsafe machinery." "We won't go near the mine," we promised and we didn't.

We went wading in the creek. We went fishing. We stuck leeches on our legs because Mary believed it purified us.

We picked Indian paintbrush and Mariposa lilies. We took our new pocketknives and made willow whistles. We watched out for rattlesnakes and bulls and we did not go near the mine.

Then one lovely hot summer's day, Mary and I decided to go huckleberrying. Dressed in overalls and straw hats and each swinging a little lard pail, with a lid, by its wire handle, we started off. It was a wonderful day. The sun was hot and the air was filled with the delicious smell of hot pine needles and huckleberry juice. We found a big spruce gum tree and pried off mildewed-looking hunks and chewed them. We found the bitter pitchy flavor of the gum mixed well with the tart huckleberries. We also found that we could lie on our backs under the huckleberry bushes and scrape the berries into our buckets. The berries went plink, plink, plunk, and it was as easy as shelling peas. We moved from bush to bush by sliding along on the slick brown pine needles. Chipmunks chattered at us and bright green darning needles darted around our heads. We chewed our big wads of spruce gum and were happy.

Then Mary saw the flume. "What's that big thing over there?" she said, rolling over on her stomach and pointing below us on the mountainside. It looked like a long gray dragon slithering down the side of the mountain. We decided to investigate. We put the lids on our little lard pails and started down the hill.

The flume, used to carry water down to the mine, had once been up on high supports, but just at this point, a small rock slide had knocked the rotting supports away and the flume had broken in two and the bottom part now sloped down the mountainside like a giant clothes chute. The inside, stained a cool green (by the water it used to carry) was actually very hot and as slippery as glass with the dry pine needles that had drifted into it.

Side by side, Mary and I knelt down and peered into the flume. I could taste the salty perspiration on my upper lip as I chewed my spruce gum and wondered if the flume was endless. From where we were it seemed to go on forever, growing smaller and smaller until it was just a tiny black square in the distance. Mary shouted into it and her voice came back to us with a hollow roar, "Ahhhhh, ooooo."

Then Mary said, her voice tight with excitement, "What a wonderful place to slide. Just like a giant chute the chutes!"

I said nothing but my stomach had a funny feeling. I backed out of the mouth of the flume and sat down on the rock slide in the hot sun. Little rocks, loosed by my feet, went clittering off down the mountain. Far overhead in the bright blue sky an eagle circled in big lazy circles. Then Mary, still kneeling, pulled herself into the mouth of the flume but holding on tight to each side. "You'd have to go belly buster," she said speculatively as she measured herself with the opening.

"What do you mean 'you'?" I said. Mary didn't answer.

"Daddy said flumes are dangerous," I said edging still further away from it.

Mary said, "He didn't mean this flume, Betsy dear, he meant flumes that go into dams or end up in waterfalls. Of course, those flumes are very, very dangerous, but this old thing," she patted the flume like an old dog, "is perfectly safe. Just look at it, Betsy."

Cautiously I again knelt and peered down into the long green tunnel and it did seem much safer. At least it was perfectly quiet and I couldn't hear the roar of any waterfalls.

"Let's just slide a little way in it and then crawl out again," Mary suggested.

"You go first," I said.

"Now, Betsy, dear," Mary always called me "Betsy, dear" when she was going to will me to do some ghastly thing. "I'm the biggest and strongest so I'd better stay outside and hold your feet and help you."

"You go first," I repeated stubbornly.

Mary said, "This is going to be more fun than anything we've ever done. We'll slide down just like a train in a tunnel. Zip and we'll be at the bottom. Crisscross your heart you'll never tell anyone about our secret chute."

As I crisscrossed my thumping heart, I had a sudden fleeting feeling that all this had happened before. Mary's eyes sparkled. She said, "We'll bring Cleve and Gammy up here and when they aren't looking we'll jump into our chute and when they try to find us we'll be at the bottom of the mountain." We both peered into the flume again. Referring to it as "our chute" seemed to make it less dangerous and it didn't seem quite so bottomless and scary now.

Mary said, "If a bear or anything should chase us we could jump right in this chute and it'd never catch us."

I said, "But where does it come out?"

Mary said, "Oh, probably in a big pile of sand." One summer when we were camping in the mountains we had played on an old ore chute that ended in a pile of sand, but I didn't think of that at the time, and thought that maybe Mary really knew where this chute ended.

"How do you know?" I asked.

She changed the subject by looking up into a tall pine tree close at hand. "I wonder if we could fix some kind of a rope that would pull us back up the hill?" she said. I said, "We could fix one of those pulleys like we fixed to send notes on."

Mary said, "Oh, Betsy, you're so smart!" That's just what we could fix and then we'd slide down, pull ourselves up, slide down, pull ourselves up. Up, down, up, down. Why we could even charge like the merry-go-round at Columbia Gardens," she added as a final persuasion. Why didn't all that up-down stuff make me remember the experiment in perpetual motion? How could I have been such a dupe and a dope?

Mary said, "Come on, Betty, hurry and get in before Gammy and Cleve get here. You know Gammy said she'd walk up this way before supper."

I climbed in headfirst. "Grab my feet," I yelled at Mary. But it was too late. The hot dry pine needles were very slick. In a second I had slithered out of reach. Down I went into the long, endless green tunnel. "Help, help, Mary, help!" I shouted and the words came roaring back at me, "Hulp, hulp!" as though I were shouting into a giant megaphone. The flume grew steeper and steeper and I gained momentum until I was whizzing along, my lard pail bumping the side, my straw hat over one eye. "Help, help, help!" I called again and again to Mary but there was no answer.

Once I slowed down and got stuck in a flat place where there were no pine needles. With swimming motions I tried to get started again but only succeeded in getting a large sliver in my thigh. I pulled my legs up under me and tried crawling. It was slow and I banged my head quite often but as my only alternative was spending the rest of my life in the flume, I kept on. Then suddenly the flume took a sharp plunge downward and I flattened out again, took the hill belly buster, rolled out (the flume was broken at the bottom) and stuck in the crack between the two parts. Slowly and shakily I got to my feet. Directly below me was the dangerous old mine. From high up the mountain I could hear Mary calling, "Betsy, Betsy, are you hurt?" as she ran toward me down the OUT-SIDE of the flume.

I grabbed my bucket and started toward her voice, determined that she was going to slide down that flume if I had to kill her first. Then from down in the valley I heard Mother calling us. "Coming," I yelled and from up the mountain Mary answered, "Coming."

The sliver in my thigh was about three inches long and as thick as a darning needle and by a series of clever questions, Daddy finally found out how I had gotten it and sternly forbade our ever going near the flume again.

From then on, as I remember, my life was reasonably safe except for a few minor things, such as the time Mary convinced Cleve and me that she had learned witchcraft and drew large quantities of blood from our veins and fed us smashed-up worms mixed with toenail parings.

And the time after we had moved to Seattle that Mary and I, then ten and twelve, were dressing after swimming and she suggested that I stand naked in the window of our bedroom and wave to the President of the Milwaukee Railroad, who with his wife was being shown the garden by Mother and Daddy. When I seemed a little reluctant to extend this evidence of Western hospitality, Mary tried to convince me and somehow in the course of the convincing she pushed her head and shoulders through the window pane and we both rolled out on the roof into the heap of broken glass, stark naked and yelping like wounded dogs.

The President of the Milwaukee Railroad and his wife, who didn't have any children, believed our story about my catching my foot in my bathing suit and falling against Mary and forcing us both through the window and were very sympathetic to us when we appeared for tea, swathed in bandages. Daddy, however, waited until his guests had left, then assigned us each a quota of five thousand stones to be removed from the orchard and dumped into the old well back of the barn.

We had just dumped our five hundred and seventy-second stone into the wheelbarrow and were morosely trying to subtract 572 from 10,000 when Mary had her idea. "I'll get all the kids in the neighborhood in the summerhouse, you tell them 'Nancy and Plum' [a continued story about two little orphans I'd been telling Mary in bed at night for years and years] and when you get to the most exciting place you stop and I'll tell them you won't go on until they each pick up a hundred stones and put them in the well." It worked too. That afternoon we got 1,100 stones dumped in the well. The next day the smarter children didn't show up but, by stopping twice in the story, we got the six that did come to gather two hundred stones each so we actually fared even better than the day before.

By the end of the week, over six thousand stones had been dumped in the well, Nancy and Plum, who had made a harrowing escape from the orphanage, had been captured by Gypsies, kidnapped by bank robbers, lost in an abandoned mine, weathered a terrible storm in a haunted house, adopted a baby who turned out to be a prince, stowed away on a boat to China, and finally come to rest with a dear old farmer and his wife who had an attic full of toys, and I felt like my bath sponge when I squeezed it dry.

Daddy's cultural program with lessons in piano playing, singing, folk dancing, French, and ballet, added further proof to Mary's theory that anybody can do anything and, in her case, without practicing.

Our favorite piano teacher among many, and the one we clung to longest, was a Miss Welcome, a very temperamental European who calcimined her arms dead white up to within an inch of her short sleeves, dressed entirely in fuchsia color, wore turbans with flowing veils when she taught, always had fish breath, counted on our backs with her strong fingers digging into the flesh, "Bun and boo and bree and bour," screamed, "Feel, f-e-e-l, FEEL IT!" as she paced around the room her veils flying, her calcimined arms beating out the rhythm like big plaster casts, often produced real tears (to our delight) when we made mistakes. "Oh, dear God, no, not B flat!" she'd moan, covering her face with her hands and sobbing brokenly.

Miss Welcome never bored us with scales or exercises or any of those stupid little Pixie-in-the-Glen or Lullaby-for-Tiny-Hands type of thing. Everybody studying with her started off the very first day on some great big hard well-known piece by some great big hard well-known composer. If, by our third lesson, we couldn't manage the full chords or the fast parts in say, Rachmaninoff's Prelude in C Sharp Minor, Miss Welcome cut them out. She cut the bottoms off octaves and the tops off grace notes without turning a hair. "Now try it," she'd say and if we still couldn't play it she'd take out her ever-ready pencil and x out the whole hard part. "Now," she'd say, "let's hear some feeeeeeeeeeling!" and with the fervor of relief we'd bear down and pound feeling into what was left.

Because I had long, thin hands and was so scared of Miss Welcome, I bawled at every lesson, she told me I was very very sensitive and gave me long sad selections with enormous chords and huge reaches. "Bun and boo and bree and bour, now come on Betsy, play, play, PLAY!" she'd yell at me and I'd begin to cry. "I can't reach the notes," I'd sob, my long, unyielding hands trying to reach the two keys over an octave so unreasonably demanded by Schumann. "You must reach it. You CAN AND YOU MUST!" Miss Welcome would hiss spittily into my tearstained face. I tried and tried. I practised one and two hours every day on my sad, great pieces but my heart wasn't in it. I didn't want to play slow, sad things with huge chords that gave me bearing-down pains. I wanted to be like Mary, who talked back to Miss Welcome, hardly ever practiced, played entirely by ear (she didn't learn to read music until after she was married), chose her own loud, showy pieces, and whose small freckled supple hands flew over the keys like lightning. Now that I think about it my sister Mary was really one of the pioneers in the field of the medley.

When Daddy and Mother had company we children usually performed. First Dede, who had perfect pitch even at two, sang "My Country 'Tis of Thee," then Cleve, until his clarinet playing had progressed to solos, recited, then Mary and I played the piano.

I would give a sweaty-fingered uninspired performance of my latest piece exactly as it was written and exactly as Miss Welcome had taught me even to the lowered wrists, high knuckles, and leaning forward and pressing heavily on the keys for depth of tone. I always knew my pieces and never made a mistake but nobody cared, I could tell from the bored rattle of newspapers, nervous scraping of chairs, even snores, so audible during the long, long waits between notes required by the dramatic Miss Welcome. "That's very nice Betsy," Mother would say when at last I finished one of those interminable D.C.L. Fine pieces where you keep playing the same thing over and over with a different ending.

Then it was Mary's turn. Up she would flounce to the piano and effortlessly dash off Grieg's "Carnival," *"Danse Negre,"* "Anitra's Dance," *"Le Papillon,"* *"Solfeggietto,"* or "Rustle of Spring," and everyone would say, "Isn't she talented?" and only I, in my envy, noticed that each was seasoned with the other and they all reflected strongly the influence of composer Mary Bard.

Miss Welcome openly adored Mary even when Mary was talking loud and trying to force her to believe that Grieg had written in that Chopin passage in Beethoven's Sonata *Pathetique,* and she always eventually gave in to her. When Mother and Daddy took us to hear De Pachmann Mary and I were so entranced with his playing of Chopin's Third Ballade that Mary decided that she would play it in the spring recital, which was only about a month away. Miss Welcome said, "Mary, darling, you are terribly, terribly talented but the Third Ballade is too difficult and there is not enough time." Mary said, "I'll practice four hours a day." Miss Welcome said, "Not enough." Mary said, "I'll practice eight hours a day, twelve, sixteen," and finally Miss Welcome gave in and with only slight encouragement sat down at the piano and played the Third Ballade for us. She couldn't hold a candle to De Pachmann in technique but she had it all over him in dramatics. For the soft parts she stroked the keys as though they were tiny dogs, and when she came to the dut-dah-dut-dah-dut-dah, dah, dada, dah, dah . . . she lifted her hands off the keys about four feet and came down on the wrong notes but the effect was very brrrright and certainly staccato. For the loud passages she used full strength and full pedal, topped off with grunting and heavy breathing. While she played, Mary and I, to keep from hurting her feelings, stifled our laughter in her purple velvet portieres that smelled of mildew.

For the next month I read the notes and Mary memorized them and by recital time we both knew the Third Ballade, but Mary played it, giving a brilliant performance if you discounted her omission of several runs and that entire, most difficult, interval near the end where the left hand is supposed to race up and down the keyboard while the right hand pounds out the original melody. Miss Welcome, to whom omission didn't mean that much, shouted, "Bravo, Bravo," from the back of her stuffy little parlor where the recitals were held and then rushed forward, kissed Mary on both cheeks and said, "Oh, Mary, Mary, I didn't think you could do it." To be perfectly honest, I wasn't sure she had.

We both took singing from our Sunday School teacher's sister, or rather Mary took singing and I played her accompaniment, but we always referred to it as our singing because it took both of us for a performance.

Mrs. Potter, our teacher, had an enormous contralto voice and was a thick singer and always sounded as though her throat was full of phlegm. She was supposed to be a very good teacher and to know Madame Schumann-Heink, which fact she just happened to mention at least ten times during every lesson. "Watch my diaphragm," Mrs. Potter would demand as she sang, "Caddy me bok to old Vugiddy. Deeahs wheah de cottod ad de sweed bodadoes grrrrow. Deahs wheah de buds waughble sweed in de sprrrring tahb . . ." At first Mrs. Potter wanted me to study singing too but Mother thought that, as I had once had very bad tonsils, it would be better for me to be Mary's accompanist, which was fine for a while.

"Pale hahnds I loved beside the Shalimah . . . ah, wheah ahhh you now, oh wheah ahhh you now?" Mary wailed at Cousin Reginald Coxe, who was painting Mother's portrait and had to endure this form of reprisal. "When the dawn flames in the sky, I love yewwwww. When the birdlings wake and cry, I love yewwwww . . ." Mary's rendition of "At Dawning" was to me the most beautiful thing in the world and always brought tears to my eyes. Mary's soprano voice was clear and true but not that good, so probably adolescence had something to do with it.

We were about twelve and fourteen then and loved romantic things but Mary's love of romance took a different turn from mine. While I wanted her to sing "At Dawning" every time we performed so I could get tears in my eyes, she wanted to swathe herself in Mother's Spanish shawl, clench her teeth, and sing, "Less than the dust, beneeeeeth thy chaddiott wheeeeel, Less than the rust, that never stained thy saw-word." Not only that, but having by this time ceased all pretense of practising, she often made up her own tunes and words and her unimaginative accompanist, often a page behind, after frantically changing keys and turning pages, would finally stop dead and point out to Mary where she was and where I was and what she had sung and what she should have sung. This infuriated the great artiste and she would assume a tortured expression and sigh heavily as we got ready to start over.

It was during this cultural interlude that my brother Cleve, who had begun ominously to refer to Mary and me as "those darn gurls" and to fill the baseboard of his room with shotgun shells, put an enormous automatic bolt on his bedroom door, spent all his free time with the Laurelhurst bus driver, and ate Smith Brothers cough drops by the box. One day Gammy interrupted one of our best recitals to show Mother a large armful of empty cough drop boxes and to tell her that it might interest her to know that while her daughter was traipsing around in her naked strip (her interpretation of the Spanish shawl) singing those lusty songs, her son had become a dope fiend.

Then Mary entered and won an elocution contest.

> "Fat black bucks in a wine-barrel room,
> Barrel-house kings, with feet unstable
> Sagged and reeled and pounded on the table . . . !"

she shouted as she sagged and reeled around the kitchen, pounding on the table so hard her fist stuck to the oilcloth.

> "Beat an empty barrel with the handle of a broom,
> Hard as they were able,
> Boom, Boom, BOOM,
> With a silk umbrella and the handle of a broom,
> Boomlay, boomlay, boomlay, BOOM."

she roared. Then suddenly half-crouching, with eyes like slits, she reached behind her and got her right arm and thrust it directly at us, the stiff index finger appearing suddenly at the end like a knife blade on a cane. Still crouching, her squinty eyes on the pointing finger, she slowly moved the arm in a half-circle and hissed through clenched teeth:

> "Then I saw the Congo, creeping through the black,
> Cutting through the jungle with a golden track."

That's the one she won the contest with and it was usually her encore and my favorite. Cleve and Gammy liked "Lasca" best.

"The air was heavy, the night was hot,
I sat by her side, and forgot—forgot;

. . . . .

Was that thunder? I grasped the cord
of my swift mustang without a word."

For Lasca, Mary wore her high laced hiking boots, her fringed Campfire Girl dress tucked up to be a riding skirt, a green velvet embroidered bolero that belonged to a Bolivian costume a friend of Mother's had left at our house, a cowboy hat of Cleve's, and carried Mother's quirt, which she flicked against the hiking boots when she sighed "for the canter after the cattle" or "the mustang flew, and we urged him on."

"That girl ought to be on the stage," Mrs. Watson, our cleaning woman, said, the first time she heard Mary do "Lasca," and I thought so too. I thought all her recitations were absolutely marvellous and was delirious with happiness when she offered to coach me.

After studying me from every angle, Mary decided that I was the "cute" type. Why she made such a decision I'll never know because at the time I was painfully thin, pale green, wore a round comb, and had a mouth filled with gold braces. Perhaps it was kindness, perhaps wishful thinking, but whichever it was, it was most gratifying to me and gave me a lot of self-confidence.

My first cute recitation was "Little Orphant Annie." Mary taught me to stick out my lips like a Ubangi, wrinkle my high forehead, roll my eyes, waggle my forefinger, and say in a kind of baby talk, "An' the Gobble-uns 'll git you, Ef you Don't Watch Out!" Then came "The carpenter man said a bad word, he said, 'Darn,'" only Mary had me say "corpenter" and "dorn" as being cuter.

The family were openly nauseated by my performances, but when I recited at school the girls thought I was cute and begged for more so I learned, "Elthie Minguth lithsps the doeth, the liveth wite croth the threet from me. . . ." Mary, terribly proud of her handiwork, took me down and showed me to her elocution teacher, who said that I should study, which we took as a compliment.

As elocution was very popular and most of our little friends studied, some of them reciting from memory, and at the drop of a hat, whole chapters from *Daddy-Long-Legs*, *Tom Sawyer*, and *Rebecca of Sunnybrook Farm*, I probably would have studied except that Daddy died that year and we stopped all of our lessons but piano and ballet. Mother could have stopped these too, as far as I was concerned.

"One, two, three, LEAP!" shouted our ballet teacher, as she pounded her stick on the floor. Mary leaped so high they had to pull her down off the ceiling but I, who had also seen Pavlova and the Duncan Dancers, rubbed my ballet slippers in the rosin and dreaded my turn.

When anything was sewed with small, hard, unrippable stiches Gammy said it had been "baked" together. I felt "baked together" at dancing class. The other girls did arabesques that made them look like birds poised in flight. I wiggled noticeably and the leg that was supposed to point up toward the ceiling hung down like a broken wing. When we stood at the bar I pulled and strained and kicked but my bones were as stiff and unpliable as pipes and I seemed to have fewer joints than the rest of the class. In spite of it all I finally got up on my toes and appeared in many recitals.

In one recital our class, clad in short silk accordion-pleated skirts with pieces of the same material tied low around our foreheads and cleverly arranged to go over only one shoulder yet cover our budding bosoms, were supposed to be Greek boys, leaping around, pretending to be gladiators and drive chariots. We were very advanced ballet students by then and the dance was such a success that we were asked to repeat it at some sort of Army-Navy celebration in Woodland Park.

We were glad to, of course; but just after we had come leaping in driving our chariots, the top of Mary's costume came off and it immediately became apparent to the audience that at least some of these dancers were not Greek boys. "Hey, Mary," I hissed at her, "your costume's broken." Mary ignored me. She leaped and whirled and stamped through the entire dance and not until we were taking our final bows did she deign to fix the shoulder strap. I was aghast. "Mary Bard," I said, "do you realize that you were dancing out there in front of all those people with part of your bust exposed?" Mary said, "My dear girl, did you think that Pavlova or Isadora Duncan would have stopped to fix a shoulder strap? After all, no matter what breaks, the show must go on." Our teacher, as well as the Army and Navy, was very pleased with Mary. In fact, the Army and Navy asked us to repeat the dance again, which we didn't, and our teacher held Mary up before the entire dancing school as an example of a true artiste.

Then we started to public high school and Mary gave up ballet and went into girls' club work, school plays, vaudeville shows, and the opera. She had leads in everything and she dragged me along with her whenever she could. Once I stumbled out of a giant grandfather clock and did a scarf dance and another time I was in the dancing chorus in an opera.

As time went on I became more and more convinced that Mary was right and that anybody could do anything, but I had sense enough to realize that it was a hell of a lot harder for some people than for others.

2

What's a White Russian Got?

WHEN WE WERE EIGHTEEN AND TWENTY I MARRIED AND WENT to live in the mountains on a chicken ranch, and Mary plunged headfirst into a business career, which eventually resulted in her being fired from every firm of any size in the city of Seattle.

Mary's being fired was never a reflection on her efficiency, which was overwhelming, but was always a matter of principle, usually involving the morale of the entire firm. "I don't give a damn if you're the biggest lawyer in the city of Seattle, you can't control my bladder," she shouted at the head of a large law firm, who had suddenly arbitrarily ruled that all his stenographers had to go to the restroom at 10:30 A.M. and 3:15 P.M.

"Labor Day is a National Holiday and I'm an American citizen and won't work if you call in the Militia," Mary announced to the front office of a legal firm whose senior partner was anti-labor and got even with the A.F. of L. by making all his employees work on Labor Day.

"Go pinch somebody who can't type," she told a surprised and amorous lumber exporter.

"Henry Ford has proven that a rest period and something to eat in the morning and afternoon raises efficiency two hundred per cent and as Henry Ford's got a lot better job than you have, I'm going out for coffee," she told the personnel manager of an insurance company.

"If you want to say 'he don't' and 'we was,' that's your affair,"

Mary told a pompous manufacturer, "but I won't put it in your letters because it reflects on me."

Even though Mary's jobs didn't last long, she never had any trouble getting new ones. All the employment agency people loved her and she enjoyed applying for new jobs.

"There are only two ways to apply for a job," she said.

"Either you are a Kick-Me-Charlie and go crawling in anxious for long hours and low pay, or you march in to your prospective employer with a Look-Who's-Hit-the-Jackpot attitude and for a while, at least, you have both the job and your self-respect." Anyone could see that all Kick-Me-Charlie's kept their jobs the longest but they didn't have as much self-respect or meet as many people as Mary.

While Mary changed jobs and met people, I raised chickens, had two children, and didn't meet anybody. Finally in March, 1931, after four years of this, I wrote to my family and told them that I hated chickens, I was lonely, and I seemed to have married the wrong man.

It was the beginning of the depression and I didn't really expect anything but sympathy, but Mary, who was supporting the entire family, replied in typically dependable and dramatic fashion by special delivery registered letter that she had a wonderful job for me and that I was to come home at once. I wrote back that I didn't know how to do office work and it was five miles to the bus line. Mary wired back, "Anybody can do office work and remember the White Russians walked across Siberia. Your job starts Monday."

It was late on a rainy Friday afternoon when a neighbor brought the telegram but I checked the bus schedule, dressed the children and myself in our "town clothes," stuffed my silver fish fork, my graduation ring, and a few other things into a suitcase, wrote a note to my husband, and leading three-year-old Anne by the hand and carrying year-and-a-half-old Joan and the suitcase, set off across the burn toward the six o'clock bus to Seattle.

It was not an easy walk. The road, following the course of an ancient river bed, meandered around through the sopping brush, coiled itself around huge puddles and never ever took the shortest distance between two points. When we made sorties into the brush to avoid the puddles, the salal and Oregon grape drenched our feet and clawed vindictively at my one pair of silk stockings. Every couple of hundred feet I had to stop and unclamp my purple hands from the suitcase handle and shift the baby to the other hip. Every half mile or so we all sat down on a soaking stump or log to rest. The rain was persistent and penetrating, and after the third rest all of our clothes had the uniform dampness of an ironing folded down the night before.

The children were cheerful and didn't seem to mind the discomforts—I was as one possessed. I was leaving the dreary monotony of the rain and the all-encompassing loneliness of the farm to go home to the warmth and laughter of my family and now that I was started I would have carried both children and the suitcase, forded raging torrents, and run that last never-ending mile with a White Russian on each shoulder.

Just before we got to the highway, the road had been taken over by some stray cows and a big Jersey bull. Under ordinary circumstances this would have meant climbing a fence and going half a mile or so out of our way, because I am scared to death of bulls, especially Jersey bulls. Not that day. "Get out of my way!" I shouted at the surprised bull and small Anne, brandishing a twig, echoed me. The bull, sulkily grumbling and shaking his head, moved to one side. If he hadn't I think I would have punched him in the nose.

When we finally reached the highway, I sat the children on the suitcase and listened anxiously for the first rumble of the bus. I knew that I would have to depend on hearing it because the highways had been braided through the thick green tresses of the Olympic Peninsula by some lethargic engineer who apparently thought that everyone enjoyed bounding in and out of forests, dipping down into farmyards and skirting small rocks and hillocks with blind hairpin turns, and at the intersection where I hoped to catch the bus, and catch was certainly the right word, the bus would be visible only for that brief moment when, having leaped out of Mr. Hansen's farmyard by means of a short steep rise, it skirted his oat field before disappearing around a big rock just beyond his south fence.

I knew that I had to be ready to signal the driver just as he appeared over the brow of the Hansen's barnyard and in my eagerness, I flagged down two empty homeward-bound logging trucks and the feed man before I heard the bus. When its gray snubbed nose peered over the hill, I rushed out into the road and waved my purse but the driver saw me too late and for one terrible sickening instant I thought he was going on and leave us to walk back up the mountains in the rain. But he screeched to a stop and waited at the big rock and I grabbed the suitcase and the children and ran down the road, and then we were aboard, in a front seat where I could urge the bus along and be ready for the city when it burst upon me with its glory of people and life.

The bus driver was not at all friendly, due no doubt to a large angry-looking boil on the back of his neck, the bus smelled of wet dogs and wet rubber, there were two drunken Indians in the seat across from us and a disgusting old man in back of us who cleared his throat and spat on the floor, but everything was bathed in the glow of my anticipation and I smiled happily at everyone.

Down the mountains, through valleys, up into the mountains again we sped. We were going very fast and the bus lurched and swayed and belched Diesel fumes but we were heading toward home. I was going to live again.

Once when we went around a particularly vicious curve, the drunken Indian woman rolled off her seat into the aisle. The Indian man, presumably her husband, peered over at her lying on her back on the floor, her maroon coat bunched around her waist, her fat brown thighs exposed, and burst out laughing. The woman laughed too and so did the other passengers. The bus driver half-turned around and said, "For Krissake, you Bow and Arrows pipe down or I'll throw you out." The woman turned over and got up on all fours so that her big maroon fanny was high in the air and a tempting target. The other Indian reached out and kicked her hard and they both began laughing again. Anne and I laughed too but the bus driver stopped the bus, pushed his cap to the back of his head and said, "For Krissake, you two, do you want me to put you off?" The Indian woman climbed back into her seat and they quieted down to only occasional silly giggles. We started up again and after a while drove onto the dock and the big bus lumbered aboard the ferry and all of us passengers got out and went upstairs for supper.

Anne and Joan and I shared our booth in the ferry's small smoky restaurant with a Mrs. Johnson, a large woman in navy blue and steel-rimmed spectacles, whose eyes very handily operated on different circuits so that while her left eye looked out the window, her right eye was fixed on the waitress or on her food or on me. Mrs. Johnson told me immediately that her ankles swelled and everything she ate talked back to her but she was going "upsound" to get recruits for Jesus. I told her that I was going to Seattle to work in an office.

She said, "The city is a wicked place full of the works of the Devil. Stay on the farm. Jesus is on the farm." I said that I had heard that He was everywhere but I hadn't noticed Him on our farm. Mrs. Johnson, who was busily fishing the lettuce out of her hamburger and putting it on a napkin beside her plate, said, "Praise His name! Praise His name! You can always count me out when it comes to greens. Just like ground glass in my intestynes."

I said, "I'm going to live with my family." She gestured with her fork and one eye toward Anne and Joan, who were quietly eating scrambled eggs, and said, "The Devil is in the city. Have those poor little tykes been babtyzed?" I said no and she said, "Throw them in. Throw them in! Wash their sins away. Praise His name."

Just then the waitress brought her apple pie à la mode and my coffee. Tapping on my cup with her spoon she said, "I like coffee but it don't like me. Binds me up tighter'n a drum. Without it I keep regular as clockwork, but let me drink one cup and I'm threw off for a week." She fixed her great big good eye on me and waited and

I was not sure whether she expected me to say, "Praise His name, praise His name," or to retaliate with a list of foods that bound me up, so I said, "Wasn't it funny on the bus when the Indian fell in the aisle?"

Mrs. Johnson swelled her nostrils until they were like twin smudge pots and said, "I am going to report that driver to headquarters. He took the name of the Lord Jesus our God in Heaven in vain." I said, "Well, he has a boil on his neck." She said, "Poison coming out of his system. Blasphemy is a stench in the nostrils of God and I'm going to report that driver."

I was pleased to note, when the ferry docked an hour or so later and we all climbed aboard the bus, that the only seat left for Mrs. Johnson, who was late, was way in the back with the Indians, by then much drunker and much noisier and destined to be a stench in the nostrils of both Mrs. Johnson and God before we reached Seattle.

It was dark and still raining when we landed. The water was gray and rough and the ferry banged into the dolphins and backed up several times before it was able to edge into the slip and the deckhands could let down the flimsy chain that had presumably kept the bus from plunging off the deck into the water.

As we rumbled onto the dock a train, bleating mournfully, and with the beam from its terrible fiery eye swinging across the water, came hurtling along the shore. The children, who had never seen a train before, were terrified. "What is it? What is it?" wailed Anne, as it streaked past, clackety, clackety, clackety, woooooo, woooooo, its lighted windows a ribbon of light in the rainy evening. "It's a train, darling. A nice choo-choo train," I told her comfortingly. She said, "It is not. It's a Mickaboo full of Bojanes."

To Anne all frightening things were Bojanes and Bojanes lived in Mickaboos, which were nailholes or tiny cracks in the floor. Now apparently Bojanes flew through the night inside fiery dragons. Anne wailed, "Take it away, Betty, take it away." And I did. I shooed it around another curve and it went wooo-wooing off into the night, jerking its red tail lights along behind it. When the red warning light by the tracks stopped blinking and the gates were raised, the bus gave a lurch and we were off.

"Going home, going home," I hummed to myself as the bus nosed its way along in the thin early evening traffic, its tires saying shhhhh, shhh to the nervous wet highway, its lights making deep hollows and sudden mounds out of shadows on the smooth pavement. We went slowly and carefully through the little town by the ferry landing, then for miles and miles the road was dark with only an occasional lonely little house peering out of the night, and we sailed swiftly along.

When we hit the main highway, small boxy houses with gas stations attached flashed by and showed cheerful glimpses of family life—mother, father, and children eating supper in the breakfast nook—father reading the paper in the parlor—a baby silhouetted at the window watching the cars go by in the rain. On the highway small tacky grocery stores and vegetable stands, open late to catch an extra dribble of trade, littered the spaces between the gas stations. Every few hundred yards or so a palely-lighted sign pleaded "Bud's Good Eats" or "Ma's Home Cooking" or "Mert and Bert's Place."

Some of the gas stations also cozily announced "Wood and Coal," and I could just make out the untidy, uncozy outlines of wet slab wood and soggy sacks of coal stacked near the gas pumps. When the houses began to be closer together and neater and whiter, the dreary gas pumps became lighted gas stations, and finally once in a while the bus would stop and pant at an intersection while a traffic light geared for a busier time of day, stopped the hurrying impatient north and south traffic and kept it teetering for a full minute at the edge of an empty highway.

At each such stop the Indians' pushing and shoving and giggling became audible but the bus driver, though he muttered angrily, kept the bus moving back and forth like a runner making false starts before a race and to my intense relief didn't take the name of Lord Jesus our God in Heaven in vain, at least not so Mrs. Johnson could hear.

Both children were now asleep, their bodies warm and soft like dough against me, and I must have dozed too, for suddenly we were in downtown Seattle and lights were exploding around me like skyrockets on the Fourth of July. Red lights, blue lights, yellow lights, green, purple, white, orange, punctured the night in a million places and tore the black satin pavement to shreds. I hadn't seen neon lights before. They had been invented, or at least put in common use, while I was up in the mountains and in that short time the whole aspect of the world had changed. In place of dumpy little bulbs sputteringly spelling out Café or Theatre, there were long swooping spirals of pure brilliant color. A waiter outlined in bright red with a blazing white napkin over his arm flashed on and off over a large Café. Puget Sound Power and Light Company cut through the rain and darkness, bright blue and cheery. Cafés, theatres, cigar stores, stationery stores, real estate offices with their names spelled out in molten color, welcomed me to the city. The bus terminal was ringed in light. Portland, New York, San Francisco, Bellingham, Walla Walla, it boasted in bright red. How gay and cheerful and prosperous and alive everything looked. What a wonderful contrast to the bleak, snag-ridden, dark, rainy, lonely vista framed for four long years by the farm windows.

The children had awakened and their glazed, sleepy eyes reflected the lights as they flashed by. Then the faces of Mary and Dede appeared right outside our windows and that was the brightest rocket of all, the *pièce de résistance* of the entire show.

According to real estate standards Mother's eight-room brown-shingled house in the University district was just a modest dwelling in a respectable neighborhood, near good schools and adequate for an ordinary family. To me that night, and always, that shabby house with its broad welcoming porch, dark woodwork, cluttered dining-room plate rail, large fragrant kitchen, easy book-filled firelit living room, four elastic bedrooms—one of them always ice cold—roomy old-fashioned bathrooms, and huge cluttered basement, represents the ultimate in charm, warmth, and luxury. It's something about Mother, who with one folding chair and a plumber's candle, could make the North Pole homey, and it's something about the warmth and loyalty and laughter of a big family.

It's a wonderful thing to know that you can come home anytime from anywhere and just open the door and belong. That everybody will shift until you fit and that from that day on it's a matter of sharing everything. When you share your money, your clothes, and your food with a mother, a brother, and three sisters, your portion may be meagre but by the same token when you share unhappiness, loneliness, and anxiety about the future with a mother, a brother and three sisters, there isn't much left for you.

Two things I noticed immediately. Mother still smelled like violets and Mary still believed that accomplishment was merely a matter of will power.

"I hear that we are sliding into a depression and that jobs are very hard to find," I told Mary about three o'clock the next morning as she and Mother and I sat in the breakfast nook eating hot cinnamon toast and drinking coffee.

Mary said, "There are plenty of jobs but the trouble with most people, and I know because I'm always getting jobs for my friends, is that they stay home with the covers pulled up over their heads waiting for some employer to come creeping in looking for them. Anyway, what are you worrying about, you've got a job as private secretary to a mining engineer."

I said, "But, Mary, I don't know shorthand and I can only type about twenty words a minute." Mary clunked her coffee cup into her saucer and looked directly at me with flashing amber eyes, "Leave the ninety words on the typewriter and the one hundred fifty words a minute in shorthand to the grubs who like that kind of work," she said. "You're lucky. You have a brain. Use it! Act like an executive and you get treated like an executive!" (And usually fired, she neglected to add.)

It was very reassuring, in spite of a sneaking suspicion I had that if put to a test I would always prove out the grub type, not the executive, and that only by becoming so proficient in shorthand that I could take down thoughts, would I be able to hold down even a very ordinary job.

"I have been planning to go to nightschool," I told Mary.

"Not necessary at all," she said. "Experience and self-confidence are what you need and you'll never find them at nightschool. Have you ever taken a look at what goes to nightschool? No? Well, they aren't executives, I'll tell you that. Now go to bed and forget about shorthand. I'll always be able to find us jobs doing something and whatever it is I'll show you how to do it." That was Mary's slogan at home. Downtown it was, "Just show me the job and I'll produce a sister to do it." And for some years, until Dede and Alison were old enough to work and she had figured how to fit Mother into her program, I was it. That night I dreamed I was going to play in one of Miss Welcome's recitals and I hadn't practised and didn't know my piece.

From two o'clock Saturday afternoon until two o'clock Monday morning, the house was filled with people. Mary, who was very popular, was being intellectual so her friends were mostly musicians, composers, writers, painters, readers of hard dull books, and pansies. They took the front off the piano and played on the strings, they sat on the floor and read aloud the poems of Baudelaire, John Donne, and Rupert Brooke, they put loud symphonies on the record player and talked over them, they discussed politics and the state of the world, they all called Mother "Sydney" and tried in vain to convince her that she was prostituting her mind by reading the *Saturday Evening Post.* Mother said, "Yes?" and ignored them.

One of Mary's favorite friends, a beautiful brilliant Jewish boy, played "With a Song in My Heart," on the strings of the piano and told me I had a face like a cameo and I grew giddy with excitement. Anne and Joan loved the laughter and the people too, and Saturday night when I was putting them to bed, Anne said, "Oh, Betty, I just love this fambly!"

Sunday afternoon, Mary's new boss, a Mr. Chalmers, who was coming to Seattle to instill some new methods into the lumber industry, called from New Orleans and talked to Mary for almost an hour. The conversation left her overflowing with enthusiasm.

"At last I've found the perfect job," she said. "Mr. Chalmers is much more of an executive thinker than I am. 'Don't bother me with details and hire all the help you need,' he said. He also asked me to find him a bootlegger, one who handles Canadian liquor, put his daughters in school, send for his wife, introduce him to the right people, have his name put up at the best clubs, get him an appointment with a dentist to make him a new bridge, open charge accounts with the Yellow Cab Company, a florist, a stationery store, office furniture company, and a catering service, and I'm to rent him a suite of offices in a building in the financial district."

We all listened to Mary with admiration and I asked her if in this new wonderful well-paid secretarial job, typing and shorthand had been requirements.

Before answering, Mary lit a cigarette, pulling her mouth down at one corner in true executive fashion, a new gesture, then said, "Betty, for God's sake stop brooding about short hand. There were hundreds of applicants for this job, among them many little white-faced creeps who could take shorthand two hundred words a minute and could type so fast the carriage smoked, but who cares? Do they know a good bootlegger?" "Do you?" someone asked, and Mary said, "No, but I will by the time Chalmers gets here. To get back to shorthand, the world is crawling with people who can take down and transcribe somebody else's good ideas. We're lucky, we've got ideas of our own." It was certainly nice of her to say we.

3

"Mining Is Easy"

MONDAY MORNING MY HANDS TREMBLED LIKE JELLO AS I ADjusted the neat white collar on the sage-green woolen office dress Mary had lent me. I was very thin, pale with fright, and with my long red hair parted in the middle and pulled tightly back into a knot on the nape of my neck, I thought I looked just like one of the white-faced creeps Mary had derisively described. Mary said I looked very efficient and very sophisticated. Mother, as always, said that we both looked beautiful and not to worry about a thing. I kissed the children, who didn't cling to me as I had expected, and started out the front door to catch a streetcar.

I had been anticipating just this moment over and over and over ever since I had gotten Mary's wire. I knew exactly how I would feel waiting on the corner with the other people who were going to work. Breathing the cool, wet spring air and listening to the busy morning sounds of cars starting with tight straining noises, of children calling to each other as they left for school, dogs barking and being called home, a nickel clickety-clacking into the paper box, footsteps hurrying grittily on cement. I was going to swing on a strap, sway with the streetcar and think about my wonderful new job. Life was as neatly folded and full of promise as the morning newspaper.

My reverie was interrupted by Mary, who called out, "Where are you going?" "To catch a streetcar," I said. "Come back," she said. "From now on we ride to work in taxis. Mr. Chalmers wants us to." "Not me," I said. "Only you." Mary said, "Betty, Mr. Chalmers couldn't have me for his private secretary if it weren't for you. Don't you forget that and I'll see that he doesn't. Now sit down and relax, I've called the cab." And that is the way we set off to inject our personalities and a few of our good ideas into the business world.

The mining engineer's office, where I was to work, was on the top floor of a building in the financial district. The other occupants of the building were successful lawyers, real estate men, brokers and lumbermen, most of whom Mary seemed to know quite well.

In the lobby she introduced me to about fifteen assorted men and women and explained that she had just brought me down out of the mountains to take her place as private secretary to Mr. Webster. In her enthusiasm she made it sound a little as though she had had to wing me to get me down out of the trees and I felt that I should have taken a few nuts and berries out of my pocket and nibbled on them just to keep in character.

When we got out of the elevator, I took Mary to task for this. "Listen, Mary," I said. "I have little enough self-confidence, and your introducing me to all those people in the lobby as the little Mowgli of the Pacific Coast didn't help any." Mary said, "You're just lucky I didn't ask you to show them some of your old arrow wounds. Anyway, what difference does it make? Most of those people have such dull lives I feel it my duty to tell them a few lies every morning just to cheer them up."

Mr. Webster's offices were luxuriously furnished in mahogany and oriental rugs and had a magnificent view of the docks, Puget Sound, some islands and the Olympic Mountains. My little office was also the reception room and after Mary had showed me where to put my hat and coat and how to get the typewriter to spring up out of the desk, I wanted to sit right down and begin to practise my typing.

Mary would have none of it. Sitting herself down at Mr. Webster's desk and lighting a cigarette, she said, "Stop being so nervous and watch me. Learn how to act in an office." I said, "I wouldn't be so nervous if I knew what time Mr. Webster gets here." Mary said, "Oh, he's out of town and won't be back for two weeks." My sigh of relief almost blew some rocks off his desks. "Does he know about me?" I asked. "Nope," said Mary, opening the mail, glancing at it and throwing most of it in the wastebasket. "You're going to be a surprise."

The phone rang. Mary answered it in a low well-modulated voice and Standard English. "Mr. Websteh's office, Miss Bahd speaking," she said. Somebody on the other end of the wire said something and Mary said, "Well, you big stinker, what do you expect when you don't call until eightthirty Saturday night?"

While she talked to the big stinker, who she later said could take her to lunch, I roamed around the office, examining the files, looking into drawers, opening cupboards, unrolling maps, reading the titles of some of the books in the enormous mining library, and looking at the view.

When someone came into the reception room, Mary, still on the phone, waved to me imperiously to see who it was. It was a large fat man who held up a little canvas bag and shouted, "Where's Webster?" I said, "Mr. Webster is out of town, may I help you?" The fat man said, "Sister, I got the richest placer property the world has ever seen!" He went on and on and on about available water, smelter reports, equipment needs, etc., and finally handing me the little bag and a business card said, "Just give this sample of ore to Webster and tell him to call me the minute he gets in town," and left.

I waited until Mary had finished three more telephone calls, one to the manager of a building across the street, demanding a suite of offices with a good view, one to a florist giving a standing order for daily fresh flowers for the new office, the other to an office supply firm for *two* executives' desks, largest size, and then I gave her the business card and the ore sample.

"The man said that this is the greatest placer property the world has ever seen," I said excitedly. "Do you suppose we should telegraph Mr. Webster?" Mary glanced at the card and with a bored look dropped both it and the sample of ore into the wastebasket.

"Mary Bard," I said, "what are you doing?" She said, "I'm doing just what Mr. Webster would have done. In other words I'm saving him trouble, which is the first duty of a good private secretary. Now I'm going to pound a few facts into that humble little head of yours. In the first place you have *two* of the *greatest assets* a mining engineer's secretary could possibly have. *A,* your father was a mining engineer; *B,* you have seen a mine and when Webster talks about an assay you don't think he's referring to a literary composition. The rest is all a matter of common sense and practice. Here's the telephone number of the smelter, here's Webster's address. Open and read all the mail and keep a record of all telephone calls."

"What about visitors like the fat man?" I asked. Mary said, "For a while you can keep all that trash and show it to Webster, after you get more used to things you'll be able to tell the crackpots from the real mining men. Or at least you can pretend you can," she added honestly.

"What about the home office," I said. "They're one of the richest corporations in the world. How will they feel about me?" "They'll never know about you," said Mary. "We're both Miss Bard and to the richest corporation in the world, a Miss Bard more or less at one hundred dollars a month in the Seattle office isn't that much." She snapped her fingers and we went out for coffee.

In spite of Mary's vehement and reiterated assurance that I possessed the *two greatest assets* the secretary of a mining engineer could possibly have, I had an uneasy feeling that Webster's reaction to a secretary who could neither type nor take shorthand, might be that of a hungry man who day after day opens his lunchbox and finds it empty.

So, with feverish intensity, I tried to remedy the situation. I practised my typing, I studied shorthand, I memorized the number of spaces to indent on a letter, I tried to remember which was the right side of the carbon paper and I prayed that Mr. Webster would begin every letter with weareinreceiptofyoursofthe, the way all John Robert Gregg's business friends did.

Mary said it was all a waste of time. She told me to read some of the geology books, to study the maps, to thumb through the files and to try and get the feeling of mining. I suggested that I might buy a miner's lamp and wear it in the office and she said it would go further with Mr. Webster than that scared look I put on every time I opened the office door.

I couldn't help the scared look, I felt like an impostor, and as the days succeeded each other and the return of Mr. Webster grew more and more imminent, every morning when I took out my key and inserted it in the lock of the door marked menacingly CHARLES WEBSTER, MINING ENGINEER, I drew a deep quivering breath and prayed that Mr. Webster's office would be empty.

Then one morning when I opened the office door there in Mr. Webster's office, sitting at Mr. Webster's big mahogany desk was Mr. Webster. I almost fainted. Mr. Webster had very brown skin and nice bright blue eyes and he called out, "Who are you?" So scared I had tears in my eyes, I said, "Well, ah, well, ah, I'm Mary's sister Betty and I'm your new secretary." He said, "Where's Mary?" "Oh, she's in an office right across the street," I said, adding hurriedly, "She said that if you wanted to dictate to call her and she'd come right over." He said, "This all sounds very much like Mary. Well, as long as she's deserted me she doesn't deserve the present I've brought her. Here," and he handed me a huge green barley sugar Scottie dog.

I took the dog and because I was nervous and felt guilty, I was too effusive in my thanks and kept saying over and over and over, "Oh, Mr. Webster, you shouldn't have done it!" as though he were trying to force a diamond anklet on me. Then, God knows why, but in an effort to offer further proof of my gratitude, I bit into the candy dog and one whole enormous green leg came off in my mouth just as Mr. Webster, who by this time was sick to death of me and obviously trying to think of some kind way to get rid of me, looked up to ask if there had been any mail or calls. I couldn't answer, I just stood there in my hat and coat, trying desperately to maneuver the huge leg around in my mouth, my eyes full of tears and green drool running down my chin. It was not a sight to inspire confidence in my efficiency. In fact, if I had been Mr. Webster I wouldn't have kept me if I'd been able to produce degrees in shorthand, typing, mining, geology, and map drawing, but Mr. Webster was very kind and had been a good friend of Daddy's so he went over and looked out the windows at the mountains while I pulled myself together.

As I look back on it now, it would have been cheaper and less of a strain for Mr. Webster to have dispensed with me and hired a cleaning woman, because, eager though I was to help, all I could do well was to dust the furniture and his ore samples and clean out cupboards. I typed a few letters but I was so nervous that I made terrible mistakes, used reams of paper, and the finished product usually had little holes in it where my eraser had bitten too deeply.

Mr. Webster, upset by the holes in his letters but not wanting to hurt my feelings, said I was much too thin and ordered a quart of milk to be delivered to the office every morning and at ten and three came out and stood over me while I drank a glass. This embarrassed me so I gulped the milk down in huge glurping swallows, which brought on terrible gas pains and several times made me belch loudly into the telephone when I was following Mary's instructions and trying to use Standard English.

The first day Mr. Webster was back he took Mary and me to lunch at a small French restaurant in an alley. While we ate goslings en casserole and drank Chablis, Mary told him that he had nothing to worry about because she had figured out everything. Whenever he wanted to dictate he was to tell me and I would call her on the phone and while she took his dictation I would go over and answer her phone. To my intense relief Mr. Webster laughed and said that he thought it was a wonderful scheme, and it did work out very well until Mary's very demanding boss arrived in town and it became harder and harder for her to get away.

Then Mr. Webster suggested that I take his easier dictation and I did and one morning when I had written "dead sir" and "kinkly yours" on a letter, he offered to send me to nightschool to learn shorthand and typing. I told him that I would like to go but I didn't think that Mary would approve and he said, "Betty, my dear girl, you and Mary are entirely different personalities and anyway she is a whizz in both shorthand and typing."

So, I went to nightschool, which Mr. Webster paid for at the rate of fifteen dollars a month, and studied shorthand and typing. My shorthand teacher, a small sandy man with a nasal voice and thin yellow lips, seemed to be an excellent shorthand teacher because at the end of three months everyone in the class but me could take down and transcribe business letters and little stories.

I couldn't learn shorthand. I got *p's* and *b's* mixed up, I couldn't tell *m* from *n* and even when I could write it I couldn't read it back. I didn't have too much trouble with Mr. Webster's letters because he dictated very slowly and I knew what he was talking about but I was such a miserable failure at nightschool that the only thing that kept me from shooting myself was the amazing fact that, although everyone in the class, and there were forty-two of them, was an expert typist and shorthand dynamo, I was the only one with a job. When I told Mary, she said, "Naturally. I told you you wouldn't find any executives at nightschool."

I never did get to feel like an executive and I never did conquer my obsession that there was a mysterious key to office work which, like holding a letter written in lemon juice over a candle, would one day be revealed to me all at once; but by the end of June I had stopped getting tears in my eyes when Mr. Webster called me for dictation; the letters I typed had fewer, smaller holes in them, I occasionally got the right side of the carbon paper so the copy was on onion skin instead of inside out on the back of the original letter; I could sometimes find things in the files and I had almost finished the maps.

The maps and the files were the worst things I did to dear, kind Mr. Webster. I never was able to figure out the filing system; why letters were sometimes filed by the name of the man who wrote them, sometimes by the name of a mine, sometimes in a little black folder marked *Urgent* and sometimes in a drawer marked *Hold*.

Of course, if I'd stopped batting around the office like a moth around a nightlight, had read the correspondence and asked a few intelligent questions, I might have learned the secret of the filing system, but I didn't. I operated on the theory that always hurrying wildly, never asking questions and shutting up Mr. Webster with "I know, I know," any time he tried to volunteer any information, were proof of great efficiency on my part. Because of this unfortunate state of affairs, Mr. Webster is still looking for things.

I'd pick up a letter, notice that the letterhead was Fulton Mining Company or that it was signed by a man named Thompson, so eeny, meeny, miney, mo—it would go either in *F* or *T.* Then Mr. Webster would ask for that letter on the Beede Mine and I would look under *B,* under *Urgent,* under *Hold,* under *M,* under my desk, under his, and finally days later, quite by accident, would find it under *T* or *F* because the Fulton Mining letter, written by Thompson, was *about* the Beede Mine.

It is hard now, for me to believe that I was that stupid, but I was, and it was easy for me. Take the matter of the maps.

One rainy, dull morning, when Mr. Webster was away on a short trip and I was flitting around the office, I happened to bump into the map case. Now there was a messy thing. Thousands of maps all rolled sloppily and stuffed in the case every which way.

"How does poor dear Mr. Webster ever find anything?" I said, opening the glass door and settling myself for a good thorough cleaning job. Now, a mining engineer's maps, like an architect's drawings or a surgeon's living patients, are the visual proof that he did graduate from college, has examined the property, and does know what he is doing.

"Here is the ore deposit," Mr. Webster would say, spreading out his maps and indicating little specks. "By tunneling through this mountain, changing the course of this river, bringing a railroad in here and putting a smelter here . . ." So, I unrolled all the maps, cleaned the smudges off them with an artgum eraser, and rolled them all up again, each one separately and each one with an elastic band around it. Then I sorted them according to size, the littlest ones on the top shelf, the medium-sized ones on the next shelf, the biggest one on the bottom. I was very tired and dirty when I finished but I glowed with accomplishment.

That night at dinner I told Mary about my wonderful progress at Mr. Webster's; how I took dictation, found things in the files and had even sorted his maps. Mary said, "I told you mining was easy."

Then Mr. Webster returned from his trip, accompanied by an important man from Johannesburg, South Africa, and for the first time since I had been working there, asked me to find him some maps. "Get me those maps on the Connor mine," he said and I jogged happily over to the map case but when I got there I realized that with my new filing system, it wasn't the name of the map that counted but the size.

I called to Mr. Webster, "What size is the Conner map?"

He answered rather testily, "What do you mean, 'what size'? It's that big bundle near the front on the bottom shelf."

My spirits fell with a thud that rattled the glass doors of the map case as I suddenly realized that the big bundle near the front on the bottom shelf was now about twenty-five bundles on all the shelves. So Mr. Webster, who had heretofore always filed the maps and knew exactly where each one had been, the man from Johannesburg and I spent the rest of the day on the floor by the map case unrolling maps. We had found most of the Conner mine by eight-thirty and I was released.

The next morning there was a note on my desk. "Betty: Have gone to Denver, will be back Monday—please return maps to their original confusion—Webster." Before I finished, however, the home office closed the Seattle office and mining was over.

4

"So Is Lumber"

"YOU THOUGHT YOU COULDN'T LEARN MINING," MARY TOLD ME when she installed me as her assistant in the office across the street. "There's nothing to lumber, it's just a matter of being able to divide everything by twelve."

"What about Mr. Chalmers?" I asked. "Does he know you've hired me?"

"He knows that I've hired an extremely intelligent young lady who has spent the last four years practically living in logging camps in the greatest stand of timber in the United States and anyway what's it to him? You're my assistant. Go sharpen this pencil."

I was worried. I hadn't yet met Mr. Chalmers and, though I knew that he didn't want to be bothered with details, I had no assurance that he would consider Mary's new assistant at $125 a month, a detail; especially when he learned that in Seattle most female office workers were paid from seven to twenty dollars a week and $125 a month was considered a *man's* salary, except in a few rare instances where a woman with years of experience showed terrific and unusual efficiency.

I was quite sure that as soon as Mr. Chalmers found out about me he would fire me, but what worried me more was a fear that he would also fire Mary for having hired me. Of course, I was reckoning without Mary or Mr. Chalmers. Mr. Chalmers was not a figment of Mary's imagination, requiring Joe Doner to prove him, but was a real, unique individual whose sole aim actually was to be the biggest-time executive that had ever hit Seattle, no matter

46

what it cost the lumbermen, and in Mary he had certainly chosen the right person to help him.

About ten-thirty Mr. Chalmers made his entrance into, or rather descent upon, the office. The door to the outer office crashed open and banged shut; the door to the conference room crashed open and banged shut; the door to his private office crashed open and banged shut; then the buzzer on Mary's desk began to buzz with short angry bursts like a bee in a tin can. I flinched nervously at each slamming door and jumped to my feet at the first ring of the buzzer.

Mary, who was checking some lumber reports, didn't even look up. The angry buzzing continued. Finally, anxiously I asked, "Do you want me to see what he wants?" Mary said, "I already know what the old stinker wants. He wants somebody to yell at because he is nasty in the morning. Come on, let's get a cup of coffee. He'll be pleasanter when we get back."

She picked up the phone, pressed a bell at the side of the desk and said, "Mr. Chalmers, I'm going out for coffee, will you please take any calls?" There was a roar from the inner office and the phone sputtered like water on a hot stove, but Mary put it back on the hook, beckoned to me and we skittered out of the office and down the stairs to the next floor to wait for the elevator. While we waited we could hear via the elevator shaft and the stairwell, Mr. Chalmers charging around on the floor above, slamming doors and bellowing, "Miss Bard! Miss BARD!"

I certainly did not look forward to meeting him and couldn't understand how Mary could laugh and talk and eat a butterhorn in the coffee shop while that monster waited for her upstairs. She said not to worry, he would be cooled off by the time we got back, and he was.

Mary dragged me, quivering, in to introduce me, and Mr. Chalmers, looking like a hair seal with a cigar in its mouth, smiled at me kindly and said, "Humph!" For the next two or three days he buzzed for me (my signal was two short) to get him drinks of water, to open and close the windows, to pick up scraps of paper off the floor, to lower the Venetian blinds four inches, and to un-lock the safe and get him his whisky. Once he asked me some questions about logging on the Olympic Peninsula and when I was able to answer he seemed terribly pleased and retaliated with stories of logging in the cypress swamps.

I still don't know exactly what Mr. Chalmers was doing or what the office was for but it was a very pleasant place to work. When I wasn't answering the buzzer and ministering to the many little personal needs of Mr. Chalmers, I was in the outer office typing reports for Mary, learning to cut stencils, running the mimeograph, or working on a story we were writing, called "Sandra Surrenders."

Then one day Mr. Chalmers buzzed for me and when I came eagerly in, dustcloth in hand, instead of ordering me to kill a fly or empty the ash trays, he announced that starting the next morning, I was to spend all my time in the Seattle Public Library reading everything that had been written on the Sherman Anti-Trust Act.

He didn't tell me what he had in mind and I was too timid to ask him, so I asked Mary. She wrinkled her forehead in a puzzled way and said, "It sounds as if I might have told him that you had studied law. Oh, well, don't worry about it, you've got as good a brain as he has, which isn't saying much for you. Go on up and read everything you can find, take notes and write a report. He'll never look at it but he'll be very pleased at your industry."

So, for the next week or two, feeling as though I were still in college trying for straight A's, I dutifully spent my days in the library reading and taking notes and when I handed Mr. Chalmers an original and two copies of the voluminous report, he, obviously having forgotten who I was or what I was doing, glanced at it and put it in the bottom drawer of his desk then gave me a long lecture on Pitman shorthand, which he wrote and I didn't.

A week after the Sherman Anti-Trust laws had been disposed of, Mr. Chalmers announced one morning that from then on I was to read the *Wall Street Journal, The Banker's Digest,* and a couple of other financial papers, pick out all items of importance and interest and relay them weekly, by means of an *interesting,* he stressed this word vehemently, bulletin to all the lumbermen in the State of Washington. Friday I was to assemble my material, write it up and leave it on his desk for him to peruse and digest (and confuse and insert "point of fact" every other word); Saturday morning I was to cut the stencils, run them off on the mimeograph, and assemble and mail the bulletin.

In actual fact, I read all the boring financial magazines, but I shook everything I had read up in a big bag and issued in my own words and well-seasoned with my own personal prejudices, a bulletin as to the state of the world's finances. I remember one bulletin that I headed, "War with Japan Inevitable!" I don't know where this dope got that dope.

Mr. Chalmers, who never took the trouble to read any of the magazines or to check my facts, used to make huge bluepencil marks around single words and then quote Matthew Arnold and Emerson at me to prove that other words would more accurately convey the exact shade of meaning I had in mind. I was reasonably sure that none of the lumbermen read my dull bulletin and I was also reasonably sure that no one of them would come storming into the office and demand a showdown because I had said money instead of pelf, or Mammon, or lucre, but I didn't dare argue with Mr. Chalmers, who was at his worst on Saturday morning.

In the meantime, or interim or interregnum, Mary took Mr. Chalmers' dictation, arranged bouquets of lovely out-of-season flowers for his desk and hers, ordered his whisky from Joe the bootlegger, and left me alone with him in the office more and more.

He would buzz for her and I would answer and he would roar, "Where's Mary?" and I would tell him that she was out paving the way for him to meet the right people and he would say, "Humph, well as long as you're here, lower that Venetian blind three and five-eighths inches, empty this ash tray, and fill my pen." When I had finished, he would say, "Betty, did I ever tell you about the time I organized the lumber industry in Louisiana?" and I would say no and he would say, "Sit down," and I would and hours later when Mary returned, he would be pouring little drinks of bourbon and tap water and I would be listening to Volume xvii, Chapter 32 of *Mr. Chalmers Is Smarter Than Anyone in the World, Living or Dead.* Lumber was a lot of fun.

Occasionally Mr. Chalmers became mildly irritated at Mary and me and threatened to tear us apart, tendon by tendon. One such outburst was precipitated by his being unusually unreasonable and hateful all week long, then leaving for Chicago by plane without his teeth, which he had carelessly left at his club. "Go to Athletic Club and airmail me bridge," he wired Mary. "You can starve to death, you disagreeable old bastard," said Mary, throwing the telegram in the wastebasket. "Mary, send bridge or you are fired!" was the next wire. Mary crumpled it up and threw it out the window. "Am calling tonight," was the next wire so Mary airmailed his teeth that afternoon and when he called that evening she was like honey and told him that she had mailed his teeth the minute she had gotten his first wire and she did hope he was chewing and having a good time.

The very closest we came to being fired was on the occasion of Mr. Chalmers' visit to New Orleans and arrival back at the office a week ahead of schedule. It was a very hot summer afternoon and Mary and I, who had received a rather unexpected invitation to dine on board a battleship, were in Mr. Chalmers' private office freshening up. We had removed and washed out our underwear and stockings and pinned them to the Venetian blinds to dry. We had steamed out the wrinkles in our silk print office dresses by holding them over Mr. Chalmers' basin while we ran the hot water full force, and had hung them on hangers on the Venetian blinds.

We had washed and pinned up our hair and finally in bare feet and petticoats were taking refreshing sponge baths in Mr. Chalmers' basin, when there were knocks on the outer door, which we had locked. Mary called through the transom, "Mr. Chalmers is in conference—who is it?" It was a telegram so she told the boy to put it through the mail slot. A little later, Mr. Chalmers' lawyer knocked and she told him that she had torn her dress and was in her petticoat mending it and he laughed and said that he had some papers for Chalmers but she could get them in the morning.

"Everything is just working out perfectly," we exulted as we felt our underwear and stockings, which were almost dry, and I ran the water for my bath. Suddenly there was a loud pounding at the outer door. "Shall I call through the transom?" I asked, taking my right foot out of the basin full of warm suds. "No," Mary said, "it's almost five. We'll pretend we've gone home." But the knocking continued, getting louder and louder and even sounding, to my sensitive ears, as if it might be accompanied by hoarse shouts. "Maybe I'd better put on my coat and see who it is," I said nervously. "I wouldn't if I were you," Mary said, "it might be some out-of-town lumberman who has read your financial bulletin." We both laughed gaily but I was very relieved when the knocking finally stopped.

Mary was patting eau de Cologne on her neck and shoulders and I was drying my left thigh on the last of Mr. Chalmers' hand towels, when I thought I heard the outer-office door open and voices. "Did you hear the door open?" I asked Mary. "No," she said.

I heard voices again and this time they sounded as if they were coming from the conference room. "Mary," I said, "do you hear anything?" Spreading her makeup out on Mr. Chalmers' desk, she said, "Stop being so nervous! You know we're going to a lot of trouble considering the fact that all the Navy men I've ever met were liars, short, and married." We both laughed.

Just then the door of Mr. Chalmers' office opened and in charged Mr. Chalmers like a bull from a chute at the rodeo. His face was pomegranate-colored, his cigar hung from his lips like brown fringe, and his voice was a hoarse croak as he roared, "Who locked the door? What in hell's going on here?"

Behind him stood the building office manager, swinging some keys and looking embarrassed. Mary, sitting at Mr. Chalmers' desk in petticoat and pin curls with all her makeup spread out on his blotter and her pocket mirror propped against his inkstand, said quite calmly, "You're not supposed to be here."

Mr. Chalmers dropped his briefcase and his suitcase and yelled hoarsely, "I'm not supposed to be here? What in hell's going on?"

Mary said, "You said you weren't coming back until next week."

Chalmers said, "I wired you this morning."

Mary said, "I didn't get it."

He said, "Of course you didn't. I found it unopened under the door. Here," and he threw the telegram at her. "Now clean up this Goddamn Chinese laundry and get out! You're fired!" He tripped over his briefcase, kicked it, and slammed through the door.

Mary and I finished dressing, wiped up the spilled bathwater and eau de Cologne, lowered the Venetian blinds, put Mr. Chalmers' mail on his desk, and prepared to leave. Perhaps because Mr. Chalmers was hot and tired and we looked so clean and fresh, he rescinded the order about firing and in gratitude we took him to dinner with us on board the battleship, where he had some excellent Scotch and sat next to the Executive Officer, who turned out to be a bigger "and then I said to Andrew Mellon" and "Otto Kahn said to me" than Mr. Chalmers.

By the end of six months, Mr. Chalmers' office force had been increased to include, besides Mary and me, a certified public accountant and a liaison man between Mr. Chalmers and the lumbermen. I was still killing Mr. Chalmers' flies and filling his fountain pen but I had to take dictation for the liaison man and so Mr. Chalmers was sending me to nightschool for fifteen dollars a month.

For reasons of pride I did not go back to the nightschool Mr. Webster had sent me to, but chose one further uptown, nearer to my streetcar. My teacher, a nice motherly woman, grew exasperated with my inability to read my notes and made me read them back aloud in front of the whole class, night after dreary night.

I grew to dread nightschool and probably would have quit if it hadn't been for the woman who sat across from me. She worked for an insurance company, dressed in black crepe, musky perfumes, and big hats and told me that every single good job in the city of Seattle required that the girl also sleep with her boss. "And they won't get me to do that for eighty dollars a month," she told me as she furiously practised her shorthand. "But they might get me for a lot less!" I told myself, as I tried desperately to figure out whether I had written pupil, purple, purposeless, billious, blurb, or babble.

The CPA and the liaison man were very nice but they kept Mary and me so busy we never did get to finish "Sandra Surrenders" and they insisted on taking sides in our fights so that they were seldom on speaking terms with each other and one or the other was always not on speaking terms with one or the other of us.

Mary and I had many violent fights, sometimes even slapping each other, but we made up instantly and it was most disconcerting to come back from lunch and find the fight of the morning still hovering around the office like stale smoke and the accountant and the liaison man wanting to take sides and talk about us, one to the other.

They thought I really meant it when I screamed at Mary, "It's no wonder you're an old maid, for twenty-five years you've always gotten your own way and you think you can boss everybody!" and Mary screamed back, "It's better to be twenty-five years old and unmarried than to shuffle through your old marriage licenses like a deck of cards," or "You haven't done a stroke of work in this office since I came—all you do is smoke and order me around like a slave," and "I will continue to order you around like a slave as long as you act like a slave, think like a slave, and smell like a slave."

By the fall of 1932, the depression was very bad and we were sure that the lumbermen weren't going to put up with Mr. Chalmers much longer. Now I grew more and more conscious of the aimlessness and sadness of the people on the streets, of the Space for Rent signs, marking the sudden death of businesses, that had sprung up over the city like white crosses on a battlefield, and I lifted up myself each day timidly and with dread expecting to find the dark despairing mask of unemployment staring at me.

Mary was so unworried about it all that she took two hours for lunch, another hour or two for coffee, and when Mr. Chalmers finally took her to task, she told him that the interesting part of his job was over and she guessed she'd leave and sell advertising.

Then for a few terrible weeks, until one of the lumbermen sent over his girl, I had to stop dusting and filling pens and take Mr. Chalmers' volumes of dictation. He mumbled so and used so many enormous and obscure words that I could never read my notes and had to bring them home at night for Mary to transcribe. She was always able to read my shorthand but finally doing both our jobs must have palled for she told me that I should quit Chalmers and sell advertising. With great tact she said that red-haired people were not meant for dull office work and instead of bawling because I couldn't learn shorthand, why didn't I use some of my many other talents.

I said that considering that Mr. Chalmers had put up with me this long and had paid my way to nightschool, I thought I should stay until the end. And I did, in spite of Mr. Chalmers' telling me many times that the depression was all my fault, the direct result of inferior people like me wearing silk stockings and thinking they were as good as people like him.

One day my brother Cleve came in to take me to lunch and caught the tail end of one of these little talks. "The only way to get rid of the poor is to line them up against a wall and shoot them," said kind old Mr. Chalmers, chewing his cigar. "I feel the same way about sons of bitches like you," said my tall, handsome, red-haired brother smiling in the doorway. Chalmers went into his office and slammed the door shut. Cleve and I went to lunch.

Two days later, the office closed and its closing, like the death of an invalid who has hovered for long wearisome months at the brink of death, brought relief rather than sorrow. I cleaned out my desk, throwing away the accumulation of half-filled bottles of hand lotion, packages of personal letters, dried-up bottles of nail polish, used cakes of soap, broken-toothed combs, and tobaccoy lipsticks, which littered my bottom drawer, and wondered how I would say good-bye to Mr. Chalmers. For, in spite of his holding me personally responsible for the depression, I was fond of him, knew

ANYBODY CAN DO ANYTHING

that his job had been in the nature of his last stand, and worried about what was to become of him.

The closing of Mr. Webster's office meant merely that Webster would be on his own instead of working for a big corporation, and we had celebrated the occasion with club sandwiches and champagne. I didn't expect anything like that from Chalmers, who had chosen to ignore the repeated warnings from the lumbermen or notice the fact that all the office force but me had left for other jobs, but I did expect him, that last day, to admit that it was all over.

He didn't though. At ten-thirty he came slamming and banging into the office, rang the buzzer furiously and demanded that I call Joe the bootlegger and order him a case of Canadian Club. Old Custer was all alone but he was still commanding, still shooting.

I dialed Joe's number and wondered if being out of business would affect our credit. Joe's wife answered. I asked for Joe. She said, "He can't come to the phone. He's dead." I said that I was very sorry and she said, "That's okay, honey, we all gotta go sometime. What did you wish?" I said, "I want to order a case of Canadian Club." She said, "All we got now, honey, is the alcohol and the labels." I wondered if she also had the sand and seaweed with which Joe used to adorn his bottles and offer as final proof that it was the real stuff brought from Canada by water. I told her that I'd talk to Chalmers and call her back and she said, "O.K., honey, I'll be here all day."

I told Chalmers about Joe and he said, "Humph!" put on his hat and left and, though I waited and waited, he never came back. At a little after one I took my package of personal belongings and went home. I never saw Mr. Chalmers again. I called his club and left word for him to call me but he didn't and when I called again I learned he had checked out and left no forwarding address.

Lumber was over.

5

"Nobody's Too Dull or Too Short for My Sister"

MOST FEMALES BETWEEN THE AGES OF THIRTEEN AND FOR-
ty-five feel that being caught at home dateless, especially on a
Friday or Saturday night, is a shameful thing like having athlete's
foot. I used to harbor the same silly notion and many's the lie I've
told to anyone tactless enough to call up at nine-thirty and ask
me what I was doing. "What am I doing?" I'd say, brushing the
fudge crumbs off the front of my pajamas and marking the place
in my book. "Oh, just sitting here sipping champagne and smoking
opium. My date had trouble with his car."

Which is why, now that I've had time to heal, I'm really grateful
to Mary for deciding that along with making me self-supporting,
she would use me as a proving ground for dates.

The first time, however, that I heard Mary, who has a great love
for people, any people, and is not at all critical, which qualities
though laudable in a friend are perfectly awful in a matchmaker,
say, "I can't go but Betty will," I protested.

Mother said, "Remember, Betsy, a rolling stone . . ." Mary, always quick to seize an opportunity, repeated, "Yes, remember a
rolling stone." Only I could tell, after just a few dates, that her real
interpretation of the old saying was, "Come out from under that
stone and no matter how mossy, you're a date for Betty."

As "I can't go but Betty will" became Mary's stock answer to any
phone call, so "Oh, please God, not *him!*" was my usual reaction.

Mary launched my business and social career the same day. The business career with mining, the social career with Worthington Reed, who when he called and asked Mary to lunch was told, "I've already got a date but you can take my sister, Betty." I was surprised and terribly thrilled when, just before twelve, Worthington appeared in a big wrinkled tweed suit, pipe, and raised eyebrow, and said, "Come on, you." He was very handsome and because of his dress, which was so casual it included a few spots and a hole in the heel of one sock, I decided immediately that he was also very intellectual. "Ah, this is the life," I thought ecstatically as I locked the office door. "A job, the city and a brilliant man to take me to lunch." Worthington took my arm as we left the elevator in the basement of the building and I swallowed uncontrollably.

The restaurant too was romantic. Dark woodwork, brick floors, real leather on the seats and backs of the booths; rich warm smells of toasted rolls, roast beef, Wiener snitchzel, and coffee; prosperous customers who looked as if they took long lunch hours; and dim lights that hid the darns in the tablecloths and the shaking of my hands as I lit cigarette after cigarette and tried desperately to assemble enough courage to cast the first stone into the deep pool of silence between Worthington and me.

Frantically I searched around in my mind for something to say. Something sophisticated enough to go with wrinkled tweeds and a pipe. Worthington, who was slouched comfortably back in the booth, seemed very relaxed. He pulled on his pipe and looked over my head at the people entering and leaving the restaurant. Finally, desperately, I said, "My this looks like real leather." "Uppa, uppa, uppa," said Worthington's pipe. "It feels like real leather too," I said, running my hand over the seat. Worthington said nothing. "It smells like real leather, too," I said, leaning over and sniffing. Worthington raised his eyebrow but said nothing.

Some people took the booth next to us. Their shoulders were wet and their faces were rosy and shiny with rain. "Why, it's raining outside," I said, as though it hadn't been for the past five months. Worthington looked at me quizzically. His eyes were a clear French blue with a black ring around the iris. There was a small brown mole in the corner of the right eye. His eyelashes were black and silky. When it seemed suddenly as if he had only one eye, one big eye with two irises, I realized that I had been staring into his eyes and blushed and looked away.

What could I talk about? What besides real leather? I tried to recall some of the brilliant witty things Mary's intellectual friends had said over the weekend but all I could remember was one remark made by an odd boy, who lay around on the floor under the furniture with his eyes closed hating everything. He had said, "Oh God, not Bizet! He's so nauseatingly rococo."

"Do you care for Bizet?" I asked Worthington hopefully. "Biz-who?" he said through his pipe, as the waitress brought rolls and butter. "Bizet," I mumbled, afraid that I had pronounced it wrong, that it should have been Busy, Bizette, or Byzay. Worthington didn't answer so I took a roll and had just started to butter it when suddenly he reached across the table, took a firm grip on my hand, looked into my eyes and said, "Do you have any sexual desires?" Needless to say, for the rest of that lunch hour I never did go back to old rococo Bizet.

"What you need is fun!" Mary said as she hung up the phone after telling somebody named Clara that of course I'd love to go dancing with her Cousin Bill.

"Not when your idea of fun is fighting for my virtue in a pitch-black taxi cab while trying to figure out the German for CUT THAT OUT!"

"Oh, Hans!" Mary said. "Europeans don't have the same attitude toward sex that we do. Anyway, he's gone back to Germany and he is a wonderful dancer."

"He's a wonderful dancer if you don't mind having your bust pinched to music."

Mary said, "Hans was simply charming at the Andersons'. He's a count and one of the Hapsburgs, you know."

I said, "Mary, there were one hundred and fifty people at the Andersons' cocktail party and I'll bet half of them have Hans' fingerprints on them some place. Do you know that he tried to pull my blouse down and kiss my bare shoulder in a *movie*."

Mary said, "Oh, Betty. That's European. They're always kissing each other's shoulders. You've seen the *Merry Widow*."

I said, "I'm not going tonight. You've never seen Clara's Cousin Bill."

Mary said, "Betty, you know Clara, and she and her husband are going. Please, Betsy, just this once and I promise I'll never get you another blind date. Anyway, I only got you a date with Hans because Helen told me that he was going to offer you a wonderful job."

"He did," I said. "Shooting wild goats in Austria. I was to tally the kill and to carry the one sleeping bag."

Mary said, "Anyway, Bill is an American."

I said, "How tall is he?"

Mary said, "He's twenty-seven and sells advertising."

I said, "How tall is he?"

Mary said, "I forgot to ask Clara about that but she says he has a sense of humor."

"I don't care how funny he is," I said. "I'm sick of looking down into some little dandruffy part."

Mary said, "Betty, you know that some of the dates I've gotten you have turned out all right. You've even had a wonderful time occasionally. Please go tonight, I've already told Clara you would and you'll never heal those wounds sitting around home brooding."

"I wasn't brooding," I said. "I was studying shorthand and I'm not worried about those old wounds, my idea is to keep from getting any new ones."

They came for me on the dot of seven. Clara, a little blonde dressed in yellow, was so sallow, so narrow and so flat she looked like a wax bean but she was sweet and very anxious for us all to have a good time. Her husband, Carmen, a large gray real estate man, had simplified the English language to just two words—"poop" and "crap." He used them as common nouns and proper nouns and then by merely adding "ed" and "y" he had verbs, adjectives and adverbs with which to describe in detail, real estate transactions, the resort where he and Clara spent their honeymoon, the "home" they were building, the music and decorations of the nightclub where we went—just everything. For punctuation he used nudges and winks. It gave his conversation a static sound like the Morse code.

Cousin Bill was exactly my height, five feet, seven inches, but we weren't twins because I had on high heels and five feet of him was torso, and his legs looked as if they'd been meant for somebody else.

Bill wore a turquoise blue suit, little pools of spit in the corners of his mouth, and a big pompadour smoothed greasily over a heavy tangle of hair, like a tarpaulin thrown over a brush pile. I thought he was the funniest-looking thing I'd ever seen but I didn't feel like laughing.

Clara and Carmen thought he was funny acting and doubled up convulsively when he pulled the tablecloth over our laps and shouted at me, "Hey, baby, no fair, you've got most of the sheet," or pretended one short leg was shorter than the other short leg when we danced or clapped his hands with the dirty fingernails together and yelled, "Hey, Garsong," to the waiter. After we had danced, we had Chinese food and Cousin Bill further convulsed Clara and Carmen by yelling, "Pass the bug juice, Baby!" or "Who'll have another piece of sea gull," or calling the waiters "Chowmein" or "Foo Young."

Louise's husband's buddy (Louise had gone to high school with Mary and me but I didn't remember her and didn't care) was tall and handsome, had beautiful white teeth, dimples, dried-blood-colored shoes with sharp pointy toes, and a yellow roadster. He took me to a country club for dinner and as he picked tidbits off my plate with his fork, told me that his Mom was his best girl and would always wear his fraternity pin, but he thought a bachelor should have a normal sex life. I told him that if he expected to have a normal sex life he'd have to get that fraternity pin off Mom and dangle it around a little and he said, "Betty, my dear, you're far too cynical for your age."

I learned during those trying times when Mary was getting me dates that most bachelors wanted a normal sex life even under the most abnormal conditions. Some were more eager about sex than others, especially Navy Officers who had been at sea.

Once Mary got our sister Dede, who is very small, a New Year's Eve date with a tiny little Navy Officer. We warned her against regular Navy procedure and her date, like a true little clinger to tradition, immediately told her she looked tired and would she like to rest in his great big old empty hotel room.

Dede told us about it at the nightclub where we convened and when we all laughed, the little Navy Officer became so incensed he crawled under the table and bit the leg of a woman at the next table. The woman screamed and her escort, who happened to be a bootlegger, threw back his coat, disclosing two little guns, and said, "Who done that?" "A member of your United States Navy," said Dede. "And I think it's pretty rotten that he has to go to another table to find a leg he can bite," said Mary's date, a captain in the Marine Corps.

Occasionally Mary would get caught in one of her own traps and for a short time thereafter would be slightly cagey about lonely friends of second cousins of switchboard operators in the offices of former customers.

One such happy occasion was the arrival in town of two young mining engineers, friends of Mr. Webster's, who had been in South America too long. Mr. Webster called Mary at Mr. Chalmers' where we were both working and asked her if we would have dinner and go dancing with his friends. Mary said yes and they could pick us up at seven-thirty at home.

At six or thereabouts, we were sitting in our bathrobes in the breakfast nook drinking coffee and complaining to Mother about how unfairly we were treated everywhere, when the doorbell rang and Alison came out to the kitchen and said that there were two funny-looking men at the door asking for Mary and me.

We went to the door and there were our dates—one with a tiny head like a shriveled brown coconut—one with a huge white melon-shaped dome; both in Norfolk jackets belted in the back, and both with pipes. It hadn't taken as long on the trolley as they thought it would, haha, and they guessed they were a little early. Mary and I asked them in, left Mother to entertain them, and went upstairs to get dressed.

While we dressed, we sent spies downstairs to pick up tidbits of information and report. "They're going to take you on the street-car!" Alison reported in a loud voice. "Oh, God, no," Mary groaned as she fastened the brilliant buckle on the belt of her long green dinner dress. "Was it the Incas who shriveled heads?" Dede asked as she came upstairs to report that little head's name was Chester and big head's Colvin. "Mother likes them, I can tell," Alison reported. "They're talking about Mexico and she's asked them for dinner on Sunday."

"If she likes them so well she can go out with them," Mary said. "I'm not going *anywhere* on the *streetcar!*"

I said, "Oh, yes, you are. You're going to get a taste of what you've been doing to me for months and months."

We went but not on the streetcar because Mary called a cab, but we did go to the Hotel and I drew Colvin with the big head and I guess he'd been in South America for a very long time because we'd been dancing for quite a while before he caught on that the man is supposed to put his arm around the girl—not vice versa. Mary said Chester held her the right way but kept springing up and down on her toes as if she were a diving board and anyway he had bad breath.

At ten-thirty Mary looked at her watch, shrieked, and said, "Mother will die if we aren't home in fifteen minutes," called a taxi and we jumped in and charged it to Mr. Chalmers.

Sunday morning we were delighted to wake up and find four inches of snow on the ground. "No trolleys, no dull little miners!" we thought exultantly. By four-thirty the snow was almost six inches thick, the house was filled with our friends, and Mary and I were giving a demonstration of Chester's and Colvin's dancing techniques, when there were thundering raps, the front door opened, and there, snowcovered and eager, were Chester and Colvin. They had *hiked* out from town. "Nothing to it," they said, stamping the snow off their big laced hiking boots. "Often hiked sixty or seventy miles in South America."

"Any chance of your getting lost?" our gentle little sister Dede asked.

"Unh, unh," said Colvin and Chester simultaneously. "We can find our way anywhere."

When they left about eleven-thirty, Cleve gave them explicit instructions to follow on the return trip, even kindly drawing them a map and explaining that he'd made a couple of minor changes in the regular route—changes involving a detour over the ice floes in the Bering Sea and along the entire coast of the Pribilof Islands. The last we ever saw of them they were standing in the snow under a street light studying Cleve's map.

As time went on and I made friends of my own, Mary had to resort to ruses other than a promise of just plain fun, to get me to go out on some date she had arranged. Sometimes it was the promise of a good job. "Now I'm taking you to this cocktail party so you can meet Pierre," she'd say. "He's very French, quite old, separated from his wife, but he needs a private secretary."

"What for?" I would ask suspiciously.

"What do you think?" Mary would say. "Because he's a very successful broker and his secretary left last week."

"Why?" I would ask.

"How should I know?" Mary would say. "And what difference does it make, do you want a good job or don't you?"

At the time I was painting photographs, or working for a gangster or a rabbit grower, I can't remember which, was eager for a good job, and so I went.

Pierre was small and nimble, smelled of bay rum, had his initials on his cigarettes and, after we were introduced, propelled me over to a corner to talk business. He began the interview by stroking the inside of my bare arm with one finger as though he were honing a razor, and talking about "loff."

After an hour of this I worked my way over to my hostess and asked her if she didn't think I'd been in that corner long enough. She said, "Have you and Pierre settled about the job?"

I said, "Unh, unh, he's been sharpening his finger on my arm and talking about 'loff.'"

She said, "Oh, he's so French. I just adore Pierre. Did he tell you about women being like violins and cellos and plucking the strings?"

"Yep," I said. "For one long hour. Will I have to take that stuff in shorthand?"

She said, "Oh, Betty! Now let's just go talk to Pierre."

We did and Pierre said, "Talk business at a cocktail party? Ne-vaire!" So I had lunch with him the next day. After we had settled ourselves in a booth in an obscure Italian restaurant and Pierre had pulled the dark red velvet curtains, I thought, "Now he'll talk about salaries and bonuses and things like that." I brightened my eyes, firmed my lips and tried to look efficient. Pierre took a bite of breadstick and said, "American women are afraid of loff. They are afraid of loff because they don't know anything about it. They are like children afraid of the dark. You are afraid of loff. You are like a child. You have been married yes, but to an American. In ways of loff you are a virgin."

The waiter brought the antipasto. Pierre took a large bite of anchovy and hot pepper then said, with his mouth full, "You are a sleeping virgin. But once awakened, Betty, my dear, you will be an exciting woman."

I took an hour and a half for lunch, almost got fired from the job I had, and I didn't learn a single thing about Pierre's job. After all, when someone is telling you that you are a potential night-blooming cereus but your insides are all shriveling up like withered vines because of lack of "loff," you can't interrupt and ask things like, "Are you closed on Saturdays?"

I told Mary that I thought I'd forget about Pierre and his mythical job. It wasn't that all his talk about "loff" had made me afraid to work for him, because I had a hunch that Pierre's virile luncheon talk was like the posing on top of a diving tower by a man who can't swim. It was just that I couldn't get him down to cases. I wanted to know how much the job paid, when it started, what the duties were, and if I got a vacation.

Mary said, "You call up Pierre and tell him you will have lunch with him tomorrow and I'll go along and we'll just settle things once and for all." So we did.

We ate in an obscure French restaurant, took two hours for lunch and settled a lot of things but they all had to do with "loff," because just when Mary was getting ready to ask about the salary, Pierre would tell her she was a flaming hibiscus and should wear perfume in her eyebrows.

After we had left Pierre and were walking down the street, Mary said, "Let's go up to his office and see if he has a secretary," so we did and he did. A dusty little woman in a gray cardigan and Ground Gripper shoes, who looked as if she had been there all her life, intended to stay, and had never been interested in "loff."

"I'll bet he's got a wife too," Mary said. And he did. A dusty little woman with gray hair and thin lips, who looked as if she had been there a long time, intended to stay, and had never been interested in "loff."

But there was something worse than having Mary get me dates, I learned; it was having a man, any man, get me a date with a pal. The thing about men is that they establish friendships on such a flimsy bases and they're so unreasonably loyal. "You can't talk that way about Charlie," Johnny'd say. "Charlie's my friend. What if he did throw up on the love seat? He said the shrimps were spoiled."

A man not only doesn't see anything wrong with Charlie throwing up on the love seat, he doesn't notice other details like black patent leather oxfords, a long bob tucked behind ears, turquoise-blue suits, maroon silk socks, or green teeth. Nor does he notice faults such as belching, dipsomania, kleptomania, or nymphomania, remembering old bridge hands, or a vocabulary of seven words, six of them dirty.

To him Charlie is, was, and always will be, "Good old Charlie who got me out of that shellhole," or "Old Fraternity Brother Charlie," or "Old Golf Pal Charlie," or "My Best Friend in High School Charlie," or "Old Outfielder Charlie." Which all adds up to the fact that men are basically much nicer than women but haven't any more idea than a corn borer what constitutes eligibility.

"Hello, Betty, this is Jock [Jock was a current fiancé of Mary's], a pal of mine from California is in town and I thought it would be nice if we all went out on the highway for dinner." This was my first experience and I said yes.

Old pal's name was Stan and his first glaring fault was no chin. None at all. I realize that this didn't keep him from being true blue or from making home runs on the baseball diamond but I had my standards and one of them was all my dates have chins. I said as much to Jock and he exploded.

"Oh, you women make me sick. Stan's one of the whitest guys that ever lived."

I said, "I don't care if he's so white he shines in the dark, he hasn't any chin and he can't dance."

Jock said, "Jesus, women!"

My brother Cleve said, "Now, Betty, John's only been in the penitentiary three times and they never did really prove he shot those seals."

I said, "I don't care about his prison record, I don't care that he sharpens his knife on his tongue, I don't care that he chews tobacco, but I do care that he hasn't seen a white woman in two years and plays tag for real prizes."

Our friend Richard said, "Betty, Osbert, an old college friend of mine, is on his way to Honolulu and I thought we'd all go dancing. I know you'll like Osbert, he's a wonderful guy."

Osbert referred to Anne and Joan as "the tykes and little folks." He called dogs "poochies"—he called Mother "Mom"—he called me "Doll Face" and he called Mary "Ginger." He didn't drink, he didn't smoke and he didn't dance, but when the floor show came on and a girl wearing three strategically-placed very small patches came walking out on her hands under a blue spot, Osbert rammed and shoved his way into the very front row and became so absorbed that he didn't even notice when the man next to him pressed the burning end of his cigar against his sleeve and set him on fire.

After the number was over, Osbert invited the eccentric dancer over to our table for a drink. She came but she turned down the drink with "No thanks, I haven't never smoked or drank." So Osbert ordered for her, at her request, "a chicken sangwidge on whoite bread with all whoite meat."

The fact that she and Osbert were practically engaged before the second floor show was over, didn't hurt my pride any. What bothered me was where he was going to pin his fraternity pin.

6

"I Won't Dance, Don't Ask Me"

FEBRUARY, 1933, WAS A TERRIBLE TIME TO BE OUT OF A JOB.
The HELP WANTED—FEMALE section of the papers offered
"Egg Candler—Piecework basis" and "Solicit Magazine Subscrip-
tions at home." The employment agencies had very few jobs but
were packed to overflowing with applicants—the overflow often
sagging wearily against the walls clear around corners and down
to the elevators.

Every day found a little better class of people selling apples on
street corners and even tips about jobs from friends were embarrassingly unreliable, I learned when I applied for a supposedly
excellent secretarial job and was coldly informed, to my horror,
that they weren't quite ready to interview new applicants as the
former secretary had only just jumped out the window.

Business colleges persisted in the attitude that getting a job
was merely a matter of dressing neatly (which according to their
posters meant wearing a small knot, a short lumpy blue suit, and
medium-heeled black oxfords), being able to write shorthand,
even words like "onomatopoeia" and "psychotherapeutic," 150
words a minute, typewriting without errors or erasures, and not
putting "he don't" or "I seen" in business letters.

Either they didn't know or were ashamed to mention to their
students that in those days when any kind of labor was a glut on
the market, an inexperienced girl, even one with a nice fresh diploma in switchboard, comptometer, mimeograph, dictaphone,
calculator, adding machine, multigraph, business law, business

English, business spelling, shorthand, typewriting, and arm movement handwriting, could seldom get an interview, especially in those low-heeled black oxfords.

How well I remembered my first experience with experience. I was sixteen, it was Christmas vacation and I didn't want to work. I wanted to stay home, paint Christmas cards, dress dolls for Dede and Alison, make Christmas cookies and be cozy. But Mary had tactlessly gotten herself a job and was clogging the Will Call section of every department store in Seattle with partially-paid-for rich gifts for the family; Cleve was delivering packages for a little gift shop and had already brought home Mother's Christmas present, a fruit basket painted gold and orange and bearing on one side, like a huge lichen, an enormous white plaster calla lily; and with such stiff competition I knew I would not be able to hold up my head Christmas morning if I gave the usual "made-it-myselfs" of handkerchief cases, sachets, or my watercolor of "Our Quince Tree in Springtime" slipped into an old picture frame. I had to get a job too.

I asked Mary how to go about it and she said, "Just go down to the department stores and apply. When they say, 'Have you ever worked before,' say, 'Naturally,' and name a store other than the one you're in."

Unfortunately I was too timid to lie and when I made the rounds of the department stores I said, "No experience but willing to learn." "No experience," they scoffed. "Run along—don't waste our time—get out!"

"You can't get a job without experience and you can't get experience without a job," I tearfully told Mother and so she called up her friend Chauncy Randolph, who owned a large department store and told him what good grades I had gotten in school and how nicely I kept my room and he said, "Of course, Sydney dear, we'll find something for Betsy to do. Send her in to see me tomorrow." So I went and Mr. Randolph, who looked and talked like "Deargrandfather," Mother's father, was gracious and charming and escorted me to his employment manager. The employment manager, even though he didn't recognize me as the little worm he had scorned and thrown out of his office the day before, didn't seem overly glad to see me.

"Ever worked before?" he sneered as soon as dear old Mr. Randolph had left.

"Not in a department store," I said humbly.

"Well, what kind of work have you done?" he asked, his pencil poised over some sort of form.

"I've taken care of children and helped around the house," I said.

"Oh, my God!" he said. "What makes you think you'll fit in here?"

I could have said, "Because my mother's a friend of the owner, yah, yah, yah," but I didn't. I got tears in my eyes and said, "I don't know." So the employment manager looked out of the window for a minute or two and then picked up his phone and told somebody named Burke that he had a new girl for the stockroom. Adding, "redheaded friend of Randolph's—no experience of any kind" (deep sigh).

He had just hung up the phone when Mr. Randolph came beaming back to see how we were getting along and to further cement our friendship by taking a little black pocket comb out of his vest pocket, running it through my hair, pinning back several loose locks with a large tortoise shell hairpin, and saying as he surveyed me, "Now we look pretty and neat and are ready for work. I've just checked downstairs and they can use you on the first floor in neck ware. How would you like to sell Spanish shawls, Betsy?"

"Oh, I'd love to," I chirped, "I'm majoring in art in college."

"I know, dear, your mother told me," Mr. Randolph said, taking my arm and leading me toward the elevators. I turned to say good-bye to the employment manager and was alarmed to find him looking exactly like our cat the day we took the baby robin away from him.

I didn't do very well in neckwear. I made many mistakes in my sales slips, especially in addition; I infuriated the buyer by advising customers not to buy the ugly shawls, and I laid away more presents than I could pay for, but I got experience.

The next year when I applied for a job I threw back my shoulders and said, "Experience, of course—two years," and was immediately given a job selling imitation leather goods.

I never did learn to enjoy applying for jobs like Mary did, and I never conquered my fear of employment managers, whose intent glances and prodding questions could crush my ego like an eggshell and expose a quivering and most unemployable me—I even hated the smell of employment offices—the hot, varnishy, old-lunch-baggy, desperate smell—"but at least," I told myself after Mr. Chalmers' office closed, "now I've got experience." I was a private secretary of almost two years' duration and could lower a blind or kill a fly with the best of them.

So I made the rounds of the employment agencies. Mary said, "Remember, tell them you can do anything, and in any language and check *all* the machines."

At the first employment agency I heard the woman at the desk turn down about twenty applicants because of lack of experience. "Sorry, kids," she said, "but these days you gotta have experience."

Instinctively I brightened. But when it came to my turn to be interviewed, the woman glanced at my card, on which I had checked typewriting, shorthand, filing, stencil cutting, legal forms, dictaphone, calculator, switchboard, addressograph, adding machine, multigraph, and bookkeeping, in spite of never having seen most of the machines, and said sadly, "Too old."

"Too old!" I said in amazement. "I'm only twenty-four."

"Sorry," she said. "For general office work, most firms want girls around eighteen."

At the next place I didn't check quite so many machines and the woman offered me a job as cost accountant for a lumber broker. I got as far as the elevator with the little white card and then I began to think about all that dividing everything by twelve to say nothing of trial balances, linear feet, and trying to remember whether it was #2 or #3 that had the knotholes, so I tore up the card and went to the next place.

The next place was crowded but there was a brisk steady movement in and out like cans on a belt going through a labeling machine. "Must be some big plant opening," I heard the woman in front of me say to the woman in front of her. "Everybody's being sent out on a job," I heard another one say jubilantly to her friend.

I filled out my card, lying about my experience and claiming proficiency in even more things like power machine operation, pattern draughting, advertising layouts, and lettering, but when my turn came I saw immediately why everyone was getting a job. The woman at the desk was taking cards out of a file box at her elbow and without looking at either the applicant or the card was sending them out. Little old ladies were handed jobs as usherettes: requirements-age 25 or under, bust 34, waist 25, hips 34; stenographers were sent out as waitresses and factory workers were sent to work in beauty parlors. As she handed out the cards, the woman rolled her eyes and mumbled, "Sure, there's a job for everybody. Sure, I'm just keeping them for my friends. I like to see people out of work, sure I do." The card she handed me said, "Chuck's Speedy Service—tire repair—boy to park cars at night—salary $12.00 a week." The card was dated July 2, 1928.

The next employment agency was across the street and was run by a woman Mary loved, who had gotten her hundreds of jobs. I showed her the card for Chuck's Speedy Service and she said, "That poor old woman's really slipped her trolley—she's always been queer but this depression has finally gotten her. Now let's see, what's come in this morning. Nursemaid, practical nurse, experienced furrier, medical secretary, waitress, and car hop. Things are tough, Betty, they really are. What's Mary doing?"

"Selling advertising," I told her. She said, "Well tell her to scout around for you. You'll stand a lot better chance of getting a good salary."

I said, "Are things really so bad?"

She said, "Things are terrible. A little girl I knew committed suicide and before the papers had been on the street ten minutes the company had had about fifty calls for her job."

I said, "I was one of the calls. A friend of mine told me about the job but neglected to mention why it was open."

"Well, if it's any comfort, the job required bookkeeping experience and I know that's not one of yours or Mary's strong points.

"Well, keep in touch with me and you know I'll call you if anything good comes up."

Even Mary's unofficial employment agency went through a slump that year but we, her steady customers, stayed close to her anyway because just being around her was so invigorating and gave us so many new slants on the employment situation.

"More girls have lost their jobs because of red fingernail polish, than for any other reason," Mary told Dede one day, pounding on the table in a tearoom so emphatically to prove her point that a muffin bounced into the cream pitcher.

"Absolutely the only way to get a job," she announced another time, "is to pick out the firm you want to work for, then march right in and announce that you are going to work there because they need you."

I said, "What if they say they do not?"

Dede said, "Show them your colorless nail polish. They'll hire you."

Another time when she wanted me to take a job as a practical nurse, Mary said that there was no point in even trying to get an office job any more—that girls in offices were past history—that from now on everything was to be machines.

Somewhere in between red fingernail polish and the machine age, Mary got me several different jobs. The first she heard about from a friend of an office boy who used to work for a shipping firm she sold advertising to. The job was described as being private secretary to a mining engineer, which at the time seemed too good to be true.

The mining engineer was staying at a small but elegant hotel and we were to meet him at two o'clock on the mezzanine. We repaired to Mary's advertising agency to wash our faces and put on fresh makeup and for a briefing on my *two greatest assets.*

At exactly two o'clock we appeared in the mezzanine lounge, rainsoaked but clean and ready to lie and say I could do anything.

The mining engineer, a Mr. Plumber, who was not only very prompt, but had aristocratic silvery hair and a firm handshake, got right down to business.

"Do you like to dance?" he asked me.

"Yes, I do," I said.

"Do you have some girl friends who also like to dance?" he asked.

I looked over at Mary and she was shaking her head and spelling something out with her lips. I said, "I thought this was a secretarial job."

Mr. Plumber reached over and patted my knee and said, "It is, haha, but, haha, you girls will work at the placer mine, haha, and the boys down there like to dance in the evenings and would a little girl like you be afraid to stay up at a beautiful mountain camp in California with a lot of handsome young engineers sitting around the campfire in the evening strumming guitars and singing?"

I was just going to say, "Haha, I should say a little girl like me wouldn't. When do we start and can I bring the children?" when Mary grabbed my arm, stood us both up and said, "Come on, Betty, we'll be late for that appointment. Mr. Plumber, the job sounds fascinating but we'll have to talk it over with the family."

He said, "Fine, fine and what about your girl friends?"

Mary said, "We'll send them down to see you."

Mary kept a firm grip on my arm but didn't say anything until we got to the lobby. Then she rushed into a phone booth and began dialing furiously. "What are you doing?" I asked. She said, "Calling the Better Business Bureau. That man's a white slaver. Secretaries, indeed. He's shipping prostitutes to California."

"How come California?" I asked. "I thought they had a lot of their own."

"The Orient," Mary hissed only now that she was on the trail of the biggest white slave ring in America she said, "Oddient."

But the Better Business Bureau didn't get the point at all. They kept talking about interstate commerce and they wanted Mary to come down and get a lot of forms for Mr. Plumber to fill out. Finally in exasperation Mary said, "Oh, my God!" hung up and went up to see a friend of ours who was a lawyer.

He said, "Probably just some lonely old buzzard who wants to meet some girls."

Mary said, "Don't be ridiculous, Andy. This man's a white slaver. Why he didn't even ask Betty if she could type. All he was interested in was whether or not she could dance."

Andy said, "Maybe he's a front man for Arthur Murray."

"No wonder this country's rotten to the core!" Mary said. "You business men are such ostriches you refuse to recognize the fact that eighty per cent of our high school graduates are being shipped to the Orient as prostitutes."

"Do they require a diploma before shipment?" Andy asked, and Mary said, "You wouldn't do anything about a white slave ring if it was operating in your desk drawer," and slammed out of the office. She was very pleased the next day to be able to call Andy and report that the Better Business Bureau had called her and told her that Mr. Plumber had checked out of the hotel, minus his brace of secretaries who could dance, and had left no forwarding address.

The next morning, I was in the store closet under the basement stairs, covered with cobwebs and surrounded by old dance programs, photographs, boxes of broken beads, all my college art work, and all our old sheet music, reading an embarrassingly pompous theme I had written for college freshman English entitled "Literary Debris" which took to task every writer since Shakespeare with the possible exception of James Branch Cabell and Upton Sinclair, the crumbs of whose works were obviously still around my mouth, when Mary called and said, "Well, I've found you the perfect job."

"Any campfires or dancing?" I asked, my spirits soaring out of my early morning black despair like eagles released from a dark cage.

"It's at the Western Insurance Company being private secretary to a perfectly darling man named Welton Brown," Mary said.

"Welton puts out the monthly magazine for the insurance company and I went in this morning to see him about an ad and he told me his secretary is leaving and offered me the job. I told him I already had a job but you didn't and so he asked about you and I told him and he told me about his job and we both decided that you are perfect for it."

"Is it a regular secretarial job?" I asked.

"No," said Mary a trifle too enthusiastically, "and that's what makes it so interesting and why, because you're so talented, you are the only person who can do it."

Instantly alerted for trouble whenever Mary started telling me how talented I was, I tried to keep my voice normal as I asked, "Just what have you told this Welton Brown I could do, Mary?"

Mary said, "Stop interrupting and you'll find out. Because Welton gets out a magazine, his secretary has to be able to type and take shorthand, know all about insurance, be familiar with advertising and layouts, draw well enough to illustrate the magazine and be able to write and edit articles. He'd really prefer someone who has been published."

"Well," I said, "*A*—I'm only mediocre to rotten in shorthand and typing; *B*—I don't know anything about advertising or layouts; *C*—I majored in art in college but we never drew anything but plaster casts; *D*—I can't write and I've never had anything published and all my insurance information is mixed up with chickens."

Mary said, "Listen, Betty, I've known you for twenty-four years and you've never thought you could do ANYTHING! Now there's a depression and jobs are hard to find and you've got two children to support and it's about time you grew up and changed your thinking to things you can do instead of things you can't do. Mull over your talents and build up your ego. *A*—You have to know insurance—you were married to an insurance salesman; *B*—You have to know advertising—you don't but I do and I can teach you; *C*—You have to be able to draw and you say you can only draw plaster casts—and what may I ask, could be more ideal training for an insurance company with all their accidents? *D*—Shorthand

and typing—if Welton Brown thinks he can get a court reporter who can do all those things he's a bigger jackass than I think he is. E—You have to be able to write and that is one thing you have to admit you can do. What about your children's stories—what about 'Sandra Surrenders'—I'll bet the *Ladies' Home Journal* would snap it up if we ever finished it."

I said, "I'll go down and I'll meet you for lunch afterwards."

After I had dressed in my office clothes, I told Mother about the job and asked her if she honestly thought that a tiny bit of talent and a great eagerness to learn might satisfy Welton Brown. Mother, who with the children was in the kitchen making vegetable soup, listening to Ma Perkins, and being unbearably hard to leave, said, "The way I feel is that anybody with a name like Welton could easily be a stinker but the job sounds interesting. However, if he doesn't hire you it's his loss, now taste this soup and see if it has enough salt."

It was raining when I left the house. A driving, drenching rain that lifted up my tweed coat and soaked the backs of my stockings, yanked straggly pieces of hair out from under my hat, and made it very difficult for me to fan the meagre flame of my self-confidence.

I walked to the corner and flattened myself against a building to wait for the streetcar but the rain and the wind followed me, clawing and nipping like playful puppies. The street around the car stop was littered with its regular debris of old transfers, gum wrappers, empty cigarette packages and sodden scattered pages from the morning paper. The gutters were filled with brown water that ran into the sewer with a strange metallic clink-clank as though it crystallized at the gratings. The downspout on an old frame apartment building was broken and rain water, with a loud gargling noise, was bubbling out and running into the entryway of the drugstore on the corner. A woman with a black umbrella pulled down over her shoulders and turned against the wind, came struggling crabwise across the street, stepped into the entrance of the drugstore, and when the water covered her ankles, gave a small scream and looked accusingly at me. I said, "It's from the broken downspout up there," but she apparently didn't hear me because she gave me another "Well!" look and went into the drugstore, banging the door behind her.

Feeling as soggy and unappetizing as leftover salad, I moved closer to the building and searched the horizon anxiously for the streetcar. There was nothing in sight but wet pavement and wet sky. I thought longingly of Mother and her hot vegetable soup and warm cozy kitchen and had just about convinced myself that my talents showed to much better advantage when dry, when the streetcar came racketing along and I climbed aboard.

The streetcar, warm and almost empty, was littered and still heavy with crowded morning smells of wet raincoats, hard-boiled egg sandwiches, bad breath, and perfume. I shuddered and opened the window a crack. Instantly rain began oozing across the sill and onto the seat. I moved over toward the aisle but the water followed me, so, putting my nose to the crack, I took a deep final breath of fresh air and closed the window.

The car stopped in the University district and a large woman with two shopping bags and an enormous wet orange fur collar that looked as if she had dipped a collie in water and flung it around her neck, lumbered on and squeezed herself into the seat beside me. "This seat's wet and I can't move over any farther," I said, looking meaningly at all the empty seats. The woman paid no attention, settled down heavily beside me, clumped her shopping bags, which seemed to be filled with old flatirons, on my feet, and leaned well back so that we shared equally in her wet collie.

A block before I got off the streetcar, I noted my bedraggled appearance in my pocket mirror, wiped off the runny mascara from under my eyes, poked some of the wet hair under my hat and comforted myself with the knowledge that most terribly talented people look as if they had just crawled out of a manhole.

Welton Brown confirmed all my worst fears about jobhunting by first giving me a talk on what a happy family they were at old Western; how they really didn't care half as much about their employees' work as they did about their fitting into the "family";

how you didn't just work at Western you "lived Western"; then suddenly thrusting a shorthand notebook at me saying, "A little test on that shorthand, just routine but part of the requirements," and dictating very rapidly in a monotone, a long very hard article on the Stock Market.

Pride made me pretend to take the shorthand and like stenographers in the movies I filled and flipped over the notebook pages with meaningless scratches and amazing rapidity, even cleverly seeming to hesitate over certain words. When I finished, Welton handed me a single sheet of yellow copy paper and told me to go to the typewriter in the corner and transcribe my notes.

To kill time and because I didn't have any notes, I took off my coat, carefully adjusted it on the back of the chair, smoothed out the fingers of my gloves, and laid them just so beside my purse, monkeyed a lot with the margin setter on the typewriter and slowly fed the single sheet of paper into the machine and adjusted its evenness to a millionth of an inch.

Finally when there was nothing left to do but to start typing, I turned and asked, "Wasn't that article from the *Financial World?*" "Yes," said Welton not looking at me. "I knew it," I said gaily as though I were already "living Western." "At the lumber office where I used to work, I had to read the *Financial World* every week and incorporate the articles in a financial bulletin we sent to the lumbermen."

"So?" said Welton, about as enthusiastically as if he had just found a fly in his coffee. Humbly I turned back to the typewriter and had just begun to type my name and the date very fast and so unevenly that all the keys stuck together, when the door opened and the secretary came in and informed Welton, in a low spy voice, that "somebody upstairs" wanted to see him. Murmuring they went out and closed the door behind them.

Quick as a flash, I leaped to my feet, grabbed the *Financial World* from Welton's desk, rushed back to the typewriter and in my hurry copied the wrong article. It didn't make any difference because when Welton returned he didn't even look at the article but told me the job paid $75 a month and my skirt was unzipped.

Mary said I should have said, "So are your trousers," and marched out. I didn't. I said, "Only seventy-five dollars a month for someone who knows shorthand, typing, insurance, and advertising and can draw and write too."

He said, "There is a depression. We are letting many of our people go."

"How, by unlocking their leg irons?" I said to myself.

After lunch I walked back to Mary's advertising office with her and she said, "I don't see why you don't sell advertising with me. You'll certainly make more than seventy-five dollars a month and you won't have to carry your toe shoes or your old report cards."

7

"Aren't We Going to Recognize Genius?"

THERE IS NO GETTING AROUND THE FACT THAT BEING POOR takes getting used to. You have to adjust to the fact that it is no longer a question of what you eat but if you eat. That when you want to go to a movie you can stay home and read the book. That when you want to go dancing you can stay home and make fudge. That when you want to go for a drive in a convertible you can go for a walk in the park. When you want to go to a concert you can play Chinese checkers with Mother.

This adjustment period didn't bother Dede and Alison and Anne and Joan because it came when they were young and pliable, or Mother, who was selfless, or me, who still grew faint at the excitement of seeing one other lighted window besides my own, but Mary grew restless.

First she became engaged to a Christian Scientist, joined the church, smiled when she was being nasty, and threw away all our medicines; then she became engaged to a Jewish boy, insisted that Mother's great-grandmother's name was not Tholimer but Tolheimer, whipped us all to a white heat against race prejudice, which we never had, and spent most of her evenings at the Temple de Hirsch; then she met our old ballet teacher on the street and started taking lessons again, only now she called it "auditing the classes," until one day she sprained her knee and for a week or two kept it enormously bandaged and dragging it behind her like a little wagon; then she became engaged to an actor, joined the repertory Playhouse, took up fencing, used Standard English even at home and began casting a speculative eye over the family for hidden talent.

Fortunately for the rest of us, the eye lit first on Sister Dede, who had, when she was fourteen, made up her mind, and Dede making up her mind is a process akin to pouring cement, that she was going to sing on the radio and for at least a year before Mary got arty, Dede had been going downtown after high school, forcing herself into radio studios and making them let her sing on the radio.

At that time she imitated Bessie Smith and was very particular about the words, which she enunciated carefully. She used to call me at Mr. Webster's and at Mr. Chalmers' and tell me when she was going to sing and I would run down to the cigar store, where they had a radio, and listen, telling anyone who would pay attention that that was my little sister singing, or, more truthfully, enunciating in a low voice. Dede sang "Mountain Top Blues," "Louisiana Low Down Blues," "St. Louis Blues," and other low down chants in her deep husky voice. She also had an enormous record collection, seemed to know the name of every musician in every band on the radio, and kept the radio or the record player going full blast night and day.

One night after dinner, she was as usual sitting by the radio listening to hot music with the volume turned as high as it would go and singing (we knew she was singing because we could see her lips moving); Mary, "with one free night from the Playhouse, thank God," was sitting by the fire reading Spengler's *Decline of the West,* and the rest of us were playing Chinese checkers, when Mary suddenly held up a hand, signaling silence from us checker players who weren't saying anything, and yelled at Dede, "Take that last note again!" Dede apparently did but nobody heard it because the radio was so loud.

Mary tossed her big boring "terribly important" book onto the coffee table, turned to us, and said, "Maybe you don't realize it but Dede has a marvellous blues voice. She also has perfect pitch and why we're all sitting around here wasting our time instead of helping her, I don't know." She got up, stalked out to the dining room and imperiously snapped off the radio. Dede snapped it on again, Mary turned it off. Dede turned it on. Mary turned it off and holding her hand on the switch said, "Listen, bonehead, do you want to sing on Fanchon and Marco or don't you?" Dede reaching for the switch said, "I'm already singing on the radio." Mary brushed this aside as being too unimportant to even mention. "Radio," she said. "Waste of time, just a fad. Now I know a man who knows the booking agent for Fanchon and Marco and I think I can get you a spot. Now let me hear you sing."

She sat down at the piano and began to play a pure Mary Bard medley of "Body and Soul," "Way Down Yonder in New Orleans," and "Mississippi Mud." Dede, firmly removing Mary's hands from the piano keys, said, "I'll sing without accompaniment," and she sang "Louisiana Low Down Blues" like Bessie Smith. Mary clenched her teeth like a movie director and said, "Goot. Veree goot." She pronounced it "goot" because she was now Dede's agent and her critic.

The wonderful thing about Mary is that only five minutes before, she had been taking Mother to task because she let a perfectly magnificent book like *The Decline of the West* lie around the house unopened while she, the matriarch, the leader of her tribe, the example for her children, read novels and the *Saturday Evening Post*. Mother had said, "I'm tired at the end of the day and I'm not going to bore myself to death with that depressing old fool of a Spengler." Mary had sighed mightily, picked up Spengler and said, "Well it's a good thing that one of us is willing to try and keep up the standards in this family."

Now the question before the house seemed to be not: "Are we going to let our mother slothfully ignore Spengler?" but, "How many people in this room belong on the stage and why in hell aren't they there?"

When Dede finished her song, Mary rushed to the telephone and called someone named Bill. With clenched teeth, she said,

"Listen, Bill, my sister Dede is terrific. Simply terrific. She sings just like Helen Morgan." This certainly surprised all of us who knew that Dede had never liked Helen Morgan and never imitated her. Mary went on, "Her voice is clear and true and she is small and dark and I think [she paused dramatically] that [another dramatic pause] with the right makeup, back drop, spots, and business she's really big time." Dede looked scared. It was one thing to be sixteen years old and singing little afternoon spots on the small radio stations but it was something else again to be a headliner on Fanchon and Marco, who put on gorgeous stage shows at our largest movie house.

As Mary talked on and on to Bill about rehearsals, traveling time, salaries, and the tryout time, we crowded excitedly below her on the stairs, where the telephone was. Except Mother, that is. She continued to sit on the couch, reading, smoking, and drinking her fourth after-dinner cup of coffee. Mother never paid any attention to Mary's brainstorms, until the fateful day when she awoke to find herself writing and directing a radio serial. But that is another story.

When Mary finally hung up the phone, she was no longer Mary pretending to be Dede's manager. She was Dede's manager. She blinked her eyes quite a lot, kept her teeth clenched, and ordered us around like stagehands. The first gesture she made toward her new position was to stalk out to the dining room and brush everything off the top of the piano, which was quite a gesture, as our piano had on its top all of the music which one of our music teachers, who had died, had left us, all of the hats and gloves which we were wearing that season, all of Alison's and Dede's school books, any games which were in vogue, like Monopoly and Chinese checkers, and a large red Chinese lacquer bowl into which, when we cleaned, were tossed bills, spools of thread, nail polish, keys, poker chips, beads, clips, pins, pencils, and odd crayons and toys belonging to my two babies.

Next, Mary took the front off the piano, made little testing noises on the strings, and ordered Dede to climb up and sit on the top. Dede said, "I don't want to." Mary said, "Now, my dear, it is not a question of what you want to do. It is a question of what Fanchon and Marco want you to do." (I'll bet that would have surprised Fanchon and Marco.) "Now GET UP ON THAT PIANO!" She folded her arms imperiously and her amber eyes flashed.

Dede's gray eyes turned black with determination. She said in her firm, deep voice, "I won't sit on the piano. I don't like Helen Morgan and anyway she doesn't sit on an upright."

Mary said, "My dear little girl, it is not the make of the piano she sits on that has made Helen Morgan great!"

Mother said, "I think that the long hard climb to the top of an upright piano might get more attention than the singing."

Mary looked at Mother speculatively and then, apparently tossing Helen Morgan down the drain, turned to Dede and asked her whose singing she admired.

Dede said, "Bessie Smith."

Mary said, "But, darling, you are so cunning and little and pretty that you aren't suited to that stuff. You should be soft and beguiling, feminine, appealing." I thought for a moment she was going to break into French, she had suddenly become so terribly soft and feminine. It wasn't French, it was a Southern accent. She sat on the corner of the dining room table, swung one leg, and sang "Judy" in a soprano voice with a Southern accent and lots of fluttery gestures.

> "If you heah heh call, in a soft Southehn drawl,
> That's Judy, Mah, Judy!
> When you heah heh sing, it's the voice of Spring,
> That's Judy, Mah, Judy!"

Mary was getting all the words and the tune wrong and "Judy" was one of Dede's favorite songs, so she gave in. She said that she would sing "Tea for Two" instead of "Louisiana Low Down Blues" and she would sing in her natural voice instead of the low down roar.

They rehearsed a little that night and for the ten nights before Dede was to try out. At each rehearsal Mary got stronger and Dede weaker until finally she was singing two octaves higher than normal and Mary had her promise to sit on the edge of the stage with her feet dangling into the footlights.

At last it was the night of the tryout. Mary brought home her makeup box from the Playhouse and said that, as she had had extensive training, she would make up Dede down at the theatre. She also picked Dede's costume, an old party dress of mine, pink taffeta with a large silver-lace bertha collar. Normally Mary would have had to chloroform Dede to stuff her into that ugly dress, but Dede had been constantly under her influence for ten days now and she was mesmerized. I will never know why Mary chose that dress. We had neither of us ever liked it and it was now old, slightly dirty and out of style, but she was in that old Southern groove and so instead of looking in the closets she had rummaged in the trunks and that was the first thing she found.

When we arrived at the theatre, at 12:30 P.M., we found that Dede's tryout was not the only one as Mary had led us to believe, but that this was the semi-annual tryout night for all Fanchon and Marco acts. Dede was very scared. Mary was in her glory. She knew everybody. She knew the piano player, who turned out to be Bill; the theatre manager whom she called "Jerry, honey," and most of the acts. This puzzled me. Mary sold advertising but had only sold it for about six months and I'm sure she wasn't handling Fanchon and Marco's stuff. I don't know where she met these people. Everybody adored her, though, and she swept back and forth backstage, laughing and talking and organizing. Dede followed her for a while then became discouraged and came and sat down in the front row with us.

There were several groups of dark men with cigars sitting in different parts of the theatre, who we supposed were friends of Fanchon and Marco, and we were, therefore, very embarrassed when Mary, carrying her makeup box, came out on the stage in front of the curtain and demanded of the darkened theatre, "Where is

Dede? Dede where are you? I have to make you up!"

Unfortunately, she saw us all just then and immediately began distributing us over the theatre like handbills. "Sydney [she had stopped calling Mother, 'Mother,' and called her 'Sydney' as being indicative of the theatah tradition] you go to the back; Betty this side, Cleve—over by that exit; Alison, you stay with Mother." We objected but she brushed us aside with, "How can we possibly tell how her voice sounds if you are all crouching in the front row?" The men with the cigars laughed and we all wanted to choke Mary. All except Sydney who said, "Wait until she goes backstage and we'll all move together again."

Dede crept up on the stage, Mary jerked her backstage and the tryouts began. First there were some adagio dancers, who had on dirty long underwear and breathed heavily; then an oily man who wore loose trousers and told dirty jokes; then a poor little juggler who dropped his tenpins and broke most of the footlights.

Then from the wings came what looked like a little raccoon, for Mary, the dramatic student, the makeup artist, had heavily blackened the underneath part of Dede's eyes as well as the lids, and had drawn Dede's dark curly hair back tight and oiled it with brilliantine. I glanced at Mary, who had slipped into a seat beside me and was smoking furiously. But she seemed well-satisfied with her work so I said nothing.

Dede walked timidly over and sat down on the edge of the stage, crossed her legs, as Mary had taught her, was immediately enveloped in the pink taffeta—all but her head—and began to sing, in the voice Mary had taught her. It was thin and eerie like cries carried on the wind and the accompaniment by "Bill honey," was the loudest thing I've ever heard outside of Sousa's band.

As soon as it was over, and it seemed like hours, we left. Dede was crying and we were all pretty mad at Mary. Suddenly Mary turned to Mother and said, "You see, Sydney, that's the trouble with having so many children. Having children is a form of selfishness like collecting jewelry, growing orchids. In your day it was fashionable—it was the thing to do. But, did you ever stop to think how or if you were going to educate them? Did you stop to think of the possibility of one of your children being a genius? How you would pay for his musical education?"

Dede had stopped crying and we were all listening to Mary, for we knew she had launched one of her attacks and it would lead to something interesting. She said, "Well, Sydney, is the entire burden of using the tremendous talent in this family to fall on me?"

Mother said, "Let's get a hamburger."

8

"You Name It, Betty Can Do It"

"WHAT DO YOU DO WHEN YOU SELL DIRECT MAIL ADVERTIS-ing?" I asked Mary.

"It's the simplest thing in the world," she said. "You get an idea, then you convince somebody who has never had one that he thought of it and it is so outstandingly brilliant, so unusual, the product of such a scintillating mentality that it should be mimeographed and sent to some long list of people. Say the Boy Scouts of America or the Teamsters' Union, whichever list has the most names on it."

"Sounds simple," I said. "But how do you know what kind of an idea they want?"

"Well, in the first place, any idea is better than none, which is most people's problem," said Mary. "In the second place, the only thing people are interested in these days is sales promotion. Ideas that will sell more butter, shoes, davenports, permanent waves, gasoline, ferry rides, or popcorn to the public. Now take Standard Oil . . ."

Which was one of my few criticisms of Mary, she was always taking Standard Oil or Sears Roebuck or some other great big important firm whose name scared me to death, to use as testing grounds for either my ability or her ideas. I didn't want to sell advertising at all. I wanted some sort of very steady job with a salary, and duties mediocre enough to be congruent with my mediocre ability. I had in mind sort of a combination janitress, slow typist, and file clerk. Not for a moment did Mary entertain any such humble idea. She had in mind for me any job up to and including the President of the United States.

The thing about selling is that you're either a salesman or you're not. I remember an insurance salesman's telling me without shame, how he followed a store executive right into his corner show window during the lunch hour and started explaining the benefits he would receive at "age 65" and was surprised but not hurt when the executive picked him up bodily and threw him into the men's wear section. He said, "Figured he must have gotten out of bed on the wrong side so I didn't go back until the next day."

If you are the type of person who remembers your second grade teacher's pinching you on the neck because you exhibited a doll dress your mother had made as your own handiwork at the school carnival; who buys brown print dresses that are too short in the waist and are unbecoming anyway, because you are afraid of the saleswoman; who could never ask the butcher for half a turkey; and can still exhibit all the symptoms of pure animal terror at the sight of any dance program; then the chances are you would be the next to the worst salesman in the world. I was the worst.

I followed Mary up and down town and in and out of offices for three days and all I learned was a lot of basic differences between Mary and me and the location of fourteen coffee shops where a butterhorn and coffee were only ten cents. Mary, who seemed to get an order with every call, used the same approach on steamship offices, bakeries, garages, oil companies, candy stores, department stores, shoe repair shops, or lending libraries.

The approach was that she was vitally interested in every single person in the organization, knew the location and condition of every tumor, sacroiliac, heart condition, bunion, and crippled relative, knew who was mistreated, how much and by whom, knew who had gone where on their vacations and who had been gypped out of theirs, who was in love, and who was lonely.

On one of our first calls she learned from a long sallow stenographer that her mother, with whom she lived, had a tumor. Mary said, "Oh, think nothing of it. I had two huge tumors. Had them both removed at once and now I'm better than ever." I looked at Mary, who had never even been in a hospital, with some astonishment. The stenographer looked avid. She said, "Where were your tumors and how much did they weigh?" Mary said, "Oh, one was here," she pointed to her appendix, "and one was here," she moved her hand around to the back. "They weighed eight pounds apiece and the operation only took twenty minutes."

As Mary, who was so vivid, so obviously bursting with health, talked on and on, the stenographer drew in every word and seemed to become firmer, to take shape. It was like watching someone stuff a rag doll. When we left the woman said, almost cheerfully, that she was going to call her mother and tell her about Mary.

Out in the hall I said to Mary, "Mary, you know that nobody in our entire family for generations and generations has ever had a tumor."

Mary said, "What difference does that make? Evelyn's mother's got one and nobody likes to have a tumor all alone. Anyway, can you think of anything drearier than that poor old Evelyn's life? She works in that stuffy office all day for that disagreeable old Mr. Felton, who has such a bossy mistress and such a nasty wife who knows about the mistress, that his only pleasure in life is kicking old Evelyn every chance he gets."

"How do you know about all these mistresses and nasty wives?" I asked. Mary said, "People tell me. I've got that kind of a face. People tell me everything. I don't know why." I did. It was because Mary was more interested in their problems than they were.

Our next call was on an automotive supply establishment. Our contact was a large fat man named Charlie, who took us into his private office, closed the door, looked under the desk and in the wastebaskets for hidden spies, and then told us he had been fired. Mary said, "It doesn't surprise me at all." Belligerently Charlie said, "How come?" Mary said, "You're too smart. You're smarter than anyone in this entire firm and it is so obvious they had to let you go. I knew the minute you were hired you wouldn't last up here."

Charlie, who was obviously slow, dull-witted, and lazy, leaned back, pursed his fat lips importantly and said, "You know I think you're right, Mary. Every time I get a good idea somebody steals it. Like that bulletin on anti-freeze I sent the dealers. That dirty little Ab Miller took all the credit for it." Mary said, "Naturally. But the thing is that you've got to learn to take things like this in your stride. You've got to learn to share your great brain with people not so fortunate." On the way out she hissed at me, "The only way he could share that great brain of his is with an atom splitter. The only work he's ever done since he started here is to wear a groove over to that coffee shop across the street."

It was fun making calls with Mary but I dreaded the day when I'd have to go alone. I didn't dread it half enough.

On Wednesday morning, Mary gave me a little stack of cards, some briefing and sent me off. My first call was on a Mr. Hemp in an automobile agency. Mary had said, "Sell him that list of Doctors and Dentists—they're about the only people who can afford cars now. Sell him on the idea of a clever but dignified letter stressing price and mileage per gallon of gas."

I left the office. It was a soft spring morning. The sky was a pale bluing blue and the breeze from the Sound smelled salty and fresh. The automobile company was about fifteen blocks uptown but I decided to walk both to save carfare and because I wanted to delay as long as possible the moment for seeing Mr. Hemp and selling him the clever idea I didn't have.

My route led me up hill, past the dirty gray prisonlike façade of the Public Library, through a shabby cluster of cheap rooming houses that advertised Palm Reading, Mystic Seances, and Steam Baths in their foggy limp-curtained windows, past wooden apartment houses with orange-crate coolers tacked to their window sills, and whose only signs of life on this clean sunny morning were a few turbaned and housecoated women scuttling around the corner to the grocery store, and a smattering of pale children listlessly bouncing balls or riding tricycles in small restricted areas, the overstepping of whose boundaries brought immediate shrill admonitions from near-by open windows.

The automobile company's wide front door was propped open with a wooden wedge and four salesmen with their hats pushed to the back of their heads lounged in the sunshine on tilted-back chairs, smoking and looking sad. Timidly I asked one of them for Mr. Hemp. The man gestured toward some offices at the back. All the salesmen watched my progress across the huge showroom, which made me so self-conscious I walked stifflegged and cut a zigzag path across the shiny linoleum floor.

The offices were guarded by a long counter, behind which several girls were talking and laughing. I asked one of them for Mr. Hemp and she said she wasn't sure he'd have time to see me but she'd ask him. She went into a glass-enclosed cell and spoke to a man who was lying back in his swivel chair, his feet on his desk, talking on the phone. He turned around and looked at me and shook his head. The girl came back and said, "Did you want to see him about a job?"

I said, "No, I don't want to see him about a job."

She waited for me to reveal what I wanted to see him about but for some silly reason I was ashamed to tell her and acted evasive and sneaky and as though I were trying to sell something either dirty or "hot."

The girl went in and whispered to Mr. Hemp and I watched him peer at me and then shake his head. When she came back she said, "Mr. Hemp's terribly busy this morning and can't see anybody."

I said, "Oh, that's all right, I'm busy myself, I've got another appointment," and I hurried out leaving my purse on the counter. I missed it after walking a block or two, and when I came back to get it the girl looked at me with such a puzzled look I didn't leave my Advertising Bureau card, which by now was quite bent and sweaty anyway.

My next card was a collection agency. As I walked back downtown, I kept glancing hopefully at my watch, praying for it to be noon or too late to make any more calls. But it was only ten-twenty when I reached the large office building that housed the collection agency.

Waiting in the foyer in front of the elevators, laughing and talking, were men without hats and girls without coats. People with regular jobs just coming back from coffee. I looked at them carefully and tried to figure out where they worked, what kind of work they did, what magic something they had that made them so employable. Only one of the girls was really pretty. She had a tiny waist, a big bun of dark hair, and was laughing with one of the men. The other girls were clean and ordinary and looked as if they might belong to business girls' groups and curl their own hair. In the elevator we all stood self-consciously, silently, staring straight ahead the way you're supposed to in elevators.

I got off at the third floor and walked uneagerly down to room 309. The door was frosted glass. Clutching my notebook of collection letters and taking a deep quivering breath, I turned the knob, pushed open the door and was immediately confronted by a pair of eyes so hard they sent out glances like glass splinters. The owner of the eyes, standing at a counter sorting some cards, said, "Wadda *you* want?" as she slapped the cards down into little piles.

I said, "'I'm from the Advertising Bureau. . . ." She said, "We don't want any more of those bum collection letters." I said, "I have a new series. I wrote them myself and I think they're pretty good." She said, "Wadda you mean new series? We already sent out one through five." I said, "Now we have five through ten," and began looking for my notebook. The woman said, "Don't bother gettin' them out. I don' wanna see them. It's all a waste of money." I said, "All right, thank you very much." She said, "Wadda *you* thankin' *me* for?" and laughed. I left.

My next call, in the same building, was on a school for beauty operators. Still smarting from the collection agency woman's laugh, I entered the La Charma Beauty School with the same degree of enthusiasm Daniel must have evinced when entering the lions' den. A woman with magenta hair, little black globules on the end of each eyelash, eyebrows two hairs wide, big wet scarlet lips, and a stiff white uniform, was sitting at a little appointment desk. The minute she saw me she shoved a paper at me and told me to sign it. So I did and she said, "Black or brown?" I picked up the paper and it seemed to be a waiver of some sort having to do with La Charma not being responsible if I went blind.

I said, "I don't understand, I'm from the Advertising Bureau." She laughed and said, "Gosh, I thought you was my ten o'clock appointment. An eyelash dye job. Say, hon, Mrs. Johnson wants to see you. She wants a letter to all the girls who will graduate from high school this June." I almost fainted. Somebody *wanted* to see me. I was going to sell something.

Mrs. Johnson, who looked exactly like the woman at the appointment desk except that she had gold hair, was very friendly, offered me a cigarette, and thought my ideas for a letter were "swell and had a latta bounce." I left with a big order and my whole body electrified with hope. Maybe selling advertising was easier than prostitution after all.

My next call was on a shoe repair shop. I went in smiling but the little dark man said, "Business is rotten. No use throwin' good money after bad. I don't believe in advertisin'. Good work advertises itself. Go wan now I'm busy." So I slunk out and went back to the bureau.

Mary, who was in giving the artist some instructions, was so very enthusiastic about the beauty shop and my first order that I didn't tell her about the other calls. We took our sandwiches, which we brought from home, unless we were invited out for lunch, and walked to the Public Market where for five cents we could get an unlimited number of cups of wonderful fresh-roasted coffee and the use of one of the tables in a large dining room in the market loft, owned by the coffee company.

The Public Market, about three blocks long, crowded and smelling deliciously of baking bread, roasting peanuts, coffee, fresh fish, and bananas, blazed with the orange, reds, yellows, and greens of fresh succulent fruits and vegetables. From the hundreds of farmers' stalls that lined both sides of the street and extended clear through the block on the east side, Italians, Greeks, Norwegians, Finns, Danes, Japanese, and Germans offered their wares. The Italians were the most voluble but the Japanese had the most beautiful vegetables.

The market, offering everything from Turkish coffee and rare books to squid and bear meat, was the shopping mecca for Seattle, and a wonderful place to eat for those who liked good food and hadn't much money. It had Turkish, Italian, Greek, Norwegian, and German restaurants in addition to many excellent delicatessens and coffee stalls.

The nicest thing about it to me was its friendliness and the fact that they were all trying to sell *me* something. Everybody spoke to us as we went by and in spite of the depression, which was certainly as bad down there as anywhere, everyone was smiling and glad to see everybody. A small dark fruit-dealer named Louis, who was a great admirer of red hair, gave us a large bunch of Malaga grapes and two bananas. "Go good with your sandwiches," he said.

The dining room was three flights up in the market loft, so we climbed the stairs, got our coffee, climbed more stairs, and sat down at the large table by the windows always saved by our friends and always commanding a magnificent view of the Seattle waterfront, the islands, and Puget Sound. Our friends, mostly artists, advertising people, newspapermen and women, writers, musicians, and book-store people, carried their sandwiches boldly and unashamedly in paper bags. Others who ate up there were not so bold.

Bank clerks, insurance salesmen, and lawyers were lucky because they had briefcases and could carry bottles of milk, little puddings and potato salad in fruit jars, as well as sandwiches, without losing their dignity. But accountants and stenographers usually put down their coffee, looked sneakily around to see if they knew anyone, then slipped their sandwiches out of an inside coat pocket, purse, or department store bag, as furtively as though they were smuggling morphine.

I must admit that I had false pride about taking my lunch and hated the days when it was Mary's turn to fix the sandwiches and she would slap them together and stuff them into any old thing that came to hand—a huge greasy brown paper bag, an old printed bread wrapping, or even newspaper tied with a string.

Mary, one of those few fortunate people who are born without any false pride, laughed when I went to a Chinese store and bought a straw envelope to carry my sandwiches in. The straw envelope made everything taste like mothballs and incense and squashed the sandwiches flat but it looked kind of like a purse. Mary said, "So we have to take our lunch. So what?" and went into I. Magnin's swinging her big brown, greasy, paper bag.

I forced myself to make calls the rest of that week but I diluted the agony with visits to second-hand book stores. I rationed myself, one call—one second-hand book store. Saturday morning I told Mary that we might as well face the fact that I couldn't sell anybody anything.

"I'll never be a salesman," I told her as she checked her accounts and figured her commission. "I'm scared to death all the time and I don't have the faintest idea what I'm supposed to be selling. Friday, when I called on that piston ring company, the girl asked me what I wanted and I said I didn't know. She thought I was crazy." Mary argued with me a little but finally had to admit that she would never get me in a frame of mind where I thought my ideas were better than Standard Oil's.

"I guess you should take an office job," she said. "Only don't try to find one for yourself or you'll end up paying them and working twenty-four hours a day. Leave it to me."

So I did and when the next five or six months were over I had certainly had all kinds of experience or experiences, to say nothing of the several new trades I had learned and could now proudly X on employment agency cards without lying.

The first job Mary got me she told me about by saying, "It's certainly fortunate you're so thin." I was so anxious to go to work I already had one arm in my coat but I stopped right there and came back to face her.

"Is this job stenography?" I asked.

"Well, in a way," she said. "It's a combination bookkeeper and fur coat modeler. That's why it's so lucky you're tall and thin."

"It would also be lucky if I could keep books," I said. Mary ignored me.

She said, "Remember, Betsy, we are in a depression. Nowadays anybody can do anything and does."

"Where is it and when am I supposed to be there?" I said.

"I told Mr. Handel you'd be down this afternoon," Mary said, writing the address on a scrap of paper. So I put my other arm in the other sleeve of my tweed coat and headed toward the manufacturing district.

The farther downtown I went the more congested the streets were with aimless, unemployed people. It had been raining all morning, it seemed to me it always rained when I was out of work, and the sky between the buildings was heavy and gray, the sidewalks were wet and everything and everybody looked cold and miserable.

The address Mary had given me was down past the Skid Road, Seattle's flophouse district and the hangout of the unemployed loggers and millworkers, as well as the gathering place for all radicals, bums, and religious crackpots.

"This will be a good place to study the unemployed and test Mary's theory that only the inefficient are out of work," I thought, but as I worked my way farther and farther downtown, my progress along the streets was hailed with so many catcalls and whistles that I had to abandon testing and keep my eyes straight ahead.

On one corner a seedy little man with small shifty eyes and a runny nose had collected a small crowd and was begging them to repent, while a tall sandy-haired man, with a high-domed head and large ascetic eyes, was shouting to the same apathetic crowd to do something about the dirty capitalists.

An old woman pushing a baby buggy full of newspapers and rags turned into an alley and began poking in the garbage cans. A drunken bum grabbed my arm and asked me for a quarter. Two Filipinos in huge belted camel's-hair overcoats, long sharply-pointed mahogany-colored shoes and hats with little feathers in them, picked their way along the street amid the jeers and rude comments of the loggers and bums.

There seemed to be a pawnshop on every corner, huge screaming banners announcing FIRE SALES, CLOSE OUT SALE, FORCED OUT OF BUSINESS SALES, every other doorway. The musty choky smells of unwashed clothes, rancid grease, fish, doughnuts, and stale coffee mingled with and overpowered the delicious sea-weedy salty smell of the Sound that was carried up every cross street by the wind.

"Complete meal—15¢" advertised restaurant after restaurant in their fly-specked windows, while unappetizing smells oozed out their doorways. I was curious to know what they served for fifteen cents and finally by walking slowly without appearing to loiter, I was able to read a menu pasted outside a window. "Stew, bread and butter and all the coffee you can drink," it said. "Soup and pie 5¢ extra." "You could live a long time on five dollars down here," I was thinking when a soft voice behind me said, "Whatsa matter, sister, are you hungry?" I turned and fled.

At the next corner, I asked a policeman where Handel's was and he kindly escorted me the rest of the way to the dark, gloomy, pleasantly-deserted manufacturing district, and pointed out Handel's sign in the second-floor window of a very old red brick building. The elevator, an old fashioned open cage, had an operator with no teeth and crusty eyes, who was too feeble to close the door and asked me to help him. I did and he said, "Shanks, lady," and wiped one of his crusty eyes on his dirty black sleeve. The marble floors of the building had a decided list to the right and I felt as if I were on board an old sailing ship as I walked down the long gloomy corridor.

Mr. Handel had apparently been crouched behind the door waiting for me, for when I timidly opened the door I almost fell over him. I apologized but he, not at all nonplussed, grabbed me, and shook my hand clear to my shoulder.

"Come in, come in," he said. "Glad to see you. Take off your coat and let's see what kind of shape you got." I disentangled my hand and arm and took off my coat and Mr. Handel looked me over very, very carefully, then said, "Kid, you got elegant lines and real class. Now let's see you walk." The office was only about six feet square but I walked back and forth and around the desk, weaving sinuously to avoid Mr. Handel's groping, stroking, clutching, fat little hands.

He said, "That's fine but don't be in such a hurry, Baby. Now I'll get a coat and we'll see how you look." He slipped through a door in the back and returned with a silver muskrat coat, a fur I had never cared for, even before it came equipped with Mr. Handel's arms as an extra dividend.

I shrugged away from him, dodged behind the desk and asked about the bookkeeping. "Oh, that," he said. "We usually do that at night." Just then a man with a tape measure around his neck and a white fox fur in his hands came to the back door of the office and beckoned to Handel, who said, "Wait for me, Baby, I'll be back in a minute." I didn't. I ripped off the muskrat, grabbed my tweed, and ran all the way to the elevator.

"Mary Bard," I yelled ten minutes later when I burst into her office, "I'll go back to the farm before I work for that Mr. Handel. He pinched and prodded me like a leg of lamb and he said we'd do the bookkeeping at night."

Mary said, "You know he used to be such an old raper I had to sell him his advertising from across the street but I thought he'd changed."

"What made you think so?" I said.

"Oh, I saw him up at the Olympic Hotel at a fur show I'd done the invitations for and he seemed very quiet and dignified. Of course, we were in the main dining room," she added reflectively.

The next job she got me was tinting photographs. She said, "This darling little woman has a photographic studio just a few doors from here and she needs somebody to tint photographs and she's swamped with work."

"Does the fact that I've never tinted photographs interest you?" I asked.

"No it doesn't," said Mary, "because I know somebody who knows how and she's going to teach you this afternoon. Her name's Charmion and she works across the street in that sporting goods store. She's waiting for you now."

Charmion had green eyes, and long black hair on her legs and arms and while she was teaching me to dip dabs of cotton in paint and rub it on photographs she also sold basketballs, golf clubs, and duck decoys and went through three husbands, four lovers, and four bottles of ergot, which she said worked like a charm on her. At five-thirty, Charmion had a date to have her palm read and I was pretty good at the photographs, so Mary and I went home.

The next morning, which was of course rainy, armed with my new accomplishment and the knowledge that we needed a ton of coal, I reported for work at Marilee's Photo Studio. The studio, which was narrow and two-storied and gave the impression of a tall thin person squeezed into a dark doorway out of the rain, was in the middle of the block on a hill so steep it had cleats on the sidewalk and all the little shops located along it seemed to be either bracing their backs against their upper neighbors or leaning heavily on the one below. There was a shoe repair shop on one side and a print shop on the other, all a little below the street level and sharing the one trash-littered entryway.

The studio had a small show window with a skimpy, rather soiled tan half-curtain across the back and a bunched-up ratty piece of green velvet on the floor. Arranged on this were tinted photographs of bold, feverish-looking girls, brides wearing glasses, and sailors and girls leaning on each other. The subjects of all the photographs bore a remarkable resemblance to each other due, no doubt, to the wholesale application of purple on cheeks and lips, red jabs in the corners of the eyes, red to the lining of the nostrils and large, white dots in the pupils of the eyes.

I tried the door but it was locked so I flattened myself against the doorway, out of the rain, and waited. I knew I was early and so was not resentful of the ten or fifteen minutes I spent watching female office workers come toiling up the hill, their chins stuck out, their behinds lagging, their faces red with exertion, or go finicking down, their black licoricy galoshes feeling for the cleats, their knees stiff so they bounced from cleat to cleat like pogo sticks.

At last the shiniest, blackest, pointiest-toed pair of galoshes turned into our entryway and I recognized Marilee instantly because she looked exactly like all her photographs, even to the rimless octagon brides' spectacles, except that she had ash-blond hair instead of the black or bright brassy yellow that adorned most of her clientèle.

Marilee smiled at me, winked, said, "Wet enough for you?" and unlocked the door. The studio, square room with walls covered with a dark brown material like burlap, and a floor of a completely patterned mustard-colored, terribly shiny linoleum, had a green-curtained doorway at one end behind which Marilee disappeared, an appointment desk in one corner, a table with a screen around it just behind the show window and hundreds and hundreds of pictures of the bespectacled brides, bold girls, and sailors and brides or sailors and bold girls. There was not one picture of a plain man, a child, or somebody's mother. Either Marilee didn't take men, children, or older women or she didn't consider their pictures glamorous enough to adorn her walls.

When Marilee appeared again, she had removed her black satin belted raincoat and black felt policeman's cap and was wearing a black pin-striped suit, a high-necked white blouse, black patent leather pumps, big pearl earrings, and orange silk stockings. She snapped on a light over her desk, checked her appointment book, winked at me and said, "Good weather for ducks. Let's see. Nothing doing till nine-thirty. That'll give us time to get you started."

She ushered me behind the screen, showed me a hook where I could hang my hat and coat, gave me a very dirty Kelly-green smock, handed me a huge stack of pictures and said, "Your sis says you was experienced so I'm going to start you right in on some orders. I take all my own photos but I send them out for developing, retouching, and printing. Now up here in the corner I've wrote the color of hair, eyes, and so forth and so on. When you get done with a photo put it over here on this rack to dry. Here's the cotton, here's the paints, here's the reducer but don't use much. I like the color strong. Now I gotta get set up for my first appointment. If you want to know anything, just holler."

I picked up the first pictures. A brunette with pale eyes, a heavy nose and a straight thin mouth stared boldly right at me. I looked at the slip of paper clipped to one corner. "Eyes—blue . . . hair—black . . . light complected," it read. I gave the girl turquoise-blue eyes, luminous white skin, a bright pink mouth, a shadow on her bulbous nose, and blue highlights on her black hair. It took me quite a while but the girl looked pretty and not nearly so hard when I had finished.

I was doing the mouth when I heard the studio door open and close and then voices. The appointment said, "I vant yust the head. Not the body. Yust the head." Marilee said, "Four dollars, payable in advance, entitles you to four poses and one five-by-seven without the folder. A tinted photo is two dollars extra. Now do you want to fix up any before I take you?"

"No," said the appointment. "Yust the head. My madder vants to see how I look before she die."

"Okay, honey," said Marilee. "Now sit right here. Look over here. Look over here. Look right at me. Now look up here at my hand. Now you're all done. You can git your proofs Wednesday." The door closed and from my worktable I watched Yust the Head's black torso go toiling up the steep hill.

My next picture was also a brunette but with brown eyes, it said in the corner. I gave her olive skin, orangy red lips, and golden highlights in her dark brown hair.

Marilee's next customer was a fat girl with scarlet cheeks, who shyly asked if she could be posed to look thinner. "The camera don't lie," said Marilee heartlessly. "Four dollars in advance, do you wish it tinted, and what type folder?"

I peeked around the screen. The fat girl was crouched on the piano bench on which Marilee posed her subjects, looking terrified as if she were about to have a tonsillectomy without anaesthetic. Marilee came out from under her black cloth and squinted at the girl. "Come on, honey," she said winking, "let's have a nice big smile, look at the birdie, now. Tweet, tweet."

She adjusted her light so that its several hundred watts illuminated the fat girl's miserable face harshly without any shadows, reduced her eyes to squinting pinpoints and changed her from a nice shiny apple to a doughy pudding. Still not satisfied Marilee clicked over on her shiny black slippers, gripped the girl by the chin and the back of her head and forced her head to the side and back into a most unnatural tortured position.

"That'll give you a neck," she said. "Now let's have a great big smile."

The girl tried again. Marilee said, "Oh, golly, honey, that was a dream and would it look good tinted. Our tinting's only two dollars for a great big five-by-seven. Now look right at me. Think of that boy-friend. Now to the left. O.K. All done. You can git your proofs Wednesday. With your coloring you should really have one tinted." The girl mumbled something and Marilee said, "That'll be two dollars. All tinting's paid for in advance." I checked my colors to be sure I had a full tube of red for those enormous cheeks.

At noon Marilee came into examine my work. I had all my finished pictures on the rack and was frankly proud of them. Marilee squinted her eyes, clicked her tongue with her teeth, and said, "God, honey, you're not gettin' the idea at all. Not enough color. When people pay for tinting they want color. Now here watch me."

She grabbed one of my best pictures, a redhead with copper-colored hair, amber eyes, and coral lips, and went to work. She changed the hair to bright unrelieved orange, the eyes to turquoise blue with large white dots in the pupils, scrubbed plenty of magenta on the cheeks and lips and then carefully, with a toothpick dipped in paint, put red jabs in the corners of the eyes and outlined the nostrils in bright red. The girl, except for the color of her hair, now looked exactly like Marilee and exactly like all the other pictures. Marilee said, "That's better, eh? Now fix up the rest of 'em."

At first I was resentful, then I thought, "How ridiculous—it's Marilee's studio and if she wants purple lips and flaming red nostrils it's her privilege." So I tinted the photographs the way she wanted them and the work went much faster.

By Saturday noon I had caught up with all the orders and Marilee and I were "real girl chums." I knew all about Mama, who was a Rosicrucian, a diabetic, and raised lovebirds. I knew all about sister Alma who was married to a sailor and followed him to "Frisco, Dago, L.A. and Long Beach." I knew about Marilee's boy-friend, Ernie, who was a chiropractor and would love to give me a treatment any night after work.

She said, "Honest to God, some nights Mama is all tied up in knots and Ernie works her over and you can hear her bones crack a block away—it's just like pistol shots. Mama says she don't think she could carry on if it wasn't for Ernie."

I didn't want any bones cracking like pistol shots and I didn't relish being worked over by Ernie but I didn't want to hurt Marilee's feelings so I said I'd call her and set a date.

She said, "Gosh, honey, it's been like a shot in the arm havin' you here. I'm real sorry the work's all caught up but I'll call you the minute I pile up some more orders."

Marilee gave me $28.45 in crumpled bills and a little package. "Open it," she said, winking and smiling. "It's a surprise. Go wan." I did and there in a little leather frame was a tinted photograph of me. I could tell it was me because the hair was orange. "Oh, it's beautiful! Thank you, Marilee," I squealed, looking with horror at the turquoise-blue, hard, sexy eyes, flaring red-lined nostrils, and purple lips.

Marilee said, "You remember that day I asked you to pose for me so I could adjust the camera?" I remembered. "I tinted it last night," she said.

I kissed her good-bye and promised to have her out to dinner but I never did, because when I went to look for her, after working for a rabbit grower, a lawyer, a credit bureau, a purse seiner, a florist, a public stenographer, a dentist, a laboratory of clinical medicine, and a gangster, I found her little shop closed, the bespectacled brides and sailors and girls gone from her show window.

I asked the shoe repair man next door if he knew what had happened to Marilee but he said, "I dona know. People coma and goa inna depresh." The printer, however, told me that Marilee's mother had died (I wondered if those treatments of Ernie's with her poor old bones cracking like pistol shots had anything to do with her sudden demise) and she and Ernie had gone to California to be with her sis. I thought that Ernie and Marilee could work out a dual business. After she had twisted and bent a customer into one of her poses, Ernie could give him a treatment to get him back in shape.

Mr. Webber, the rabbit grower, who was tall and thin and had a high-domed forehead like pictures of the Disciples, was raising Chinchilla rabbits and trying to organize the other growers. For two weeks he laboriously wrote out reports and letters in longhand and I copied them. In the afternoons he made tea over an alcohol stove and as we drank it he told me how much he admired Mary. He said that she was a flame in this burned-out world.

Mr. Webber was as gentle and soft as his rabbits and never ever pointed out my mistakes but secretly, behind his arms, wrote over them in ink. At the end of the two weeks he gave me a check for seventy-five dollars, which was twenty-five dollars more than I expected. The extra money, I knew, was a tribute to Mary rather than an appreciation of my efficiency.

After Mr. Webber, I was out of work for three days but I wasn't as sad as I might have been because of that extra money, so I painted the kitchen, using a very remarkable yellow paint which never dried. It looked very nice but it grew more and more irritating as weeks and weeks went by and we still had to pry dishes off the drainboards and peel the children out of the breakfast nook.

On Wednesday night Mary told me she had found me a job with a darling old lawyer. I protested that I didn't know anything about legal forms but Mary said they were easy. All you had to do was go through the files and copy. She also explained that the old lawyer used a dictaphone and gave me a demonstration on the coffee table of how to use one, which wasn't too helpful as I'd never even seen one.

However, the next morning I reported for work at Mr. O'Reilly's law office, which was in an old but very respectable building in the financial district. Mr. O'Reilly had thick gray hair, an oily manner and a most disconcerting habit of appearing behind me suddenly and soundlessly.

By the trial and error method I got the dictaphone to work, learned about legal forms and phraseology, but I needn't have bothered. Mr. O'Reilly had very little work and the little he did have he didn't attend to. All he really wanted me there for was to talk about sex. He edged into it gracefully and gradually and by constantly referring to cases tried to make it seem as if he were merely discussing business. When I left he promised to mail me my salary but he never did.

Mary finally admitted that she had never seen Mr. O'Reilly but had been told about the job by an elevator starter in another building.

Then I went to work in a credit bureau typing very dull reports implying that everybody in Seattle but the President of the First National Bank had rotten credit. One day when my boss was out of his office I sneaked over and looked up our family's credit. We took up almost a whole drawer and from what I read it sounded as if the credit bureau not only wouldn't recommend us for credit, they wouldn't even let us pay cash. This, however, didn't make me feel too badly because I knew they didn't like anybody.

The next job Mary got for me was taking dictation on a dock for a purse seiner, who was trying to settle an estate involving hundreds of relatives all named Escvotrizwitz and Trckvotisztz and Krje and living in places called Brk, Pee, Plav, and Klujk. My shorthand, feeble enough in English, collapsed completely under Mr. Ljubovija's barrage of Serbo-Croat mixed with a few By Gollies and Okays, which he fondly thought was English. Finally, I told him that if he'd give me a general idea of what he wanted to say and would spell out all the names, I would write the letters.

I could not understand why he wanted the letters in English when there was a good chance that, as none of the family including him, spoke it, not one would be able to read it, but he was insistent. To him, writing in English was synonymous with success. He was a very nice man and I loved sitting in the sun on the dock listening to the raspy-throated gulls, smelling the nice boaty smells of creosote and tar and watching the purse seiners work on their nets.

I ate my sandwiches on the dock and then walked up to a little restaurant for coffee. The restaurant, run by two enormously fat blond women who dressed in stiff white uniforms like nurses and always had beads of sweat on their upper lips, catered to the fishermen and specialized in Swedish Meat Balls, Veal Sylta, Potatis Pankaka, Ugnspannkaka, Mandel Skorpor, Kringlor, Hungarian Goulash, and terrible little fruit salads filled with nuts and marshmallows and canned grapes, which they served with every order and seemed to believe gave the place an air of refinement.

My next job was working for a public stenographer, a large woman who wore wide patent leather belts around her big waist and had a most disconcerting habit of sniffing her armpits, reaching in her bottom drawer for her deodorant and applying it via the neck of her dress, when she was talking to clients.

The first time I saw Mrs. Pundril go through this little routine was when she was talking to a lumberman from Minnesota. He was in the midst of explaining a report, when suddenly she sniffed her right armpit, grabbed out her Mum, took off the lid, gouged some out with her right forefinger and with a great deal of maneuvering managed to apply it even though her blouse had a very high neck. As he watched, the lumberman's face turned a dull red. I laughed so hard I had to stuff my handkerchief in my mouth and Mrs. Pundril was as unconcerned as though she were filling her pen.

After one week, Mrs. Pundril fired me. She said I wasn't fast enough for public stenography and I made too many errors. She pronounced them "eeroars." I didn't blame her for firing me, but it didn't do my self-confidence any good. Then for a few weeks I typed bills for a florist, a dentist, and a laboratory and then Mary got me the job with the gangster.

His name was Murray Adams, he had an office in a funny old building that housed beaded-bag menders, dream interpreters, corn removers, and such, and I still don't know what he intended to do. He was big and dark and handsome and wore an oyster-white fedora and a tan camel's-hair overcoat even in the office, which was hot.

Mary met him in some oil promoter's office and he asked her if she knew of a girl to sit in his office and answer his phone. Mary naturally said of course she did, her sister Betty, and so there I was.

Murray, he told me to call him that, told me that he'd been a member of a mob in Chicago and a rum runner on the Atlantic Coast and had "a bucket of ice in hock in Washington, D.C." He was very sweet to me and used to take me out for coffee and tell me about different "dirty deals" he had gotten from different "babes," but he used to make me nervous when he sat by the office window, which was on the second floor, pretending that he was holding a Tommy gun and mowing down the people in the street.

"Look at that bunch of slobs," he'd say. "Not one of 'em got anything on the ball. Jeeze I'd like to have a machine gun and ah, ah, ah, ah, ah, ah, [he'd make motions of moving a machine gun back and forth] I'd let them all have it. Especially the dames."

I don't know why Murray had me and I certainly don't know why he had a telephone because whenever he left the office he told me to tell whoever called that he wasn't in and whenever he was in the office he said to tell whoever called that he was out. I had a typewriter but nothing to type so I wrote letters to everyone I had ever known. Murray paid me in crisp new bills, twenty dollars a week, for three weeks and then left town owing his rent, telephone bill, and for his furniture. I never heard of him again.

"This is the best job I've ever gotten you," Mary said. "You get twenty-five dollars a week for being Mr. Wilson's private secretary and you have a chance to make thousands more on the dime cards."

So I went to work for Mr. Wilson and his dime card scheme, which was the depression version of the present-day Pyramid Clubs.

Mr. Wilson, an advertising man, thought up the dime card scheme and if Seattle hadn't been such a stuffy city he might have made a million dollars and I might have made about ten thousand.

The idea, as I remember it, was that you bought a printed share in Prosperity for two dollars—you turned your share and a dollar more into the Prosperity office, where I worked, and got an envelope containing a dime card (cards with round slots for ten dimes each and ten places for signatures)—and two more printed shares in Prosperity. You sold your two shares for two dollars each, kept three of the four dollars to pay yourself back for the two dollars you spent on your original share, plus the one dollar turned into the office, had the other dollar changed into dimes, inserted them in the dime card, and passed it to the person you bought your share from. That person took one dime from the card, signed his name and passed it back to the person he bought from. That person did the same, etc., etc., etc.

Because I was the originator of several chains I got ninety cents from the first four, eighty cents from the next eight, seventy cents from the next sixteen and so forth. As each share was turned into the office I entered the name on a chart so that I knew who had bought from whom and where the dimes were or weren't.

After the first week the office was a madhouse, and I had to hire four girls to help me and every night at home all the family sat around and picked dimes out of Mary's and my dime cards. One night we counted seventy-two dollars' worth of dimes. All day long people stormed into the office demanding a share in Prosperity and then rushed out again to sell their shares and start their chains. I knew that there had to be an end to this delightful game some time because Seattle only had about 300,000 citizens, but I didn't anticipate how or when it would come.

One day after the office had been running for about six weeks, a fat man came in and asked me to explain the dime card game to him. I did, slowly and succinctly and he said, "That's it, sister. I'm closing up this joint!" Whereupon he called in a huge task force of policemen, who came loping in swinging their billy clubs. All the girls who were working for me began to bawl, and I tried vainly to locate Mr. Wilson, who had gone to the bank.

"I'm from the D.A.'s office and I'm going to take you all to the station house," the fat man said. I said, "You are not. We only work here and anyway what's the matter?"

"Plenty's the matter," said the fat man.

Then a photographer took a lot of pictures of the policemen seizing the files, which was pretty ridiculous as nobody was holding on to them. Finally in an hour or so a small pleasant gray-haired man appeared, dismissed the fat man, sent all of us home, and that was that.

"Crime is too nerve-racking," I told Mary. "Just get me a plain job." So she did. Typing estimates for an engineer. The work was dull and so was the engineer but it was a job.

9

"All the World's a Stage and by God Everybody in This Family Is Going to the Foreign Movies and Like Bach"

IT SEEMS TO ME, AS I LOOK BACK, THAT WHEN WE WERE THE poorest we had the most fun. Our ability to enjoy ourselves in the face of complete adversity was astounding to the people who believed that you had to have money to have fun; appalling to those others who believed that it is an effrontery for the poor to laugh. I am not sure that individually we would have been so "happy in spite of it all," but together we felt we could survive anything and did.

The world was a very sad place, in those days. The people who had jobs were so obsessed with the fear of losing them that they balanced precariously on each day of employment like a hummock in a quicksand bog, and the people who didn't have jobs had their eyes so dimmed by the fear of hunger, sickness, and cold that they walked right over golden opportunities without seeing them. I belonged to the latter group—Mother and Mary to neither.

Mary, one of those fortunate people who are able to bring forth great reserves of strength and fortitude during times of stress, accepted the depression as a personal challenge. She always had a job, she tried to find jobs for her family and hundreds of friends and, while she was looking, propped up everyone's limp spirits by defying big corporations.

When the telephone company threatened to disconnect our telephone because the bill hadn't been paid, Mary marched right down to see the president and told him that if he cut off our phone and left us with no communication with the outside world, she was going to sue him personally. Her exact words, which she recounted to our amusement at the dinner table, were, "I told him a telephone and telegraph company is a public service operating under a special grant from the state. If you cut off my telephone you will not be performing a public service and I will sue you. In fact from this day on I'm going to be known as the biggest suer in the city of Seattle." It did keep the telephone from being disconnected and it certainly bolstered our morale. She tried the same thing with the power and light company, but they turned off the lights anyway and for a week or so left us to burn old Christmas candles and not iron.

During this interlude, Mary, who was inclined to keep up with our friends of private school days, brought home to dinner a terribly snobbish young man who remarked, as we sat down to our candle-lit vegetable soup, "You Bards absolutely delight me. You have a simple meal of vegetable soup and toast and then you make it elegant by serving it by candlelight." He was so elegant, of course, that he didn't go out into the kitchen to note that we were also washing the dishes by candlelight. When he left he amused us greatly by standing by the front door for a full ten minutes flipping the switches and trying to make the porch light go on. Finally he called to Mother, "Sydney darling, I hate to mention it but your porch light's burned out. Have one of the great beasts who come to court your daughters put a new one in." When we all laughed he thought he'd been witty and repeated his asinine remark.

When we ran out of fireplace wood, Mary unearthed a bucksaw and marched us all down to a city park two blocks away, where we took turns sawing up fallen logs. We were just splitting up the first cut on our first log when two park gardeners came up and asked us what the hell we thought we were doing. Mary told them exactly what we were doing and why we were doing it and to our surprise and relief they helped us saw and carry the wood up to the house, and after that saved logs and bark for us.

During the depression we all came home right after work and Mary brought home to dinner, to stay all night, or to live with us, everyone she met whom she felt sorry for. Some of these people were brilliant, talented, and amusing. Some were just ordinary people. Some unconscionable bores. Mary didn't care. They were alive, or at least pretended to be.

Every night for dinner we had from two to ten extra people to tax Mother's ingenuity in stretching the meatloaf, macaroni and cheese, spaghetti, chili, tuna fish and noodles, vegetable soup, park wood, and beds. After dinner we played bridge or charades or Chinese checkers or the piano, rolled old cigarette butts into new cigarettes on our little cigarette-rolling machine, drank gallons of coffee which was seventeen cents a pound, ate cinnamon toast, read aloud Mark Twain, made fun of each other and all our friends, sang songs, played records, followed the dance marathons on the radio, and complained because our bosses tried to stifle our individuality by making us work.

We were in love most of the time, but being in love in those days didn't seem to be such a crystallized state as it is today. Nobody had enough money to get off by themselves, let alone get married, so grand passions flamed and were spent in front of the fireplace reading Rupert Brooke, listening to "Body and Soul" on the radio, or walking up by the reservoir to watch, across its flat black surface, the lights of the city made teary by the rain.

Every Saturday in the fall, Mother made a huge kettle of chili and we all sat around and listened to the football games. Mother, an ardent fan, kept a chart, groaned in agony over the stupidity of the announcers who commented on the crowd and didn't tell where the ball was and invariably told us that there was no football spirit in the West, we should go to a Yale-Harvard game. When our side made a touchdown we all shouted at the top of our voices, which made the dogs bark, the children wake up from their naps and bawl, and our neighbors pull aside their curtains and peer over at us.

I always looked forward to Saturday. I loved the tight expectant feeling I had as I opened the front door and wondered who would be there. I loved Saturday's dusk with the street lights as soft as breath in the fog or rain, the voices of the children, filtering home from the matinee, clear and high with joy and silliness; the firm thudding comforting sound of front doors closing and shutting the families in, the world out; the thick exciting sound of a car door slamming in front of the house; the exuberance of the telephone bell. Everybody came over Saturday night, brought friends, and stayed until three or four Sunday morning.

Sundays were always marked by a strong smell of gasoline and meatloaf and tremendous activity. First we got the children ready for Sunday School, which always meant a wild hunt for matching socks, misplaced mite boxes, and Sunday School lessons, then we all pitched in and cleaned the house, Mother made an enormous meatloaf (hamburger was only twelve cents a pound), then Mother and Dede left for church, while Mary and I repaired to a small covered areaway by the basement door, filled a little washtub with cleaning fluid and sloshed our office dresses, our skirts, even our coats in it then hung them slightly less spotty and dripping gasoline, on a line under the porch. The cleaning fluid was twenty-five cents a gallon and could be strained through flannel and used over and over again and doing our own cleaning, beside being an economic necessity, burned our hands and made us feel so virtuous that we often cleaned things that didn't need it. Big washings gave me the same terrific feeling of godly accomplishment and sometimes I'd get so carried away I'd wash old oriental rugs, doll clothes, big lumpy comforters, and a pair of Bagdad portieres we never used, just to be sure that every single thing in the house was clean.

By dinner time the house had been scrubbed and the smells of shampoo and scorch from the iron were mingled with the gasoline and meatloaf. Sunday evenings, which usually drew the biggest crowds of all, ended earlier than Saturday but not as early as they should have considering that Monday was a workday and on Monday night we usually went to the movies because Monday was family night at our neighborhood theatre and an unlimited group arriving together and appearing reasonably compatible could all get in for twenty-five cents.

Tuesday nights we went to bed early unless someone was giving a party. Parties were indistinguishable one from another. They were always given in someone's apartment; the food was always spaghetti, garlic bread, and green salad; the drinks were either bathtub gin and lemon soda or Dago red; the entertainment sitting on the floor and listening to Bach or sitting on a studio couch and listening to Bach. I didn't care much for Bach, even when partially anaesthetized by bathtub gin, but redhot nails in my eyeballs wouldn't have made me admit it, because Mary had made it very clear to me that everybody who was not down on all fours liked Bach, Baudelaire, Dostoevski, Aldous Huxley, Spengler, almond paste on filet of sole, Melochrino cigarettes, and the foreign movies.

I liked Baudelaire, Huxley and Dostoevski, I loathed Spengler, felt that almond paste on filet of sole had a lot in common with chocolate-dipped oysters, Melochrino cigarettes tasted like camel dung, and the foreign movies would have been dandy if only they hadn't been foreign.

There is a certain state of ennui in which I become engulfed almost immediately when confronted by a flickering, speckled film and a lot of unfamiliar actors batting their eyes and saying, *"A bisogni si conoseen gli amici,"* or *"Adel sitzt im Gemuthe nicht im GEBLUTE,"* or *"A pobreza no hay verguenza,"* or *"Battre le fer pendant qu'il est chaud,"* or *"da svidanya."*

The foreign movies were on Wednesday nights at eleven-thirty at a University district theatre. The reason I kept going, aside from a false pride that made me say I thought they were "magnificent," "a new approach," "delicately directed," etc., when I really thought most of them were boring and dull, was the fact that after each one the theatre management served little cups of black coffee and free cigarettes.

"An amazing picture, grrrrreat photography," I announced loudly in the foyer of the theatre, as I stuffed my pockets with cigarettes, after having slept through *Rocket to the Moon,* a ridiculous picture in which the poorly made-up actors and actresses had themselves shot to the moon and were shown lurching around in its barren craters, speaking German, and being otherwise hysterical about a questionable achievement.

We saw a French film of Joan of Arc which showed only the heads and shoulders of the actors. "Terribly new approach," I said, grabbing at the cigarettes and trying to shake off the stiff-necked feeling of having spent the evening peering over a high board fence.

The Constant Nymph, however, an English picture starring Elizabeth Bergner and Robert Donat, I still consider the best adaptation of a book and the most delightful moving picture I have ever seen. Mary also liked it but our friends were not enthusiastic—"Pleasant little thing," they called it, ashamed because they had enjoyed it and it had been in English.

One winter Saturday afternoon, quite by accident, as we were walking through the University district, my sister Dede and I discovered what was to become one of our chief and most enjoyable forms of free entertainment.

"I wonder why all those people are going into the basement of that church?" I asked Dede, as we strolled along the street. "Let's go in and find out," Dede, always one to face things, said. So we did and found that Miss Irma Grondahl was presenting her pupils and herself in a piano recital. Having nothing else to do we decided to stay and seated ourselves on folding chairs in the front row. Immediately Miss Grondahl, in a long gold velvet cape, appeared and assuming that we were relatives of some performer, solicited our help in moving the upright piano over to the left side of the stage and arranging large bouquets of dusty laurel leaves along the footlights.

The recital began and was more or less routine, except that all the performers made mistakes, swayed back and forth like pendulums as they played and even a baby only about four years old, who played "Baby Bye See the Fly, Let Us Watch Him You and I," standing up, used the loud pedal.

Then Miss Grondahl announced that she would play "Rustle of Spring" and "Hark, Hark the Lark." She had shed her gold cape and was simply clad in a sleeveless black satin dress and some crystal beads. She settled herself on the piano bench, folded her hands in her lap and began to sway. Back and forth, back and forth, back and forth and then suddenly, like running in backdoor in jumping rope, she lit into the first runs of "Rustle." Miss Grondahl was a vigorous very loud player but what made her performance irresistible to Dede and me were the large tufts of black hair which sprang quivering out of the armholes of her dress each time she lifted her hands at the end of a run or raised her arms for a crashing chord.

After that we rarely missed a recital. We watched the neighborhood papers and clipped out the notices and attended every single singing, dancing, elocution, or piano recital that didn't conflict with working hours and was within walking distance. We grew very partial to modern dance recitals whose uninhibited antics, often resembling the pangs of childbirth or someone who had just been stung by a bee, so delighted us that we were sometimes asked to leave, but singing was our favorite.

We learned almost immediately that, as we invariably became hysterical with mirth at the first frenzied shriek of the first performer and singing teachers were wont to salt their audience with friends and relatives, the very back row was the safest place to sit. If we were fortunate enough to locate and attend a voice recital where one of the performers was tone deaf or there were some thick mashed-potato contraltos, our joy was complete.

Our attendance at recitals so stimulated our appetite for simple pleasures that we began clipping out and attending other little functions. The Annual Tea of the Northwest Driftwood Society was remembered for its few guests and enormous platters of open-faced sandwiches which we wolfed down as we exchanged opinions on patina, good beaches, and time of year to look.

Most groups of Penwomen had very little food but lots of cigarettes; we were too young and regarded suspiciously by most garden clubs; but North American Indian Relic Collectors, the Society for the Protection of the Douglas Fir, and the Northwest Association of Agate Polishers, etc., were glad to see anybody.

Another simple pleasure we enjoyed in those poverty-ridden days was looking at real estate. My brother Cleve through a long involved series of trades, beginning, I believe, when he was ten years old with a saddle Mother had had made in Mexico, had acquired a long low cream-colored Cord convertible with dark blue fenders and top. On spring Saturday afternoons we would all climb in the Cord and go househunting.

I suppose in a way it was taking an unfair advantage of the real estate dealers, who invariably, when they saw our gorgeous car drive up, often primed with Mary's and my cleaning fluid, came careening out of their offices brandishing keys and carrying fountain pens and a contract. But on the other hand they tried awfully hard to take advantage of us.

"This magnificent structure," they would say, as they tried to force open the sagging door of some termite-infested old mansion, "was the home of one of Seattle's finest old families and is being sold for taxes. Just given away, really." In we would all troop, the children racing up the stairs or down to the cellar, the rest of us walking slowly, examining everything and noting with amusement the empty whisky bottles, lipstick-smeared walls, and other irrefutable evidence that this fine old family must have been supplementing their income by making whisky or dabbling in white slavery.

Sometimes we found wonderful bargains. One was a huge brick inn, north of the city, about an $85,000 structure, on sale for $5,500. There were thirteen bedrooms, a living room eighty feet long, a dining room, breakfast room, library, music room, and billiard room, every room with a fireplace, magnificent barns, a stream, and ten acres of land, and we had many violent fights over who would have which room and how we would furnish it. The real estate dealer finally got so sick of taking us out there that he gave us the keys and we used to take picnics and make plans while we ate our peanut butter and pickle sandwiches. The real estate dealer was more than anxious to make an even trade for our very salable house in the University district and we were all ready to move in when Mary, distressingly practical, pointed out that the nearest bus line was five miles away, the nearest school about eighteen miles and the former owner had, upon questioning, admitted that it cost from $200 a month up to even take the chill off the lower floor.

We were all so disappointed that Cleve went right out and rustled up an enormous yacht which was on sale for almost nothing and would really be a much more economical home for us because it would eliminate real estate taxes, light, gas, and telephone bills, we could catch fish from it, and we could pull up the gangplank when bores or bill collectors approached. The yacht unfortunately was in Alaska and Cleve never did get around to sailing it down.

Once we found a whole block of brand-new empty houses, each uniquely hideous, each on a forty-foot lot and each priced at $40,000, which at that time would have bought the Olympic Hotel with Puget Sound thrown in for good measure.

When we stopped by the first one, the owner who lived in the middle house popped out of his front door and came running up to the car before Cleve had turned off the motor. "Wonderful buy, wonderful buy," he said rather thickly, swallowing the last of a doughnut but not bothering to wipe the powdered sugar off his chin. "Come on in, all of you. Go through them. Lots of time." We all trooped out and into the first house.

Hours and hours later we were only on the next to the last and it was dark, the children were hungry and we were all surfeited with bad planning, unrelieved ugliness, chromium, peach plaster, and maroon tile. Mother, pointing to the miles and miles of woodland stretching away in all directions, asked the eager little builder why he had put such expensive houses on such small lots. He said, "Big development out here. Gatta make room for everybody." We drove away then and left him in front of his big development whose only signs of life were a single lighted window in his own house and the hoot of a night owl from one of the trees across the road.

10

Nightschool

UNTIL I STARTED TO NIGHTSCHOOL, MY LIFE WAS ONE LONG sweep of mediocrity. While my family and friends were enjoying the distinction of being labeled the prettiest, most popular, best dancer, fastest runner, highest diver, longest breath-holder-under-water, best tennis player, most fearless, owner of the highest arches, tiniest, wittiest, most efficient, one with the most allergies, or highest salaried, I had to learn to adjust to remarks such as, "My, Mary has the most beautiful red hair I've ever seen, it's just like burnished copper and so silky and curly—oh yes, Betty has hair too, hasn't she? I guess it's being so coarse is what makes it look thick."

Then I started to nightschool to learn shorthand and after ten years of faithful attendance, realized that now I was eligible for some kind of a medal for being the slowest-witted, most-unable-to-be-taught and longest-attender-at-school-studying-one-subject.

I went to every nightschool in the city of Seattle, both paid and free, studied under expert teachers, but I couldn't learn shorthand. It had something to do with my coordination I believe, because I was never able to learn arm-movement writing in school either.

Mary, as I have pointed out, was never in favor of my attendance at nightschool. She thought it was a waste of time and she was right, but learning shorthand got to be an obsession with me, like swimming the English Channel. I bought a book of stories in shorthand and for years mouthed them out on the streetcar riding to and from work—I worked at memorizing the Gregg dictionary, symbol by symbol—I spent from seven to nine or six to eight of most of my Mondays, Wednesdays, and Fridays for ten years in some shorthand class. But at my jobs the minute anyone ever said to me, "Take a letter," or "Get your notebook, Miss Bard," I would get such a case of buck fever I'd make wiggly little scriggles instead of smooth curves and little lines and would get far behind trying to remember whether "a" went on the inside or outside of the angles.

Nightschool differed from dayschool, I learned, not only in time of day but in atmosphere and type of students. Dayschool students, who were usually young, career-conscious people, eager to get jobs and get started (the fools), exuded an air of cheerful self-confidence. Nightschool students, predominately young foreigners and old Americans suddenly faced with the necessity for earning their own livings, were even in times of great prosperity badly handicapped by language difficulties, the wrong color of skin or old stiff fingers. Nevertheless they zealously, gallantly, and in spite of the inadequacy of their tools, tried to carve niches for themselves in the stone face of the business world.

Often when I attended the Public Evening School, which was almost free, my shorthand class would be comprised entirely of old ladies and young Japanese girls. The old ladies worked feverishly at their speed studies and over and above the teacher's precise nasal dictation of dull business letters I could hear their labored breathing and creaking joints, like old hulls straining at their moorings during the stress of a storm.

The frustration I experienced over my inability to master shorthand was overshadowed by the tragic realization that even if those little old secretaries and young Japanese ones learned to take shorthand five hundred words a minute and could type faster than the speed of light, nobody would hire them. Not just because of the depression but because of a horrible practice in American business of seldom hiring any female office worker who does not have white skin and is not under thirty.

The little Japanese girls were wonderful at shorthand. Naturally quick, studious, and imitative, the rapid accurate transcription of someone else's thoughts was just their dish. When the teacher gave us final impossible tests of long articles, read at two hundred words a minute, and then asked for the hands of those who had gotten it all, only the little tan hands shot up and waved eagerly. "Read your notes, Miss Fukiyama," the teacher would say and Miss Fukiyama would read in her soft, sweet little voice, with only a little hesitation and giggling, exactly what had been dictated. But when Miss Fukiyama went to apply for a job, all she was offered was housework.

The Public Evening School was housed in a large gray stone building that smelled of old bodies, stale sandwiches, and chalk. My shorthand classes were usually from six to eight, which meant that I could go right from work and eat dinner when I got home. Sometimes, however, I would have to take the seven-to-nine class and then to kill time and to avoid the long trip home and back downtown again, I took another subject from six to seven. Once I took French, another time Speech, and another time Creative Writing.

The Speech woman, who wore a big brown felt tam and rough tweed suit, said, "Korrrrect speeeeeech is more eemportant than korrect post-eur. A person is eemeejutly judged by hees speeech." As she talked she rolled back her lips, swung them to the sides, or pulled them down so she looked like a red snapper. I used to imitate her at home at night for the pleasure of the family but I left after the sixth time.

Each session of the Creative Writing class was jam-packed with frustrated people who wanted to be writers and live Bohemian lives. Almost every student carried a large briefcase bulging with manuscripts which either the publishers were too timid to publish, were too crooked to publish, or else had kept just long enough to steal the idea and give it to some big writer. After about the fourth session I began to wonder if frustration produced bad breath because halitosis accompanied so many of these unpublished writers.

In addition to their frustration and bad breath, most of the students were violently jealous of each other. The teacher, who confided to me one night that trying to teach people with nothing to say how to write it down was a sad business, had us write stories and little articles and then read them aloud and invite criticism.

Before the unfortunate victim had read his last word, the stiff upraised arms of the criticizers were as numerous as wheat stalks on a stubble field. The criticism ran to: "I don't like your style and nothing you said was true to life," "I don't like to say this, honey, but your grammar is terrible," or "I think that the author of this piece of material should put in deeper meanings and make the material a thing of lasting importance and more general import so that when the material is read by intellects other than those of this community they would have something to recall in the material," or "I don't think that fella would have married the girl after she treated him like that, I know I sure wouldn't have," or "I think the story wonderful and I don't think we should be so hard on our fellow authors because think how you're going to feel when you get up there," or "I noticed that in one place she said that the cabin was twenty feet long and in another place she said it was eighteen feet long." There were a few poets whose works were of the:

> "Oh beautiful waters of Puget Sound
> You are bluer and softer than the hard dry ground,
> Oh, Mount Rainier so majestic and pink
> Every night in your beauty I drink"

school and got much less criticism and more praise than the works of the fiction writers.

I noticed that the people with the worst breath were the ones most anxious to corner you and outline their trilogy on the life of a Butter Clam. The consensus of opinion seemed to be that all successful authors owed their success to illicit relations with their publisher and/or dirty books.

A large florid woman, who sat across from me at each session and had a terrible time forcing her stomach behind the school desk, was interested only in religious poems, several of which she gave me as keepsakes. One of my favorites ran, as I remember,

> Here I am, Jesus, take me to your bosom,
> You didn't bleed for nothing, Jesus,
> Nor from the grave was risen.
> Now I am all alone, Jesus, You are my only friend
> I want to come home to you, Jesus,
> So an angel down for me send.
> I want to be with Papa
> He's up there with you too
> So are Johnny and little Mildred and Bertha
> They all died of the flu.

The woman's name was Mrs. Halvorsen and according to her she had buried everyone she could get her hands on. In addition to Johnny, little Mildred, Bertha, and Papa, who had all gone out just like lights and within minutes of each other during the flu epidemic after World War I, there had been innumerable little Charlies, Dannys, Carls, Helwigs, and Irmas who smothered in their beds, swelled up and died, choked to death on baby teeth, or just came in and announced they were going to Jesus and did.

Talking to Mrs. Halvorsen was the equivalent of attending hundreds of funerals but she was very kind and brought me little bags of Sirup Spisser, Fattigman, and Sand Kakers, which I ate during shorthand so that that winter my notes were not only wrong but always crumby. Mrs. Halvorsen was one of the very few of us students who had been published. Her poems had been published in religious papers both in Norway and the United States and though she hadn't been paid anything we were all very proud of her.

Another friend of mine at Writing class wrote personal experience stories, all very depressing, about how she was fired and not paid, about one place she worked where the woman was so stingy they only bought a half a pound of hamburger for dinner for themselves and their two servants, and about the time she slipped on the sidewalk and broke her hip and the city wouldn't pay her. She had a stack of rejection slips about nine feet high and couldn't understand why.

"I tell de trut," she said. "Dere is not vun vord I write dat is not de trut." I told her that I thought she should write about happier things, not be so sad, and cited Mark Twain as an example. She said, "You mean I should make yokes?" I said yes and so she went home and laboriously inserted Pat and Mike "yokes" here and there in her sad little manuscripts.

A little fat Greek man thought the idea behind successful creative writing was quantity not quality and he came staggering into each session with about a hundred pounds of badly written, greasy manuscript in pencil on scratch paper, about a moronic detective and an even stupider police captain who could never catch a big gang of killers and robbers who continually robbed a little Greek grocery store run by the cleverest little fellow ever to appear on a grubby piece of scratch paper.

The class criticizers were so relentlessly cruel to him they almost made him cry, so Mrs. Halvorsen and I invited him to have coffee with us and we told him we thought he was a genius. He said, "I got lotsa ideas. I write all night lotsa times." We told him that someday he would be famous and he was so grateful he brought us each a bottle of Metaxa brandy.

One time during the depression I tired of the regular Public Evening School and registered in one run by the WPA. This nightschool had one shorthand teacher, who for some strange reason held the class in a different room every night and lived in mortal fear of Government spies.

When I had dates pick me up at the school, as I often did, and they came early and signaled at me through the door, she would jump up from her desk, shout, "Who's out there? Who is he—what does he want?" in her excitement dropping her books and her pencils, even her glasses, which she stamped on one night. Once, when she seemed more upset than usual, a friend of mine, a shy young lawyer, appeared and she threw open the door to the hall and shouted at him, "Let me see your credentials. If you're going to snoop around here you've got to show your credentials."

Mary was right, I never met any executives at nightschool, and it didn't improve my shorthand much, but there were many times when I found it most comforting to look around a big class and feel that we were all failures together.

11

Bills! Bills! Bills!

A BILL IS A THING THAT COMES IN A WINDOWED ENVELOPE AND causes men to pull in their lips and turn the oilburner down to sixty degrees and women to look shifty-eyed and say, "Someone must have been charging on my account."

A bill collector is a man with a loud voice who hates everybody. A collection agency is a collection of bill collectors with loud voices who hate everybody and always know where she works.

I could no more have a complete feeling of kinship with someone who has never had bills than I could with someone who doesn't like dogs. Owing money is not pleasant and undoubtedly stems from weakness, but those of us who have known the burden of debt; have spent our long wakeful night hours peering into that black sinkhole labeled "the future"; have grown wild with frustration trying to yank and pull one dollar into the shape and size of five; have flinched at the sight of any windowed envelope; have cringed with embarrassment at the stentorian voices of bill collectors; have been wilted by money lenders' searing questions; and have often resorted to desperate dreams (in my case usually involving scenes where a beautifully dressed, charming, red haired lady says to a lot of different people, "Your pleading just bores me—close my account!"), emerge finally, if we are able, kicked and beaten into a reasonable facsimile of a human being and/or dogliker.

Which is why, I guess, I've never felt very close to bankers. Bankers remind me of a little girl I used to play with in Butte,

Montana—a little girl named Emily, who always had a large supply of jelly beans which she carried in a little striped paper bag, the top of which she kept closed and tightly twisted. When Emily wanted a jelly bean she untwisted her bag, reached in, took one, put it in her mouth, retwisted the bag, and told us, her loyal playmates drooling on the sidelines, "Gee, kids, I'd like to give you some jelly beans, I really would, but my mother won't let me."

Experience has convinced me that all bankers are little Emilys. The only time they untwist their little striped bags and take out a jelly bean or two is after you have proved conclusively that you already have plenty of jelly beans of your own and aren't hungry anyway. When you don't have any jelly beans and are starving they say, "Gee, kids, I'd like to give you some jelly beans, I really would, but my Board won't let me."

The best pal I'd like to have least after a banker, is a credit manager. Credit managers are people who, by birth or training or both, live entirely in the past, have no faith in the future, are not interested in the present, hold grudges indefinitely or at least for six years, never forget old slights, and are always ready and eager to rehash old quarrels. Credit managers collect, the way other people collect recipes, all the nasty things anybody has ever said about anybody else.

If you were two payments behind on your vacuum cleaner in 1943, the year Mama got that fishbone stuck in her throat, Bobby broke his arm, and the sewer backed up, and apply for credit in 1949, the credit manager shuffles through his neat stack of white cards, swells his nostrils, and says, "I'm sawry, but it says here that you didn't live up to your contract on your vacuum cleaner and your attitude was sullen." The rest of us are taught that every day is a clean slate but a credit manager is taught that every day is an old bill.

The only person ever able, to my knowledge, to completely confuse credit managers is my mother. Mother, a truly charming and most talented woman, has no more financial sense than a hummingbird, arguing with her about money is like trying to catch minnows in your fingers, and what is worse she adopts a reasonable attitude toward bill paying.

When a credit manager would call Mother and shout accusingly, "You promised to be down here on Monday and you didn't show up," Mother wouldn't cringe or get tears in her eyes, but would say pleasantly, "I know but I was busy with something else."

When the credit manager said, "Why didn't you come down on Tuesday, then?" Mother would say, "Would you mind holding the phone a minute, the cat seems to have a fur ball in her throat?"

Sometime later, having disposed of the cat, Mother would pick up the phone and resume, "Hello, Mr. Crandall, I'm sorry to have kept you waiting. Let's see, Tuesday, oh, yes, there was a program at school."

"What about Wednesday?" Mr. Crandall would ask.

"Wednesday is a very bad day to get someone to take care of the children," Mother would say.

"What about Thursday?" Mr. Crandall would ask irritably. "Couldn't you have come down Thursday?"

"No," said Mother, "I couldn't. I was having the chimney cleaned and I had to get Mrs. Murphy's lunch." Mrs. Murphy was the cleaning woman but the credit manager, whose head was beginning to buzz, thought she cleaned the chimneys.

"Then will you be down today?" he would finally ask wearily.

"Oh, not today," Mother would say. "I'm making Alison's dogwood costume."

"Next Monday then?" he'd say, still with hope.

"All right, next Monday," Mother would say, adding after he had hung up, "If my primrose woman doesn't show up."

Mother employed the same infuriatingly reasonable tactics with Mary and me.

"Mother," I'd shout in exasperation, "I gave you twenty-five dollars Thursday to pay the gas bill and they called me today and said it hadn't been paid."

Mother, intent on frosting an applesauce cake, would say, "Which man did you talk to?"

"A Mr. Ellsworth," I'd say.

Mother would say, "Is Mr. Ellsworth the one with that lump behind his ear?"

"I don't know about the lump," I'd say, "but he has a Southern accent."

"Oh, then the one with the lump must be Mr. Hastings," Mother would say. "Mr. Ellsworth is the one whose daughter failed her college board examinations and he is awfully upset about it."

"Which college was she going to?" Dede would ask.

"Wellesley," Mother would say, "and I told him that I had a very dear friend who teaches at Wellesley and promised to write to her and see if anything can be done."

"Who do you know at Wellesley?" Alison would ask.

"Charles Horton's sister, Mabel," Mother would say.

"Is she old 'there is rhythm and grace in every pore of the human body' who used to sit on the couch with her skirts clear up around her thighs?" Dede would ask.

Mother would say, "She wore tweeds she wove herself and she is very nice."

"Oh, that old bore," Mary would say. "She's not coming out here is she?"

Dede would say, "She's probably packing her loom right now."

Mother would say, "I think Mabel is very charming."

Mary would say, "You do not. You think she's a great big bore but you won't admit it because she's from Boston."

I would yell, "WHAT ABOUT THE TWENTY-FIVE DOLLARS FOR THE GAS COMPANY?"

Mother would say, "Lower your voice. I gave it to the egg man."

"But I promised it to the gas company and the egg man isn't due until next week," I'd wail. "Why did you give it to him?"

"Because," Mother would say, gently and with great reasonableness, "his wife has arthritis. Now let's eat this applesauce cake while it is hot."

Mother's approach to any direct unpleasant question is to pick out the least important word in the question and make an issue of it. I can best illustrate this by an incident depicting a similar type of mind. When Anne and Joan were nine and ten, we overheard the following conversation one day as they sat on the back steps discussing school.

Anne said most dramatically, "Do you know that Janice Price is only ten and she *smokes!*"

Joan said, "What brand?"

Mother, a strong believer in and supporter of the small business, made keeping the household accounts more confusing than world government. Mother had an egg man, a bread woman, a rabbit man, a chicken man, a spice man, a vegetable man, a butter man, a milk man, a laundry man, a coal man, a slabwood man, an alder man, an old forest growth man, a good plumber, a punk plumber who would come on Sundays, a painter, a primrose woman, an electrician, a Fuller brush man, five magazine men, an ice man, a chimney cleaner, a sewing woman, a bulb man, an orange man, a dahlia woman, an apple man, a regular manure man, a well-rotted manure man, a pots-and-pan woman, a mothball-and-potholder woman, a wire toecover man, a little old needle woman, a Christmas wrapping woman, and a downspout man.

All of these "at the doors" as Gammy used to call them, had regular times to appear but both because they all loved Mother and because her method of payment was so erratic, they dropped in whenever in the neighborhood. On payday they swarmed around the house like yellowjackets around a rotten apple.

Occasionally when Mary and I would try to bring order into our lives and live on a budget, we would gather the family together for strength and try to take Mother to task for her "at the doors."

"Can't you get rid of some of them?" we'd wail.

"I'll do my best," Mother would say. "Now which ones do you want to eliminate?"

"The potholder-and-mothball woman," we'd all shout together.

"Why?" Mother would say.

"Because," we'd say, "her potholders are no good. She makes big mistakes in her crocheting and when you try to grab anything hot you burn your fingers in the holes and you know as well as we do her mothballs make the whole house smell like a Chinese whorehouse and contain some sort of special breeding stimulant for moths."

Mother would set her lips stubbornly. "Mrs. Twickenham," she'd say, "makes mistakes in her crocheting because she needs new glasses which she can't afford. I know her mothballs are no good and smell horrible but I always try to throw them right away."

"Why do you buy them, then?" we'd groan.

"Because I had Cleve drive her home one rainy day and she lives in a little one room shack and she looks like Gammy."

So Mrs. Twickenham stayed.

"All right," we said. "What about that awful wire toecover man? You know we've never been able to figure out a use for one of his inventions."

Mother said, "I have. I'm using his egg basket to keep the dogs off my camellia cuttings."

"What about his butter slicer, his bread cutter, his fruit basket, his soap dishes, his lettuce bag?" we said. "They none of them work and whenever you open any cupboard in our kitchen, one of them lunges out and snags your stockings."

Mother said, "Yellow Belly had her kittens in the fruit basket and anyway Mr. Muster's wife has t.b."

Mother, a completely selfless person herself, has her own means to combat selfishness. When my sister Mary married a doctor all the rest of the family, via Mother, immediately became well supplied with expensive vitamins. It was simple. When Mother stayed with Mary she loaded her suitcase with different bottles from Mary's medicine cabinet and distributed them to the other members of the family.

Occasionally, of course, there would be slipups, like the time we all took, with excellent results, quantities of a Kelly-green bile-priming pill in the belief that it was a newer, stronger vitamin A. Or the time we all took, for several months, a great many bright red cinnamon drops in the belief that they were some wonderful new all-in-one vitamin, enormous quantities of which Mary always seemed to have on hand. "No wonder Mary gets so much done," Mother told us, as she came staggering in with a new supply. "I've never felt better in my life." "What energy, what vitality—hooray for vitamins!" we told each other over long distance and when Mary's husband heard about it he said, "Chalk up another for Christian Science."

When I moved to the country, Mother arranged summer outings for all the family at my house and saw to it that Don and I dug lots of clams for distribution among the drylanders. When one of us married an Italian the others got plenty of olive oil, when one acquired an orchard the others all got fruit, when one got chickens we all got eggs. If one of us has a rare rock garden plant, Mother snips it up, roots the pieces and distributes them to the others.

As I write this I am convinced that the Government could use Mother but I'm not exactly sure where, unless it would be to confuse the Russians.

My first experiences with debt were mild and vicarious but they fostered in me a strong and lasting belief that bills were shameful things and should always be kept secret.

When my brother Cleve was about twelve he decided one desperate day that his only hope in a world which seemed to be peopled entirely with females (Mother, Grandmother, sisters, cats, dog, cows, horses, even the turtle and canary were she's) was to answer an advertisement in a magazine and become, with nothing down and plenty of time to pay, a "high-paid executive" and show a few people!

To his chagrin, immediately upon receipt of his evasively filled out coupon, he received from the advertiser, not a magic formula, not explicit instructions for brain control, not one darn thing that overnight would enable him to emerge suddenly from his messy, cough-drop-boxy, gun littered room, a suave, smooth, high-paid executive in a blue, pin-striped suit, but a great big, thick arithmetic book labeled *First Steps in Accounting* and filled, he discovered to his disgust, after he had thumbed through a few pages, with nothing but "thought problems"—that most detested of all types of arithmetic problems. Cleve immediately abandoned all idea of becoming an executive, tossed the accounting book under his bed and returned to his job as unofficial assistant to the Laurelhurst bus driver.

Unfortunately, the Executive Builders didn't give up so easily. They had started to mold a high-paid executive and by God, man, they were going to finish. Every week or two for months they deluged Cleve with courses, ledgers, notebooks, examinations, books of receipts, and mimeographed letters on character-building, co-operation, don't be a quitter, and forging ahead. Surreptitiously Cleve garnered them from the mailman and shoved them under the bed.

Then one day the courses stopped and the letters began.

"Mr. Bard," said the President of the Executive Molders, his long admonishing finger appearing across the entire face of the letter, "have you no honor? Don't you know that buying things and not paying for them is STEALING?"

"Mr. Bard: Cheat is a terrible word. Honesty and GOOD CREDIT are a high-paid executive's most *important* assets."

"Mr. Bard: If there is some reason why you cannot pay, tell us what it is. We want to be FAIR WITH YOU! We want to give you every CHANCE!"

"Mr. Bard: PLEASE REMIT!"

"Mr. Bard: Unless full payment is made AT ONCE, this long over-due account will be turned over to our attorneys."

Mr. Bard, who by this time was scared to death, appealed to Gammy, who kept all her money in her Bible and could always be counted on to bail us out of any monetary difficulties. Gammy heard the story, read the advertisement, saw the accounting book, and said, "Only robbers take things they can't pay for. Never buy anything unless you have the money in your pocket. Now go gather everything up and we'll send it back to these people. Imagine en-rolling a boy your age. The big grafters."

So Cleve and I started hunting up the stuff but somehow or

other most of the paper had been marked on with crayons or used for scratch paper, the books and notebooks all bore traces of apple core or puppy's teeth, and somebody had spilled a cup of cocoa on one of the biggest ledgers. So Gammy wrote and told the Big Grafters that she would pay for the books and supplies but not one cent for the instructions. She wrote, "In the future, I think you had better check on the qualifications of your high-paid executives to be, the one in question is only in the seventh grade and has never to my knowledge, shown the slightest aptitude nor liking for numbers" (Gammy's name for arithmetic in any form).

After that we children sailed along with pretty good credit until my sister Dede got to be nine and answered a most enticing advertisement which said, "Sell these exquisitely colored, beautiful Christmas seals and EARN MONEY! Fill in your name and address and we will send you without charge these beautifully colored, gorgeously designed Xmas seals." The whole tone of the advertisement led Dede to believe that it wasn't going to be a matter of her selling the gorgeous, exquisite Christmas seals, but rather a question of whether or not she would be strong enough to hold off the eager excited mobs who would be trying to grab them away from her.

The first disappointment was the seals themselves, which, when they came, proved to be neither gorgeously colored nor exquisitely designed but sheets of poorly perforated, ugly, dun-colored seals, so carelessly printed that angels and wise men wore blank faces while their eyes and mouths appeared like large black flies on the flanks of Santa Claus' reindeer gracing the seal just above.

The next tragedy was when little sister Alison found the seals, tore them apart in spite of their faulty perforation, licked most of them and stuck them to the doll bed and the wallpaper. Then last, but not least, Dede, who at nine had not had a great deal of business experience, thought that the money made from the sale to a kind neighbor, of the few that were left, belonged to her and spent it.

Around January second, the mailman delivered the first big white business letter addressed to Daisy Bard. Mother, resigned through the years to being addressed as Mrs. Daisy Bard, instead of Mrs. Darsie Bard, thought the letter was for her and opened it. It was a stern but straightforward request for three dollars.

> 4 pkg. of Xmas Seals @ $1.00 ea ... $4.00
> Less Commission 1.00
>   Balance Due $3.00

it read. Mother was mystified and asked the family that night at dinner if they knew anything about any Christmas seals. Nobody did.

The next month there was another bill marked PLEASE REMIT. Again Mother asked us if any of us knew anything about these mysterious Christmas Seals. Nobody did.

In the meantime my sister Dede, who was a very nervous little girl and often thought she saw Jesus with a candle walking around her room at night, began having big black circles under her eyes and crying for no reason at all! Mother took her to a pediatrician, who said to put her on buttermilk, which didn't help, and Gammy said that milk had nothing to do with it, Dede's trouble was too much talent in music, so Mother stopped her piano lessons, which didn't help either because Dede still kept seeing Jesus at night only now he was carrying Christmas seals instead of a candle.

Then one day a letter came addressed to Miss Daisy Bard and it was threatening. "Are you playing the game on the square?" it said. "We have done our part—Daisy, why don't you do yours? . . . Where is your money? Unless action is taken on this matter immediately, we will take steps."

Mother sat right down and wrote the company and told them that they had made a mistake and nobody in our family had bought any Christmas seals and would they please not bore us with any more of their bills or letters. By return mail came a letter from the company enclosing a labored little penciled request for the Christmas Seals and signed, "We remain cordially yours, Darsie Bard." Mother, in true Mother fashion, said nothing about the Christmas seals or the three dollars but asked Dede why in the world she had signed her letter, "We remain cordially yours." Dede, who was crying, said, "That's the way we sign our invitations to the PTA."

Mother paid the Christmas seal company and accompanied her check with a few pointed comments on the quality of their merchandise and the age of the commission salesman they employed. Gammy told Dede that only robbers took things they couldn't pay for.

Years passed and then I came winging in from a farm, where budgeting had been simply a matter of subtracting the feed from the eggs, adding the sacks, subtracting the gasoline, adding the potatoes, subtracting the buttermilk, and adding the pig, and tried to cope with a system where I was paid every two weeks, the main bills came once a month, Mother's little business men came every week or every day or by the seasons, insurance payments were quarterly, taxes were yearly, and no matter how many times we had macaroni and cheese there was always somebody left over. Somebody who came at dinner time and announced in ringing tones, "Collect for the *Times!* . . . Collect for the sewing machine! . . . Collect for the slab wood! . . . Collect for the sheep guana! . . . Collect for the *Saturday Evening Post!* . . . Collect for the Belgian hares!"

We all pooled our money and Mary and Mother and I distributed it to the best of our ability and Mother's reasons, but it was a losing game. Like climbing up a rock slide. We'd just get to the top and the front porch would sag, or the toilet would overflow or the downspouts would leak or Christmas would come and down we'd go to the bottom again.

Then of course there were things like the five green party dresses I charged in the course of one winter.

My darkest memories are of that spring after my first winter of charge accounts. For months, as I rode to and from work on the streetcar, I had been confronted at exactly eye level with advertisements that pleaded "Use your credit! Don't go without! Buy from us—take a year to pay! NEVER SAY HOW MUCH—SAY CHARGE IT!"

So one day I did. I opened a charge account at a large department store and bought a handwoven tweed coat on sale for fifteen dollars. "A charge account," I told the family, "really saves you money. This coat was a marvellous bargain and I never could have gotten it if I hadn't had a charge account. After this we'll charge whatever we need and pay at the end of the month."

"Good idea!" "Sound reasoning!" "Oh boy," said the family.

At first we were very careful and limited our charges to pots and pans, stockings, water glasses and bathmats. The small bills came in, I paid and said, "You see, a charge account makes life much simpler." So I opened a few more, and a few more and a few more and then came Christmas. "Charge it, charge it, charge it," I said all over town and if I hesitated the least little bit the clerks said, "Don't worry, honey, things bought in December aren't billed until February." In December, February seems as far away as July and so I staggered through the Christmas crowds, my arms loaded with rich gifts, the smells of fog and pine tingling my nostrils, certain disaster dogging my heels.

Then Christmas was over and so was Lumber and bearing down upon me as surely and relentlessly as death, was February tenth. Mother said, "Go down and talk to them. Explain that you have lost your job and won't be able to pay until you find something permanent." I said, "Yeah, something permanent that pays about five thousand dollars a month. Somebody *must* have been charging on my accounts."

Mary said, "Pay each one a little bit. That's what I do. Even fifty cents lets them know that you owe the bill and intend to pay."

How could I give Mr. Beltz of the fishy eye, reluctant credit, and five green party dresses, fifty cents? I said I'd handle it my way.

My way was to lie awake all night in the bed I shared with Mary, flinching as occasional raindrops bounced from the sill of the open window to my face, and watching the street light through the window make prison bars on the wall. My way was to toss and turn and beat my brains and wail, "Why did I do it? What was I thinking of? What will I do now?"

The raindrops hitting the ground at the bottom of the narrow black crevasse between our house and a neighbor's with a heavy spull-lit! spull-lat! plup, plup, plup, like ripe fruit falling from the trees, seemed to my tortured brain to be saying, "Charge-it, charge-it, charge-it—payup, payup, payup."

The drops that went splink, splink, as they bounced off the window sill, and ploop, ploop, ploop, as they searched for and found the empty flower pots Mother kept underneath the cutleaf maple at the corner of the house, seemed to be saying, "The clink, the clink, the clink, you Fool! Fool! Fool!"

I turned my pillow over and over trying to find a cool side and was resentful of the rest of the family blissfully suspended above reality in their hammocks of sleep. The house was as quiet and depressing as a vault, but outside the rain, apparently to make up for the fact that it couldn't be heard on the roof, splashed noisily on the sills, splatted down between the houses, hissed on the pavements, slurped into the drainpipes, raced in the gutters, and finally went gulping into the sewer. How harsh and unmusical were its noises compared to those of country rain. Country rain thrummed like a woodpecker, pit-a-patted across the roofs with quick light strokes like bird's feet, swished moaning through the orchards, slid like quicksilver from leaf to leaf, thudded hopefully against windows like June bugs, and plopped in the dusty roads like small toads. City rain sounded businesslike and as though it were metered and I hated it—I hated everything about the city. Why had I ever left the farm? What would I do?

Mary had said, "You are a victim of circumstance and you are not alone. There are millions of Americans who have suddenly lost their jobs and owe bills. I imagine the people we owe money to, owe money themselves to someone else. Think of that."

I did and it wasn't comforting because I reasoned that if Mr. Beltz, for instance, was as worried about the bills he owed as I was, then he'd get the money out of me for those party dresses if he had to chisel it out of my bones. Five green party dresses. What had I been thinking of? I must have been crazy. I hardly ever went to formal parties and even if I did was there any reason I always had to be in a charged green?

I finally got through February, which was a short month, but I lost twelve pounds, was as jumpy as a cricket, and had such circles under my eyes I looked like a marmoset. I had to do something immediately.

Then one day I was walking along the street and right up ahead of me on a huge signboard was an awfully nice-looking man. His outstretched hands were filled with ten and twenty dollar bills and in a big white bubble to the right of his head he was begging me to come on down to the Friendly Loan Company. "We want to help you," he said. "We want to make life easy for you. Stop worrying. Come down and let us share our money with you." There it was. The answer.

I hurried right up to the small, dark office housing the Friendly Loan Company.

"Whaya want?" said the friendly little lady at the desk, whose mouth should have been set out in the woods to catch raccoons.

"I want to borrow some money," I said, adding with a gay little laugh, "a lot of money."

Miss Friendly Loan looked at me coldly, threw her lips over to the left and yelled, "Chawrlie! Customer!"

Chawrlie, who had close-set, pale green eyes and a small head, took me into his office and shot questions at me for about an hour. I had intended to lie about my job, my salary, my bank account, my bills, everything, but I found that I couldn't lie to Chawrlie. He caught me up every time, picked the lie up in two fingers, handed it back to me still wriggling and told me to keep it.

When I had finally told all, Chawrlie had me sign a note for a hundred dollars and then handed me only sixty-two. The other thirty-eight, he said, went for carrying charges, upkeep, risk insurance, and probably that great big advertisement. The interest was twelve per cent and I was to pay five dollars every two weeks. I thanked Chawrlie profusely and skipped out to distribute the sixty-two dollars among my charge accounts and to make rash promises about future payments.

When I got home, I bragged to the family about my great financial acumen, told them about darling old generous Chawrlie and that night slept soundly for the first time in weeks.

It was fortunate I did, because from then on my life became the living hell. My jobs were all temporary—a week here, a week or two there, and though I was almost always paid, there was something about that temporary money, usually in cash, that made it seem as if I'd won it on a punchboard. I'd use my salary to buy little presents for the family, a string of gold beads, take us all to a show, buy candy, and pay Mother's "at the doors," and tell myself, "When I get a permanent job I'll start in on the big bills."

It was the other way around, of course, the big bills started on me. Each of my charge accounts had a collector, equipped apparently with second sight. They knew about my jobs before Mary had found them for me and would often be milling around the door before I'd been properly hired.

"Who in hell are all those people?" one of my short term bosses asked me.

"Bill collectors," I told him humbly.

"All of them?" he asked in amazement.

"Yep," I said, "and I've more that haven't found me yet."

"And I thought I had troubles," he said and was very kind about my shorthand.

I might have been able to duck a few of my bill collectors if it hadn't been for Mother. When they called at the house, she invited them in for coffee and they told her about their wives and children and sicknesses and ambitions and Mother retaliated with where I was working, had worked, hoped to work, and could no longer work.

"Don't tell them *anything*," I used to scream at her.

She'd say, "Now, Betsy, you're taking the wrong attitude entirely.

Mr. Hossenpfiester knows all about Mr. Chalmers' office closing and what a hard time we've had this winter and about having to buy a new gas heater and taking Sandy [our collie] to the veterinary and all he wants is for you to talk to him and explain when you can pay and how much."

"He's very nice when he's drinking your coffee," I said, "but when he comes to my office he yells and calls me 'sister.' Don't you dare tell him about this job."

But Mother did and pleaded with me to go down and talk to all my creditors. I wouldn't. Only too well I remembered what Gammy had said about only robbers buying things they couldn't pay for. I was ashamed of owing money, I was scared to death of all credit managers, and I hated my bill collectors. I sneaked around town, jumping six feet if anyone touched me on the arm, getting tears in my eyes every time I was called to the phone and dashing for the restroom if a stranger came into my office.

Then I got behind on the payments to the Friendly Loan Company and I learned what trouble really was. The Friendly Loan collectors were everywhere. They yelled at me in the lobby of movie theatres when I had dates, shouted at me on the streetcar, and the woman with the coontrap mouth called me on the telephone three or four times a day no matter where I was working.

One time I lied to old Coontrap and told her that she had called me so much I'd been fired. I went up to her office after work and cried real tears and she said she was sorry, but the next day at work she called and when I answered the phone she said, "Well, hello, you dirty little sneak. You better come up here tonight after work or else."

Then I went to work for the Government and the first week so many bill collectors came roaring into the office or called me on the phone that I expected to be fired but instead my boss took me down to the Federal Employees Union and they not only loaned me the money to pay all my bills, but paid them for me.

They paid the Friendly Loan exactly twenty-seven dollars—the difference between the thirty-five I had paid them, which they had apparently credited to cleaning the rugs, new draperies, etc., instead of the principal, and the sixty-two dollars I had actually received, and told them that if they didn't like it they could come into court and fight charges of usury.

In all my life I will never forget the deliriously free, terribly honest feeling I had the day the Federal Union notified me that all my bills had been paid and that from that day forward, except for a little matter of several hundred dollars I owed them and was to pay back so much out of each pay check, I was solvent.

Is it any wonder that I love the Government and don't mind paying my income tax?

12

———•———

Bundles for Bards

I READ THE OTHER DAY THAT SOME WOMEN SOLVE THE CLOTHES problem by giving a designer $100,000 a year to dress them. All I can say for that designer is that he must be sewing together old hundred dollar bills and using them for interlining. Clothes are a problem to almost every woman but sans a designer and a check for $100,000, the problem is usually how to turn the dentist bill money into a tweed suit without a certain party noticing.

Naturally during the depression clothes were more of a problem. If it is hard to be well dressed on $100,000, imagine how hard it was to be well dressed on nothing. Fortunately, we could all wear each other's clothes (the first one up was the best dressed) but our wardrobe even when combined had nothing in common with the "early evening," "country living," "an afternoon at the museum" or "something for the symphony" categories depicted by the fashion magazines. Our clothes had categories but they were "clean," "dirty," "work," "date," and "terrible" (which we wore around the house).

Our problems were not the knotty ones of trying to choose between a Dior or a Carnegie, or deciding whether to wear a peplum even if it made our hips look big. Our problems were first getting something, anything, and then trying to keep it away from Alison and her high school friends, who descended on our closets like moths, the minute we left the house. We threatened Alison with torture, we ordered her friends from the house, we even yelled at Mother, but it was all wasted effort and for Alison's four high school years, nothing Mother or Mary or Dede or I owned ever got really cool.

I would clean and press a dress and have it neat and ready for work in my closet, but when I went to get it, it would be gone and in its place would be a wrinkled, milk-shake spotted tweed skirt and a blouse ripped under both arms.

"Alison," I'd yell. "Where is my brown dress?"

"Which brown dress?" Alison would say, her eyes shifting from side to side like a metronome.

"My office dress," I'd say. "It was brand clean and pressed and now it's gone."

"I haven't seen it," Alison would say, slipping through the front door and signaling to whoever had it on not to go past the house. That night when I got home the dress would be back in my closet, reeking with some musky perfume and still warm.

But even with Alison and the depression, Mary and Dede and I never attached the desperate importance to our work clothes some girls did, as we learned one night at a roadhouse north of town.

A large group of us were sitting in a booth drinking terrible drinks and eating old boiled chicken that had been slightly heated in deep fat, when we became aware of a commotion next door. A heavy thumping, a few curses, and then little moans. One of the men in our party peered around the curtains and reported that a man in the next booth was throwing his lady-friend against the wall like a hand ball. "How terrible," we all said as we climbed up on our chairs and peered over the partition.

Sure enough, a rather small but strong man was hitting a girl and sending her crashing into the wall. Each time as she hit she'd straighten up, say, "Aw, honey," and he'd hit her again. Finally, however, there was a ripping noise, and when the girl looked down, saw that her dress had caught on the corner of the table and torn, she immediately burst into tears. "Stanley Johanson," she sobbed. "Now look what you done. You tore my office dress!"

For a long time we bought our clothes at nice stores, waiting until they were marked down for the last time, which usually meant that we were just buying our summer clothes when the rest of the world was getting ready for snow. But "it's not your clothes but you, yourself that counts," Mother told us and so we whetted our personalities and patched our petticoats and dreamed of the day when we'd be rich and could be beautifully dressed and dull.

Then Dede and I found the Bargain Mart, a funny little dark store with funny little dark clerks; store hours geared for musicians and gamblers; clothes that often bore in addition to labels from other stores, little traces of other occupancy, such as a little grease and powder around the neck, a forgotten clip, even a handkerchief in the pocket; and dusty, cluttered show windows displaying, even in summer, children's dirty white fur coats, heavily embroidered Chinese mandarin coats, and big waterproof work shoes. Dede and I never could decide whether the Bargain Mart sold stolen clothes, bought up leftovers from other stores, or dealt in white slavery in the back and sold the clothes of their victims in the front. Whatever it was we liked it.

We first found the Bargain Mart one evening about ten-thirty when walking down the street after a movie. I had caught and torn my only pair of stockings on the seat of the movie and was wondering what I would do about work the next day, when Dede said, "Look, a store! And it's open. Maybe they carry stockings."

We went into the Bargain Mart and for a few minutes just stood and waited. There didn't seem to be anyone there. Everywhere were counters piled high with underwear, hats, dolls, men's hunting jackets, purses, silk scarves, jewelry, satin nightgowns, kimonos—but no clerks and almost no lights. Finally, nervously I said, "Maybe the door wasn't supposed to be open. Maybe there are burglars in here."

Dede said, "So what. There's enough junk here for all of us. Look, I've found a pair of stockings."

She had been digging down under a counter and had come up with a pair of pinkish tan silk stockings, so old they crackled like tissue paper and were faded on the creases. There was no price mark on them. Dede took them toward the back of the store and yelled, "Hey!" Instantly from somewhere up front near the door a tiny little dark man appeared and said, "Something?" "Yes," I said. "These stockings. How much?" "Dollah," he said. "These stockings are old," I said. "Look they're faded." "I'll get new ones," he said, reaching under the counter. "What size, please?" "Ten," I said and he pulled out a box and produced a pair of sheer, new, beautiful silk stockings. So I gave him the "dollah" and we left.

A few nights later Dede and I were going home from work and happened to pass the Bargain Mart. A little dark woman waited on us, or more truthfully, stood in the shadows and watched while we pawed through the dresses, suits, and coats, which were hung among and on top of the men's suits and coats and gave the back of the store the look of a crowded coatroom.

After some searching and no help from the woman, I found a very smart, three-quarter-length mouton coat with a plaid wool lining, marked, for heaven's sake, $35. I tried on the coat and it was most becoming. I showed Dede the price and she said, "If it hasn't got somebody else's initials where they'll show, take it." So I did. "Oh, what a darling coat, where did you get it?" everyone said and I, looking as dishonest as the Bargain Mart clerks, said, "My aunt sent it to me."

The thing about the Bargain Mart was their boxes, which were bright magenta with ENORMOUS gold letters on both sides screaming BARGAIN MART at anybody within a radius of twelve miles who didn't carry a white cane. Dede and I loved the Bargain Mart but we certainly hated those boxes which were made of such punk cardboard they tore when we stopped in the alley and tried to turn them wrong side out.

We didn't take Mary to the Bargain Mart because we knew that she'd be more interested in what they were doing in the back than in the good bargains, but we took Mother and she bought, for seventeen dollars, a gray tweed coat with a "Made in England" label in the sleeve and a fountain pen in the pocket.

Mary didn't miss being taken to the Bargain Mart because she had her own ways of being well dressed on no money. In the first place, she liked, and had the courage to wear, high style clothes and so when she had to lengthen a dress by inserting a girdle of a different material, people didn't look at her and say, "I'm sorry!" as they did to me. They said, "Mary, how smart!"

Then Mary had a dressmaker who charged very little and could copy pictures in the *New Yorker* and *Vanity Fair*. The only problem was to get the finished article away from her before she had a chance to embroider it. She wanted to embroider wool flowers on coats, big birds on dresses, and leaves and flowers on suits and the reason she charged so little for her sewing was because she intended to charge a lot for the handwork we wouldn't let her do.

Then Mary made good use of our trunks and when asked to a cocktail party would rummage in the trunks, grab the garden scissors and often emerge in an hour or two looking at least different. One Saturday afternoon she took our black taffeta evening dress with the huge full skirt and our white high school graduation dress and by cutting off the sleeves and lowering the neck of one and removing the skirt from the other evolved a very smart ankle-length black jumper dress with a white dotted-organdy blouse with enormous puffed sleeves, real lace on the collar, and a demure little black velvet bow at the neck. Mary's only trouble was that she made so many of her major changes with pins that sitting down in one of her creations made you feel like one of those Hindus who lie on spikes.

One time a Mrs. Schumacher, a very rich friend of Mother's, met Mary at a cocktail party and admired her dress, and when Mary told her how she had made it not ten minutes before out of some old portieres and a few potholders, Mrs. Schumacher was so impressed by Mary's cleverness that the next day she sent over a huge box of clothes accompanied by a note which said, "Some things I've hardly worn and thought you and your brave little family might use."

"Hooray!" we all said, diving in, jerking things out and throwing them over our shoulders. But when we'd looked at everything, we knew that we would all have to be a great deal braver than we were to wear Mrs. Schumacher's hand-me-downs which were big blouses and big party dresses, of chiffon, satin and beaded fringe, all orchid or fuchsia.

"Here," we said tossing them to Anne and Joan and their friends for "dress ups," and for years afterwards we could hear them in the playroom quarreling and saying, "Now, Joan, you know Tyrone Power wouldn't wear a beaded Schumacher," or "How can I be Sonja Heine when you have on the chiffon Schumacher."

Last year at an autographing in southern California, a large woman in a beaded purple chiffon Schumacher came up to me and said, "I'll bet you'll never guess who I am," and I wanted to say, "I don't know who you are but I know what you've got on." But I said, "No, I'm sorry, I don't."

She said, "I'm Mrs. Schumacher from Seattle," and I said, "How wonderful! You're the woman who gave us all your old clothes during the depression," and to my surprise she wasn't at all pleased but got very red in the face, said, "I don't remember any such thing," and went flouncing off, ashamed because I had been poor.

Another friend of Mother's, a woman so rich that she could afford to wear brown dresses trimmed with black tatting, like our cleaning woman whose son gathered their coal off the railroad track (only the rich woman's dresses were labeled Florence original and the cleaning woman's St. Vincent de Paul), came to tea one Sunday afternoon bearing over her arm a beautiful gray coat with a collar and reveres of blue fox. "I'm tired of this old thing," she said, tossing it at Mary and carefully undoing the fastenings of her own manure-color-trimmed-with-black-Persian-lamb creation. Mary said, "Oh, how beautiful, Aunt Alice. May I try it on?" "Of course dear," said Aunt Alice smiling benevolently. "I want you to have it."

"Oh, my gosh, what a pretty coat," said a friend of Alison's who had just dropped in to return my skirt, Mary's blouse, Dede's jacket, and Alison's shoes. "Can I try it on?"

"NO!" screamed Mary, Mother, Dede, and I together.

"Well, all right," said Alison's friend. "Gee, Alison did I tell you how mad my sister is? Yesterday was her birthday and her boyfriend gave her a cross with a head on it."

"Some sort of religious medallion?" asked Aunt Alice.

"Uh, uh, it's a red color and has long hair," said Alison's friend.

"A figurine?" asked Mother.

"Gosh, no," said Alison's friend. "It's one of those fur scarves with a head on it. You know."

"Oh, a cross fox," said Aunt Alice.

"That's it," said Alison's friend. "I think it's ugly. It looks just like an animal. Well, bye, Alty, thanks a lot for the clothes."

"Heavens what a silly little girl," said Aunt Alice. "Now, Mary, that coat is a Charlie Petcock original and my, it is becoming to you. Just made for red hair."

I said, "Let me try it on." Mary did. I looked in the glass and felt like a movie star. Then Dede, Alison, and Mother tried it on and we all looked like movie stars.

"Oh, Aunt Alice, it's beautiful! Thank you, thank you!" we said when she left.

She said, "Remember it's a Charlie Petcock original. Take good care of it."

Monday Mary wore the coat to work. Monday night I wore it to a movie. Tuesday I wore the coat to work. Tuesday night Dede pinned up the hem and wore it on a date. Wednesday Mother wore the coat downtown and Mary wore it to a party. Thursday I wore the coat to work and Friday we got the bill from Aunt Alice. "One Charlie Petcock original—$75.00."

"Why that stinking old skinflint!" we screamed. "That rich horrible old grafter!" and kept the coat and wore it over the weekend.

Monday night Mary returned the coat and Aunt Alice, after going over it with a magnifying glass said, "I think you're being very silly, Mary. You couldn't even buy the fur for that."

Mary said, "In the first place I thought you gave me the coat and in the second place seventy-five dollars would buy winter outfits for our entire family."

Aunt Alice jammed the coat into one of her bulging closets and said, "Seventy-five dollars is very little to pay for a Charlie Petcock original."

Shoes were also a depression problem. First there were the children who delighted in greeting me at the end of a weary day by lifting a foot and displaying either a large new hole or a sole flopping up and down like a panting dog. "Not another pair?" I'd groan and they'd say, "Um, um, and my play shoes have come unsewed and my party shoes are too short." You could get very good children's shoes for $2.50 in those days but $2.50's didn't grow on trees and I longed to bind the children's feet.

Mary and Dede and I got our shoes in cheap stores that carried pretty good imitations of Andrew Geller and I. Miller for $1.98 if you could stand the pain and didn't go out in the rain. The $1.98 Andrew Geller's and I. Miller's required a great deal of breaking in, in fact almost complete demolition before you achieved anything approaching comfort, but they looked very nice. I remember a pair of green Lizagator pumps I bought that lasted well, but took over two months of breaking in by the whole family before I could walk across the room in them without fainting from the pain.

We had a little shoemaker in our neighborhood who would do anything to our shoes, short of half or whole soling, for fifteen cents and many's the morning we waited in our stocking feet in the breakfast nook while Anne or Joan or Alison ran up to Mr. Himmelman's with our shoes.

"There," Mr. Himmelman would say, polishing the shoes on his sleeve after he had sewed up the side or put on heel tips. "Just like new, eh?" And Alison or Anne or Joan would bound up the front steps, slam the front door, and hand us our shoes saying "Just like new, eh?" no matter what they looked like.

One time I bought myself a pair of brown suede ties which looked very nice but were apparently made of suedefinished scratch paper because the first day I wore them it poured and rained and my feet got soaked and the next morning when I went to tighten the laces of my new shoes the holes came out and hung on the lacings like little gold beads.

"Hurry and take these to Mr. Himmelman," I told Alison. "Tell him to bore new holes or something."

But Mr. Himmelman told Alison, "These are not shoes. These are just imitation shoes. Bah, no good. Tell your sis I'm sorry I cannot do a thing."

Last winter I paid $49.50 for a pair of real alligator pumps and though they are comfortable and have stayed sewed even in snow, I miss those old exciting days when a sudden storm might mean the dissolving of my brand-new pair of brown simu-calf pumps and leave me standing at a busy intersection in my stocking feet.

13

"Now Listen, Mother, It's Only a Fifteen Minute a Day Program"

DURING THOSE YEARS WHEN WE WERE ALL LIVING AT HOME, Mother managed to keep reasonably busy. She took care of my two children, made beds, washed dishes, cut the lawn, gardened, washed, ironed, cooked, marketed, sewed, darned, fed, and administered veterinarily to our household pets, which included at one time three dogs, four cats, a canary, two guinea pigs, a white rabbit, and a mallard duck, and fed and administered homeopathically to her five children, our house guests who often stayed five years, and an adopted sister.

For recreation Mother listened to dreams, helped with homework, heard long, often dull, stories about jobs and lovers, listened to the radio, made sketches, grew primroses, read all the new books and almost every magazine published, attended family-night movies, and entered contests.

For years we all saved wrappers and box tops and Mother wrote twenty-five words or less on Why I Like Ivory, Lux, Camay, and Oxydol, and had gentle unselfish dreams of what she would do with the ten thousand dollars or the new cars she would win. But not until the Old Gold contest came along and she accompanied her entry with a letter stating, "I am a little old grandmother who smokes two packages of Old Golds a day" (and coughs constantly) and won fifty dollars and a flat of Old Golds, did she have any success.

With the fifty dollars, Mother bought a new clock for her bedside table and paid off some of her more insistent "at the doors." The clock, which had numerals that shone in the dark, immediately began pointing out to Mother how late she was going to bed and how early she was getting up, so she put it in Mary's and my room, in which location it became a symbol of her cleverness instead of a reminder of her hard lot.

We were very tolerant about Mother's contests but we were not at all nice about her radio programs. "How can an intelligent woman listen to that drool?" we would yell as we turned off Stella Dallas, who in spite of years spent with the finest families in Boston still said "we was" and "I seen it" and called her daughter "Lolly Baby."

When we turned off Mother's programs, she would sigh and say, "Oh, well, they'll be doing the same things tomorrow, anyway."

"But Mother," we'd wail, "they're so corny."

"I don't remember asking you for your opinion," Mother would say. "And I find them very relaxing. It's like having someone read aloud to me while I do my borish housework."

The one serial we didn't object to was "Vic and Sade," an extremely witty, very original little program that had none of the kidnappings, killings, trials, bawling, poisonings, or dreadful little children that graced the other daily droolers. In fact, was so clever and cheerful it was finally taken off the air.

Then there came the day when Mary switched from direct mail to radio advertising and we were sorry we had ever made Mother turn the radio off and were grateful for every minute she had spent with Ma Perkins, who said, "Upuratah, upuratah" when she wanted to telephone, with Helen Trent, who was trying to find romance, though over thirty-five (by actual count about fifty-two), or "Just plain [dull] Bill."

As soon as Mary had launched herself in radio she started in on the rest of us. First it was merely a matter of listening. Every afternoon Mary told Seattle housewives about good bargains in half soling, denture cleaner, and rat poison and every evening told her family that we were indifferent, uncooperative, unappreciative, and unprogressive because we forgot to listen to her. "Did you listen to my program?" she'd ask us at dinner, and we'd all say yes whether we had or not and then she'd check on us. "What was today's big bargain?" she'd ask and if we didn't know she'd slam her napkin down beside her plate and say, "How can I expect to reach the ears of a million housewives when I can't even get my own family to listen to me?" and we'd feel ashamed of ourselves and vow to do better. The one time we all did remember to tune in on Mary she said, "You must come down and see our imported English tin setter sweats," which fact we joyfully reported to her.

Then through her own program, Mary got some singing spots for Dede, whose voice was so beautiful when she sang "Boy of Mine" in an attempt to get people to come down and buy boys' underwear on sale for forty-nine cents that we all cried, and Dede, who got seven fan letters, began wearing green eyeshadow in the daytime.

Naturally, after such a start, Mary expected Dede to go right to the top in radio, but though she got her many auditions for regular programs, invariably the sponsors, a most unprogressive lot, would listen to Dede and then choose some wiggly soprano singing "From the Land of the Sky-Blue Water" to advertise their chocolate syrup or flea powder.

In the interim Mary found Dede a job folding horoscopes and stuffing them into envelopes and though the horoscope company was within walking distance of the house and didn't object to Dede's singing occasional radio spots, they only paid her eight dollars a week and they didn't have a restroom.

"I'll have to have either a better job or a better bladder," Dede said finally, and so Mary again began scouting around and at last got her an interview with the head of the continuity department for one of Seattle's biggest radio stations.

Dede, who had spent ten of her seventeen years crouched in front of a radio, displayed, in her initial interview, such an amazing knowledge of all radio programs, especially who played what, how, and where, that she was immediately hired and given the full responsibility of writing flowing sentences about biscuit mix and bread dough to be read by throaty-voiced announcers in front of a musical back drop. Because of her vast experience and the high calibre of her work she was paid ninety dollars a month and given an occasional sack of flour.

Mary naturally turned next to her old standby, her most faithful jack of no trades and master of nothing, me. "Canada Dry wants you to write them a terribly funny radio program," she told me one night at dinner.

"Why me?" I said. "I never drink ginger ale."

"Radio," Mary said, "is the most important discovery of all time. It is the greatest advertising medium of the age and offers the most magnificent opportunities to all talented people. For anybody to sit home and not take advantage of radio is so unbelievably stupid I don't even wish to contemplate it."

Dede said, "Anyway look at me. Do I eat biscuits?"

I said, "Who shall I talk to in Canada Dry?"

Mary said, "Oh, you won't have to see anybody in Canada Dry because actually they don't even know about the program yet. The point is that we have a half-hour spot we want to sell them and I told our production manager that I'd get him a program if he'd arrange the audition."

So I wrote two skits which were probably not very funny but were certainly not improved nor abetted by the services of the two no-sense-of-humor "drahma" students imported for the audition.

"Hahnd me that cahn of peppah, Chollie," intoned the female drahma student speaking from her diaphragm and tossing her lips back from her clenched teeth. "Wheech cahn, deah?" replied her cohort, raising one eyebrow and stroking his pimply chin. If the Canada Dry people were there they were certainly nice about it and left quietly without any fuss at all.

Then one day Mary sold a large department store on the idea of a daily radio serial, to be cast from their employees, directed by Mary, and written by er . . . uh . . . er . . . Mother—Mary decided on the spur of the moment as she sold the program.

When the advertising manager asked to see the script, Mary said, "I left it at the office, but we'll start auditioning tomorrow morning and you can read it then."

He said, "Fine, fine," and Mary rushed to the nearest phone and called Mother, who was out raking leaves, watching the children and exercising the mallard duck, which someone obviously not familiar with the family had given us alive and expected us to kill and eat.

Mary said, "Mother, could you write a fifteen minute a day radio serial?"

Mother said, "Why, I don't know. I've never given it much thought."

Mary said, "Well, dear, I've just sold the program and I have to have a script tomorrow. It's for a department store and you can have as many characters as you want because we're going to cast from the employees. The program should have suspense and it should be funny. The girl who is the lead at the Playhouse works in the book department, which is a help. Will you do it, Mother?"

Mother said, "How much is fifteen minutes' continuity?"

Mary said, "Gosh, I don't know. You're the one who listens to the 'daily droolers.' Anyway, there should be only about twelve minutes of continuity—the rest of the time is for introduction, advertising, etc."

Mother said, "Well, it would certainly be easier if you could give me an idea about how many pages I'll have to write. I can't tell much from the 'droolers' because they can drag a choking spell out for two weeks."

Mary said, "Well, write the first episode and we'll all read and time it tonight. We can add or subtract what we need."

Mother said, "I wish we could afford to have the lawnmower sharpened. It just chews the grass off."

Mary said, "You write this program for me and you can afford to have it sharpened every day if you want to."

"Oh, am I to be paid?" Mother asked, cheering up considerably.

"Naturally," Mary said. "You'll get twenty-five dollars a week."

"My," said Mother, "it's just like winning one of those one-hundred-dollars-a-month-for-life contests."

"I always knew that some day I'd find a job for you, Sydney," Mary said, laughing.

So Mother laid aside her rake, put the duck in the basement, fed the children, put them down for their naps and then sat down in the breakfast nook and wrote the first episode of "Schuyler Square."

It was charming, it was funny, and it had suspense. After dinner that night we read, Mary timed, and Mother made the necessary changes.

The next day the advertising manager signed the contract and for the next year, five nights a week, about ten or eleven or one or two o'clock, Mother would slide into the breakfast nook to drink coffee, to smoke millions of cigarettes, to cough and to write, in her absolutely unreadable handwriting, her twenty pages on both sides of radio continuity.

We never had meatloaf again.

14

"Let Nothing You Dismay"

OUR FAMILY ARE GREAT ONES FOR CHRISTMAS AND EVEN during the depths of the depression we managed to indulge in our annual Christmas-tree-getting excursion and accompanying fight, carol-singing and oyster stew on Christmas Eve, and a Christmas morning with a nice little pile of presents (usually ninety-nine per cent made-it-myselfs and often still warm from the hands of the maker) under the tree for each member.

Every year we talked about starting our Christmas shopping or present-making in August, but inevitably two or three o'clock Christmas morning would find some of us, aided by Mother, putting the finishing touches on a doll dress or a blouse or an apron, knitting a pair of mittens or wrapping up a little rock-hard fruit cake, the biggest surprise about which when opened was that though it felt and cut like it, it hadn't been wrapped in the pan after all.

I was so sentimental about Christmas that I used to feel my heart swelling and filling my whole chest when at last it was Christmas Eve, the Christmas tree was dragged into the living room, and the wonderful woodsy fragrance from its bruised branches mingled and eventually displaced the regular family smell, or one of the children excitedly announced carolers and we all rushed out and stood shivering on the front porch while high eager distant voices sang "Silent Night" and "Joy to the World."

My skin drew tight and I would get a gulpy feeling in my throat as Mother read the first words of "'Twas the night before Christmas and all through the house . . ." and even now with just a little thought I can taste that peculiar flavor somewhere between wintergreen and hair oil (so aptly described by Gammy as "assabass") that distinguishes those log-shaped hard candies with a flower stamped in the middle found only in the little mesh bags distributed at church, school, or community Christmas parties.

All my memories of Christmas are happy ones except for the one in 1933, just after I had begun to work for the Government.

It was in October that Mary came bursting through the front door and announced, "This is the biggest thing that has ever happened to any of us. Western Trucking has given me carte blanche to put on the most enormous Christmas party I can think up. I'm going to have a Christmas tree that will reach to the ceiling of the Civic Auditorium; I'm going to have door prizes of cars, washing machines, radios, bicycles, dolls, sets of dishes, and wristwatches; I'm going to have all the Betty Jeans and Charma Lous in the state on the stage singing, dancing, reciting, or playing their a-cordeens; I'm going to have the A Cappella Choir singing Christmas carols; I'm going to send calliopes and sound trucks tootling all over the state; I'm going to put spot announcements on every radio station; I'm going to invite everybody; I'm going to provide transportation for all shutins; and *every single person in this family is going to help.*"

"My tap shoes are rusty and Mother gave away my violin but I'll do my best," Alison said.

"Just hand me a microphone and ask me," Dede said, clearing her throat.

"We can sing 'Silent Night' in German and we know all the verses of 'Away in a Manger,'" Anne and Joan said.

Cleve said, "Betty'll be glad to cut your Christmas tree when she gets ours. What did you have in mind, something with a trunk about four feet in diameter or do you want one as big as ours?" (I have a weakness for large Christmas trees and a loathing for either table trees or the one-stalkone-picker kind sold in most lots—Cleve's bitterness stemmed from his usually having to yard my trees out of the woods.)

I said, "I'd love to help, but when? What about my job?"

Mary said, "We'll do the whole thing after work and on weekends."

"Will we have a chance to win any of the cars or wristwatches?" Mother asked.

"I'm afraid not," Mary said. "Members of families are always excluded. However, I'll get twenty-five dollars a week extra while I'm working on this and a two-hundred-and-fifty-dollar bonus when the party's over, which will come in very, very handy for Christmas."

"Then can I have ice skates?" Alison asked.

"I wouldn't be surprised," Mary said. "In fact I think this year we'll all have quite a few 'boughten' presents." My but we were excited and eager to help.

So, one rainy Saturday afternoon in November Mary escorted me to a large empty warehouse owned by Western Trucking and located on the waterfront, rolled aside one of the huge front doors, took me into the murky interior, switched on a feeble light, showed me a mountainous stack of announcements of the Christmas party, and said, "You can start folding these announcements and putting them in these envelopes." She indicated boxes holding several hundred thousand envelopes. "I'm going out to round up some calliopes."

"Ugh, what a depressing place to work," I said, looking at the eleven-watt globe suspended from the dim distant ceiling and the enormous cavernous interior of the warehouse.

"It's the best I could do," Mary said. "Western didn't want a lot of strange people tramping around in their offices over the weekends, so they offered me this."

"Didn't they have something just a little larger?" I said looking down the five-hundred-foot vista of emptiness and gloom. "This seems so cramped."

Mary said, "Usually this building is jammed with stuff but this month they've nothing in it but apples and rats, the watchman told me. Which, of course, is why I'm putting on the Christmas party. I'll bring them so much business they won't be able to handle it all."

"Wharf rats carry bubonic plague," I said, settling myself sadly on the high stool placed in front of an empty wooden packing box which was to be my office.

Mary said, "Rats don't come near light."

"In which case," I said, "would you mind if I lighted matches to supplement that flashlight bulb up there?"

Mary laughed, picked up her gloves and said, "I'll hurry as fast as I can. If you hear someone walking around don't be nervous, it's the watchman."

She left and I set to work. The announcements were pale green and on paper of a blottery texture which harbored no errors in folding. However, by crumpling three I learned just where to fold and crease to make each announcement fit exactly into its envelope and come out announcing. The light was very bad, the small single suspended globe only lighting, or rather making barely visible, an area about four feet in diameter. The warehouse was unheated and so draughty my hands soon grew woodeny and unskillful, my feet icy lumps at the bottom of my legs. All around me there was an intermittent tapping noise which could have been either rain on the roof or rats. Over all hung the thick, sweet, sickish smell of rotting apples.

As with all monotonous jobs the work seemed to go with incredible slowness, so I invented little ways to spur myself on. I timed myself. I counted the announcements. I folded in time to music I hummed, and finally I said, "Now I'm going to put little markers about six inches apart on this stack and I'll see if I can get to the tenth marker before Mary comes back."

I was on the twentieth marker and it was after five o'clock when, at last, with a low rumbling one of the huge doors was pulled back and I made out the outline of a female figure slipping through the opening. In great relief I called across the darkness. "Mary, is that you? Where have you been?" My words swooshed around in the empty building like dry leaves in a barrel. There was no answer. I could hear the click of high heels and could make out a dim approaching shape but though I called again, "Mary, is that you?" there was no response.

It was not far from the doorway to where I sat under my suspended firefly of light but I strained my eyes in the gloom and waited long minutes for my mute visitor to identify herself. She certainly wasn't hurrying. Was in fact almost sauntering, which seemed somehow sinister.

When at last she came into my small circle of light she revealed herself to be a total stranger in a leopard coat and looking unpleasantly like a seagull. The same grayish white skin, close-set pale gray eyes, thin curved nose, slit mouth, and no chin. To further the illusion she had covered her small narrow head with a white woolen knitted scarf pulled tight and knotted under the chin and was wearing white string gloves. Emerging from the scarf and clinging wetly to her forehead was a fringe of lustreless jet-black hair. I waited for her to speak but for a minute or two she just stood and looked at me with her pale gull's eyes.

Finally desperately I said, "Who are you? What do you want?"

She said, "Who are you?"

I said, "I'm Betty Bard."

She said, "What are you doing here?"

I said, "I'm mailing out announcements for the Western Trucking Company's Christmas party."

She said, "Oh."

I said, "Who are you?"

She said, "I'm Dorita Hess. I work for Western Trucking. How much do you weigh?"

I thought she must be joking, but her voice was as monotonous, as devoid of inflection as a taxi meter, so I couldn't tell.

"Why do you want to know how much I weigh?" I asked.

"I like to know about people," she said. "I always ask questions."

"I weigh one hundred and twenty-three," I said, laughing. "I wear a seven shoe and I don't like meatloaf."

Dorita didn't smile. She said, "Is there another stool? I'm supposed to help you."

I said, "I'll look around." I stood up, stretched to get some of the stiffness out of my back and clumped off into the darkness on my icy feet. After a bit my eyes became accustomed to the gloom and I could see a little but I walked slowly and gingerly, listening for rats. At the back, along one side, I found a few wooden boxes but they were filled with trash and I was afraid to touch them for fear they also held rats. Once I thought I had found an empty box and I turned to call to Dorita. She was sitting on my stool fumbling for something in her purse.

"I think I've found an empty box," I called loudly. At the sound of my voice Dorita jumped up, dropped her purse, grabbed up one of the announcements and began studying it. I kicked at the empty box and something dark leaped smoothly, fluidly over the side and melted into the darkness. That was enough. I ran back to the light and said to Dorita, "I'm afraid to look any more. A rat jumped out of that last box." Dorita laughed. It was a gulping mirthless sound more like sobbing than laughing.

"Here," I said. "You take the stool and I'll sit on some of these envelope boxes."

"Okay," said Dorita, sitting down on the stool and not offering to help me move the envelope boxes.

By shifting and moving things I fixed us each a place to work. Then I showed Dorita how to crease the announcements. "Make the first fold on the word 'welcome' and the second on 'Come all,'" I said. "That way it will just fit the envelope." Dorita was humming tunelessly and looking over my left shoulder.

I said, "Do you see what I mean?"

She said, "Millions of rats. I can hear them everywhere."

"That's rain on the roof," I said not very convincingly.

"It is not," she said. "It's the rats. I see their eyes shining in the dark."

"Where?" I said nervously.

"There," she said. "Behind you."

As I turned to look I saw out of the corner of my eye one of her white-gloved hands flash out as quick as a snake's tongue and knock my stack of announcements off the packing box. But Dorita said, "Oops, look what you did."

The announcements slapped to the floor and fanned out into the darkness. I didn't relish the thought of kneeling down and feeling around on that dark floor with my bare hands for them. I put on my gloves and seeing that Dorita still had on hers I asked her to help me. She laughed the gulping ugly laugh and said, "You spilled them. You pick them up."

I said, "I saw you knock them off the table, Dorita."

She said, "You did not. You never did." Her voice held no conviction—in fact no inflection of any kind. She might have been saying, "Hand me the ink."

I said, "Dorita, I saw you spill those announcements. What was the idea?"

She said, "I did it for a joke," then made the funny gulping noise which from the floor where I was kneeling sounded so much like something stemming from grief that I looked up at her sharply. There was no joy in her face but her eyes blazed and her gloved hand covered her mouth. She was laughing all right.

I said, "I don't think it's funny. I'm tired."

She said, "I've got ten fur coats. You can borrow them any time."

I said, "No thanks."

She said, "Here, put on this leopard." She yanked off her coat and dropped it down on my shoulders. I tried to shrug it off but she leaned over, grabbed the two lapels and began pulling the coat tight around my neck. I could feel the warmth from her body still in the coat. I could smell her oily body smell; I could feel her breath in my face not unpleasant but sweetish and warm like a dentist's assistant's. I stood up, jerked the coat off, and threw it at her, just as Mary called out from the front door, "Hi, Bets, I'm sorry I'm so late."

Like a flash Dorita slipped into her coat, buttoned it and was demurely folding announcements when Mary got to our lighted spot. Mary said, "Oh, Dorita, I didn't know you were coming down here."

Dorita said, "Mr. Ajax asked me to help."

Mary said, "That's wonderful, it's awfully lonely for Betty down here."

Dorita said, "Betty doesn't like me. She doesn't want me to help her."

I said, "That's not true. I just don't like your knocking my announcements off on the floor."

Dorita said, "I didn't knock them off. You knocked them with your sleeve."

Mary looked puzzled. She said, "You two aren't quarreling are you?"

"Heavens, no," I said.

Dorita said, "Let's all go and get a cup of coffee. I know a little place just a block from here."

I said, "Wait until I pick up these announcements."

Mary said, "Here, I'll hold a match. Oh, darn, I've only got one. Have you got any, Dorita?"

Dorita said, "No, I didn't bring a purse."

I was fumbling in my purse for matches when it suddenly dawned on me that if Dorita didn't have a purse, then it must have been my purse she was looking in while I was back in the warehouse trying to find her something to sit on.

I looked up at her but she was busily smoothing the fingers of her string gloves. They were crocheted in ridges and looked like the skin on chickens' legs.

Mary said, "Oh, let's let the old announcements go until tomorrow."

I said, "You and Dorita go ahead. I'll turn off the light."

They started toward the door, I knelt down, hurriedly scooped up the spilled announcements, then reached up, turned the switch and plunged the warehouse into thick impenetrable blackness. Like a tightrope walker I started feeling my way through the darkness toward the thin strip of pale light that marked the door. I was about halfway there when suddenly at my elbow I heard the gulping laugh. Panic-stricken I ran toward the door calling, "Mary, Mary, wait for me."

When I got to the doorway, Mary said, "What in the world happened? Did you step on a rat?"

"Almost," I said as Dorita sauntered slowly out of the darkness.

As we walked along the waterfront in the rain, the waves slurped under the pilings, the sharp prow of a Japanese freighter loomed dark and sleek, like a huge shark; trucks zoomed past, belching Diesel fumes, taxis screeched to sudden stops, and people passed us with their heads down to avoid facing the storm.

I loved the waterfront any time, especially in the rain when the salt and tar smells were stronger, but this night it seemed sinister to me. Filled with dark corners, rats, and people who looked like seagulls. I had gotten thoroughly chilled in the warehouse and my teeth were chattering when we finally got to the small, warm, brightly-lighted cafe. Dorita laughed and talked with the funny old Norwegian who ran the place and ordered us all sugar doughnuts and coffee.

Under the pretext of getting out my cigarettes I opened my purse and went over the contents. Everything seemed to be there. Had I imagined that I had seen Dorita looking in a purse? Had it been some trick of light and shadow? I looked again to make sure that Dorita wasn't carrying a purse. She wasn't. I drank my coffee and as its comforting warmth took the knots out of my stomach, everything that had happened began to take on the aspect of a bad dream.

Mary and Dorita were making plans to meet at the warehouse at two o'clock the next day, which was Sunday. Mary gave Dorita her key saying that she knew the watchman and wouldn't need it if we got there first. It was when I was wondering why Dorita didn't have a key of her own, why Mr. Ajax hadn't given her one, that I noticed that she was eating the sticky, sugary doughnuts in the white string gloves.

"Normal people don't eat sugar doughnuts in gloves," I told Mary excitedly on the way home. "Only people who are afraid to leave fingerprints keep their gloves on all the time."

Mary said, "Oh, Betsy, you're just imagining things. You know what a vivid imagination you have. Dorita works for the Western Trucking Company."

"Doing what?" I asked.

"I don't know exactly," Mary said. "She's queer-looking but she's awfully nice."

I said, "She's queer-looking and she's queer-acting. I caught her fumbling around in my purse; she deliberately knocked over my stack of announcements, she asked me how much I weighed, and she tried to choke me with her leopard."

Mary said, "You're just tired, Betsy."

The next afternoon when we got to the warehouse, Dorita was already there. Sitting on the stool under the dim light, industriously folding announcements and stuffing them in the envelopes. The afternoon was uneventful except that I thought it odd both that Dorita should have worn such a beautiful mink coat to work in a dirty old warehouse and that the fringe of hair under her scarf should have changed from jet-black to magenta.

As we worked we talked, but at the end of the afternoon I realized that although Dorita knew almost everything about Mary and me, we not only didn't know what she did at Western Trucking, we didn't even know where she lived.

Monday I called Mary at work and told her that I could not face going down to that lonely warehouse and couldn't I bring the rest of the announcements home.

She said, "Well, I told Dorita you'd be down at five-thirty."

I said, "That's just why I don't want to go. I'm afraid to be in that old warehouse with her. Anyway it's terribly stormy and will probably be as cold as the dead down there. Call Dorita and tell her we're going to do the rest of the announcements at home."

Mary said she would and at five-thirty I took a cab to the warehouse, told the driver to wait and went in to get the announcements. Dorita in a gray squirrel coat and blond hair was sitting under the light folding announcements.

I said, "Didn't Mary call you?"

She said, "No."

I said, "Well, I'm going to take the rest of the announcements home and do them."

She said, "You're not. I won't let you. Are you a Catholic?"

I picked up a big stack of the announcements and started toward the door. Dorita ran after me, grabbed the front of my coat, and hissed at me, "I asked you if you were a Catholic?"

I said, "No, I'm not and let go of my coat."

She said, "You're lying. You're lying. You're lying."

The cab driver called from the doorway, "Need any help, lady?"

I said, "Yes."

Dorita let go of my coat and said, "Here, honey, I'll help you load the stuff in the cab."

I didn't say anything but I must have given her a very cold look for she pretended to shiver, said, "Brrr, it's cold in here," then laughed.

The cab driver and I made three trips and when we had everything in the cab I told him to drive me home. As we drove off I saw Dorita standing in the doorway of the deserted warehouse. She waved to me. When Mary came home she insisted that she had called Dorita and told her not to go to the warehouse.

That night as we all sat around the dining room table folding the announcements, I told the family everything about Dorita. They all agreed that she sounded both crazy and dangerous but not for a moment did they want me to give her up. They agreed that the warehouse was too lonely and scary a place to see her but they thought we should move our operations uptown.

About eleven-thirty we were in the breakfast nook drinking coffee and listening to the storm howl around the house when the doorbell rang. Dede went to the door and reported nobody there but the wind. The next morning I found the identification card with my signature which I always carried in my wallet, slipped under the front door. I hadn't even known that I had lost it. I told

Mary that I thought that Dorita had taken it the day I saw her opening my purse.

Mary said, "Well let's go right down and ask her. She's going to meet me at the radio station at ten o'clock."

I said, "I have to go to work but we'll all have lunch together and I'll ask her then. Mary, I think you should find out more about Dorita. Ask Mr. Ajax about her. I know there's something peculiar about her. Something almost sinister."

At a little before twelve Mary called to tell me to meet them in the coffee shop of a small hotel way uptown. I said, "Why so far away? I'm terribly busy and I have to get back on time."

Mary said, "Dorita says that she has something important to show us in this hotel. She asked me if we wouldn't please meet her there."

I said, "Did you ask Mr. Ajax about her?"

Mary said, "He was too busy and so was I. I'll do it tomorrow."

We got to the hotel at twelve-thirty sharp, and Dorita, in a beaver coat and black hair, was waiting for us in the coffee shop. The minute we sat down she said, "My uncle works for Scotland Yard. My father is the head of the Pinkerton Detective Agency. For years they've been on the trail of the biggest diamond smuggler in the world. She is here working in the florist shop of this hotel. Mary, you go in and ask the woman in there if her name is Martha Heath. Tell her a friend of yours wants to know. Don't tell her who you are. Don't talk to her, just find out and come right back." Her eyes blazed but her voice was as unemotional as gravy.

I said, "Why don't you go?"

She said, "Because Martha Heath would recognize me. Go on, Mary. Hurry."

I said, "What good will it do even if she says she is Martha Heath?"

Dorita said, "You'll see. Scotland Yard has been after her for years and years."

Mary said, "Order me a tomato sandwich on dark bread and a cup of coffee. I'll be right back."

Her eyes were shining and I knew that she loved this assignment for Scotland Yard and Pinkerton. After she had gone I said to Dorita, "What do you do down at Western Trucking?"

She said, "Are you a Catholic?"

I said, "I asked you what you did at Western Trucking?"

She said, "I check on other trucking companies for Mr. Ajax, and I check on the employees of Western."

"What kind of checking?" I asked. "You mean what time they get to work and how long they stay in the restroom?"

"Oh, no," said Dorita. "I check on employees they think are stealing. There's a lot of room for stealing in a trucking company. Our cargoes are very valuable sometimes. Saturday I had to have a man fired."

"How did you get your training for this job?" I asked looking pointedly at the black fringe and thinking of the other colors of hair.

Dorita said, "I was trained by Pinkerton but I worked for Scotland Yard."

I said, "Is that why you asked me how much I weighed that first day?"

She said, "Yes. I have to know everything about people."

I said, "Is that why you went through my purse? I saw you, you know."

She said, "Honey, I didn't go through your purse. You shouldn't say things like that about people. Is Mary in love with Mr. Ajax?"

"Heavens, no!" I said. Mr. Ajax, the president of Western Trucking was short, bald, about fifty and married.

Dorita said, "They're both Catholics."

I said, "Mary is not a Catholic. We're Episcopalians."

Dorita said, "Why does she wear that big silver cross then?"

I said, "That cross belonged to our Aunt Louise who was a sister in the Episcopal Church. Mary wears it because it looks smart with that plain black dress."

Dorita said, "You're lying and you're both Catholics." Then she opened her purse and took out a framed miniature of a doughy-looking little baby. "This," she said, flashing the picture in front of my eyes, "is your precious Mr. Ajax when he was a baby."

"Who cares?" I said.

Just then Mary came back and excitedly reported that the woman in the flower shop looked like a tired algebra teacher instead of a famous diamond smuggler, but had admitted that she was Martha Heath.

"What do we do now?" Mary asked.

"Nothing," said Dorita, putting the miniature in her purse. "I'll cable England tomorrow."

Even Mary thought it was funny that she ate her tuna fish sandwich without taking off her brown suede gloves.

Mary's Christmas party had snowballed and snowballed until it was now a good-sized avalanche. Mary was getting wonderful cooperation from everyone and had had so much stuff donated that it began to look as if there would be a wristwatch and a vacuum cleaner for every shut-in in the state, but the millions of details of such a promotion kept her running about eighteen hours a day. After all the announcements had been mailed, I volunteered to go to her office in the radio station for an hour or two every night after work.

"I can write spot announcements, answer the phone, write letters, even take dictation from you," I told her. She accepted joyously and so each night I left the office a little early and was at the radio station at five minutes past five.

The first night, when I walked in through the reception room, the door to the continuity department was ajar and I could see through into the salesmen's room. Dorita was sitting at Mary's desk typing on her typewriter. I remember being mildly irritated because Mary had also solicited Dorita's help with her clerical work.

When I went into Mary's office after stopping to tell the switchboard girl I would take all Mary's calls, Dorita was sitting across the room looking at a magazine. From the speaker overhead Bing Crosby was mellowly intoning, "God rest ye, merry gentlemen, Let nothing you dismay."

"Hello," I said unenthusiastically to Dorita. "Did Mary ask you to come down and help too?"

"No," she said. "Mr. Ajax told me to drop in and see if there was something I could do."

I said, "Well, if you want to help, type this list while I go through this huge pile of telephone messages."

Dorita said, "I can't type."

I turned and looked at her unbelievingly. She smiled at me and lit a cigarette. The telephone rang. I answered and a woman wanted to know if Mary would raffle off her cow at the Christmas party. I said I wasn't sure and for her to call the next day.

The phone rang again as soon as I had hung up and it was a churchwarden in the southern part of the state volunteering the voices of his choir if we would furnish the transportation. I told him to call the next day. The phone rang again and a woman asked if I would lend her little boy an accordion so he could play at the Christmas party.

By the time Mary finally came in I had forgotten all about Dorita and was desperately trying to fend off a very drunk fat man who wanted to play Santa Claus at the Christmas party and wanted to practise there in the radio station by having me sit on his lap. Mary got rid of the fat man, put Dorita right to work alphabetizing some cards, and put me to work typing the lists and answering letters. We worked until after eight, Dorita without taking off her gloves.

On the way home I told Mary about seeing Dorita typing at her typewriter. Mary said, "Oh, darn, I forgot to ask Mr. Ajax about her. Say, did that man call about the popcorn balls?"

"Yes and he says he'll make them in all colors," I told her. "Let's go down and talk to Andy about Dorita. There is something evil about her that I don't understand. Anyway where does she get all those fur coats and why is her hair a different color every day?"

Mary said, "Well, of course if her uncle is the head of Scotland Yard and her father is the head of the Pinkerton Detective Agency that would account for the fur coats and the hair too, I suppose. I mean she probably has lots of wigs and things."

"Mary," I said. "We aren't living in the days of Sherlock Holmes. Anyway I'm not sure I believe that stuff about her uncle or her father."

Mary said, "As a matter of fact I'm not sure I do. I think she's a lonely, ugly, slightly crazy woman who is probably taking a correspondence course in detecting. Did that man call about the buses for the shut-ins?"

"No," I said, "he left word for you to call him at ten tomorrow morning. Mary, I think we should have lunch with Andy tomorrow and tell him about Dorita. Just in case anything should ever happen."

"What do you mean just in case anything should ever happen?"

"I don't know," I said. "I just have a funny feeling. You didn't work down in the warehouse with her. She's evil, Mary. I know it."

Mary said, "We've had twenty-five bicycles donated. Isn't that wonderful?"

I said, "Will you have lunch with Andy and me tomorrow?"

Mary said, "I'm supposed to go out to the auditorium but I'll meet you at twelve."

Andy listened carefully while Mary and I told him everything we could remember about Dorita. Then he had us go back to his office and repeat the entire story while his stenographer took it down. He said, "Just to be on the safe side I would suggest that every night you write a report of everything Dorita says and does and mail it to me."

As we walked up the street festooned in rain-soaked cedar and Christmas lights, I said to Mary, "Now I feel better. If an important lawyer like Andy had thought I was just imagining things he would have said so."

One of Mary's sound trucks turned the corner. From its twin horns Bing Crosby's velvet voice filled the air with "O tidings of comfort and joy . . . ti . . . i . . . dings of co . . . om . . . fort and joy! Comfort and joy . . . o, o, ti . . . i . . . dings of co—omfort and joy!"

Mary said, "I'm going to give Mother a double waffle iron for Christmas."

I said, "I suppose I'll have to give her housedresses again. I wish to God she'd revise her Christmas list."

Mary said, "Christmas to Mother means Quelques Fleur toilet water, new housedresses, and a pair of blue felt Daniel Green bedroom slippers. You'll never get her to change. It's like her hats. A hat to Mother is a sailor. If it's spring it's straw, if it's winter it's felt."

Bing Crosby had turned and was coming up the street. "God rest ye, merry gentlemen, Let nothing you dismay," was coming at us from behind now. Suddenly there was a Christmasy feeling in the wet hurrying crowds; a Christmasy look on their wet intense faces. I supposed it was a result of the relief I felt.

Every night Dorita was in Mary's office in the radio station when I got there. I never actually saw her at the typewriter again but sometimes when I felt the chair it would be slightly warm. She did help some with little routine jobs but she never took off her gloves and mostly she just smoked and asked questions.

I did my Christmas shopping during my lunch hours and it got so that no matter where I went, into what store, I saw, or thought I saw, Dorita. Once at the very crowded perfume counter in a department store, I was smelling and admiring a perfume I couldn't afford, when there was a terrific crash at my elbow and an enormous bottle of the perfume was knocked off the counter. Nobody knew how it had happened, the clerks all looked suspiciously at me and when I turned to see who had been standing next to me I saw a woman in a leopard coat dart into the next aisle and disappear in the crowd.

Another time I was in a ten-cent store buying Christmas tree ornaments when someone behind me pulled my hair so hard my eyes watered. I turned angrily to see who it was and a beaver coat was just going through the revolving doors.

Another time I was in the meat market near our house buying lamb's kidneys when I happened to look at the front window and there was Dorita standing with her face pressed to the glass looking in at me. She stayed there while the butcher weighed the kidneys, wrapped them and I paid for them, but when I came out she was gone.

"Maybe she also lives in the University district," Mother said when I told her, but I didn't think so.

Mary reported coming home on a terribly crowded streetcar one night and having her silver cross and chain get caught on the button of someone's coat and being almost choked to death. I asked Mary if she saw the person whose button the chain was caught on and she said how could she when there were thirty people jammed into a place meant to hold two.

I noted all these facts in my nightly reports to Andy but it didn't quell my uneasiness.

Two nights before the Christmas party, Mary and I went to the auditorium to supervise the decoration of the Christmas tree. It was a very foggy night and our taxi crawled along hugging the curb and honking loudly at intersections.

"Did you ever ask Mr. Ajax about Dorita?" I asked Mary. She said, "I haven't seen Mr. Ajax for days. I think he's out of town."

I said, "Oh well, the party'll be over in two days and then we'll be rid of her for good, I trust."

Our cab drew up before the front entrance of the auditorium and as we got out, Dorita in a black sealskin coat and blond hair, came sauntering along the street and joined us.

"Where did you come from?" Mary said.

Dorita said, "Oh, I live near here and Mr. Ajax asked me to help you decorate the tree."

Mary said, "I thought Ajax was out of town."

Dorita said, "That's what everyone thinks but he isn't."

Mary nudged me. We walked up the steps and into the auditorium.

The eighty-foot Christmas tree had already been set up at the left of the stage and electricians on extension ladders were festooning it with lights. The edge of the stage, and the front of the balconies were looped with garlands of cedar and pine and there were huge heaps of trimmings and unhung garlands here and there on the floor, which when stepped on or moved gave off a wonderful spicy aromatic Christmasy smell. One of the workmen had brought down a portable radio and between shouts of "Hand me that hammer, Mac!" or "Key-rist, Charlie, watch where you're throwin' them branches!" Bing Crosby mellowly intoned, "God Rest Ye, Merry Gentlemen, Let Nothing You Dismay" and "*Adeste Fideles.*"

There was nothing for me to do so I sat on the edge of the stage and told the workmen how beautiful the tree was and how artistic they were. Mary spent most of her time in a little office telephoning or answering questions. Dorita leaned against a doorway and smoked.

About eleven-thirty, when they were almost through and ready to go home, one of the electricians asked Mary for her telephone number so he could call her the next day about some fancy lights he thought he could get donated. Mary opened her purse to get one of her business cards and seemed slightly upset when she couldn't find one. "I distinctly remember putting twenty-five cards in my purse less than a week ago," she said. "Did you take any of them, Betty?"

"I took one for that man who printed the tickets and one for the popcorn man, but that was two weeks ago," I said.

Mary said, "Oh, well, remind me to grab another handful tomorrow morning."

After the workmen had gone Mary and I walked around and admired everything. We switched on the Christmas tree lights and stood and looked up through the branches to the blazing star at the top, and the love of Christmas and everything Christmasy burned so brightly in me, I could feel myself melting like a candle.

"Wouldn't it be terrible not to have a family at Christmas time? To be all alone?" I said to Mary.

"Perfectly horrible," said Mary. "Imagine being all by yourself in a hotel room on Christmas Eve. Sitting by the window watching everyone else hurrying home to their children and gay families."

I said, "Imagine getting up Christmas morning to open your one present from you to you."

"Speaking of which," Mary said. "What happened to Dorita?"

"I guess she went home," I said. "She disappeared about an hour ago."

"Thank heaven for small blessings," said Mary. "Let's turn off these lights and go home. I'm exhausted."

When we got out to the main entrance Mary said, "Damn it all, I forgot to call a cab. Wait for me, I'll be back in a minute." She ran back into the building and I waited on the steps.

The fog which was rolling in thicker than ever, smoked around my feet like swamp mist. From all over the city came the irritable frantic honking of automobile horns and from the Sound occasional anguished groans as freighters warned the little ferries to look out. A car burst suddenly out of the fog, its pale, impotent headlights like cataractcovered eyes, its body almost invisible. A faint yellowness in the mist and the hissing of tires were the only evidences of its progress up the street. When I turned my head to watch it turn the corner, I saw Dorita standing in the dark by one of the building's pillars, smoking.

I said, "I thought you had gone home."

She said, "Did you?"

I said, "Why didn't you speak? Why did you stand there silently in the dark?"

She said, "I was watching the fog. I love fog. It reminds me of London."

I said, "Did you live in London?"

She said, "Yes, about five years."

"Recently?" I asked.

She said, "How would you feel if something happened to your children?"

I said, "What are you talking about? What do you mean?"

She said, "Oh, nothing. I was just wondering how you would react if something happened to your children."

I said, "In the first place nothing is going to happen to my children and in the second place if something should, I'd find the person responsible and kill her."

Dorita said, "Here, Betty, I brought you a present."

I said, "I don't want a present from you."

Ignoring me, she quickly unwrapped a brown paper bundle she had been carrying and shook out a long dress. "Here," she said walking over and tossing it at me. "Merry Christmas from me to you."

As I caught the dress, I noticed a price tag swinging from one sleeve. It was hard to see the dress in the dark but I could feel it was silk. I threw it back at Dorita. "I don't want a Christmas present from you," I repeated.

She said, "Okay, honey," and began wrapping the dress up again. When Mary came out she had it all wrapped up and tucked under her arm.

Mary said, "Hi, Dorita, I thought you'd gone home."

Dorita said, "I just came out to watch the fog. I love the fog."

Mary said, "I do sometimes."

Dorita said, "Here's a Christmas present for you, Mary." She tossed the package to her.

Mary said, "Why, thank you, Dorita. How sweet of you."

I said, "Don't take it, Mary. She tried to give it to me. It's some kind of a dress with the price tag still on it."

Mary said, "Betty, I think you're being awfully rude."

I said, "I am not. Don't take that dress."

Mary said, "Betty, I've never seen you act like this before."

The taxi drove up. Mary offered Dorita a ride but she refused. As Mary and I walked down the steps I could hear Dorita laughing. I grabbed the brown paper package from Mary, turned and threw it at Dorita, pushed Mary into the cab, got in and slammed the door. Then I told Mary what Dorita had said about the children.

Mary said that she would see Mr. Ajax the next morning, but not to say anything to Mother as it might worry her.

The next morning about ten Mary called me and told me that she had just talked to Mr. Ajax. She said, "He says he knows absolutely nothing about Dorita. He thought she was working for me. He said that two days after I agreed to put on the Christmas party,

Dorita appeared in the Western Trucking offices and announced that she was working for me. However," Mary said, "he looked embarrassed every time he mentioned her name and he was awfully anxious to get me out of his office." So Mary and I had lunch with Andy and he said to forget the whole thing, that we'd probably never see Dorita again. And we didn't.

The Christmas party was magnificent, stupendous, gorgeous and so well attended it seemed to include everyone in the entire state, but Dorita was not in evidence. When Mary and I left the auditorium, and we were among the last, we expected to find her leaning against a pillar waiting for us. But she wasn't. She just disappeared. "Probably climbed back into one of those boxes of rubbish down in that warehouse," I told Mary.

Christmas Eve we were all around the piano singing carols and when we got to "God Rest Ye, Merry Gentlemen," Mary and I both said, "Please, not that one, ever again," then laughed.

By February Dorita was a story we told unbelieving friends. "But who was she, what did she want?" they always asked and we didn't know. "Maybe her father was the head of Pinkerton Detective Agency and maybe her uncle did work for Scotland Yard," we said. "Maybe she was hired to see that we didn't steal any of those donated bicycles or little bags of hard candy. Maybe the reason she never took off her gloves was because she didn't have real hands."

By March, Dorita was no longer real, but a character in something we had read. I got so I hardly even flinched when I saw a leopard coat.

Then came March fifteenth. Mary and I were in her office getting ready to go to lunch when the switchboard operator dialed and told us there were two men to see us. Mary told her to send them in and said, "Darn, it's those apple men!" But it wasn't. It was two perfect strangers in light covert cloth overcoats and carrying brown snap brim hats. One of them had piercing brown eyes. The other had heavy-lidded blue eyes. The brown-eyed one said, "Are you Mary and Betty Bard?"

"Yes," we said.

"Will you please come with us," he said.

"Where?" we asked.

"To the Post Office Building," said the heavy-lidded one, opening his coat and showing a gold badge.

"What in the world for?" Mary said.

The brown-eyed one said, "We'll talk about it when we get to my office." His voice was deep and throbbed with sadness.

Mary and I put on our coats and the four of us marched solemnly out of the radio station.

It was a beautiful March day. Bright and blowy and with air that smelled like clean clothes. There was an old woman selling daffodils on the corner.

"Daffys," she said. "Big bunch for a quarter. Daffys, girls?"

"No thank you," I said, and she winked at me and thrust a big bunch of the daffodils at the Government men. "No, no," they said curtly, dodging around her.

At the next corner we had to wait for the light and we couldn't have felt more conspicuous if we had been handcuffed to our captors. Everybody seemed to be looking at us.

Just in front of the Post Office Building an old Southern friend of Mother's, a Mrs. Carstairs, spotted us and came running up. "Mary and Betty Bahd," she said looking appraisingly at our escorts. "I do declah ah haven't seen you in yeahs and yeahs. How is youh deah mothah and youh dahling little ole family. We'ah all sick as dogs. Colds and grippe all wintah. It's the dampness. Ah declah ah just despise all this rain." She dimpled and smiled at the men and Mary and I shifted our eyes, turned red and were embarrassed because we couldn't introduce her.

She said, "Nellie Louise is havin' beaus now and Carol Anne has turned as big and fat as a mountain. Poh lil thing. 'You'll outgrow it, honey,' I tell her, but she just cries and cries, that is when she's not eatin'. I declah that girl eats moh than George and you know what a pig he is. . . ." We finally broke away just as she was giving us a recipe for pecan pie.

The Post Office Building had an old-fashioned cage elevator with an old-fashioned shirt-sleeved operator, who when he saw us enter in the company of the two Post Office inspectors, looked us over carefully, from every angle, before starting the elevator. We got off on the third floor, walked down a corridor and went into an office. The office had a window looking out on a court, a mahogany desk, and at least a dozen dark green steel filing cases.

Heavy-lids carefully closed the door, they both took off and hung up their coats and hats and then turned to us. Mary immediately said, and I could tell she was upset because she talked exactly like Mrs. Carstairs, "What is all this? Why have you brought Betty and me up here?"

The man with the brown eyes said, "I can't understand it. Two nice young girls like you. Why did you do it?"

"Do what?" Mary said.

The man reached down in his desk, pulled out a Manila folder, opened it and showed Mary and me about twenty letters, all either signed with a very poor imitation of my signature, with one of Mary's business cards pasted to the bottom, or Martha Heath. The letters were all addressed to Mr. Ajax and were all very obscene.

Mary glanced at the letter and said, "May I use your phone?"

"Of course," said heavy-lids pushing it towards her. Fiercely, rapidly, Mary dialed a number. While she waited for an answer she drew her lips into a thin line and tapped her fingers on the desk. When Andy answered she said, and she had the clenchiest teeth and the spiest voice she had ever had, "Well, this is it. It has happened. Betty and I are up here in the Post Inspectors' office and we are UNDER ARREST!"

Andy said something and Mary said, "Never mind why, just get up here fast and bring that entire file on Dorita Hess."

When she had hung up I said, "What did Andy say?"

Mary said, "Never mind. He's on his way."

While we waited for Andy, Mary and I stood by the window and looked down into the sooty court. I felt exactly as though I had already been sent to prison. Again I said, "Mary, what did Andy say?" She pursed her lips together and shook her head meaningly toward our captors.

When Andy came in he introduced himself, looked at the letters, told the postal inspectors all about Dorita Hess, and told Mary and me to go home. The Post Office Inspectors apologized to Mary and me and we didn't know what to say. The usual answers to an apology, such as "Think nothing of it," "A natural mistake," "Don't mention it" seemed both inadequate and rather inappropriate. So we just shook hands and left.

A week later there was a very small notice in the Seattle papers to the effect that one Dorita Hess had been arrested, and had confessed to sending obscene matter through the mails.

We never did learn what happened to her, where she was sent, or for how long, but every Christmastide when I hear "God rest ye, merry gentlemen, Let nothing you dismay!" I think of Dorita in one of her ten fur coats and many colors of hair, eating sugar doughnuts with her gloves on.

15

"Just Like Flying"

I KNOW THAT MOST PEOPLE THINK THAT THE WORST PITFALLS in the path of a working girl are low salaries and sex. I don't. I think the worst pitfalls in the path of a working girl are shorthand and office parties.

Office work is dull enough, God knows, with all its taking down and transcribing of someone else's thoughts, usually boring, endless making of copies, and stamping of dates. But office play is much worse. Why don't people realize that it is as ridiculous to try to get all the people who work together to meld socially as it is to expect everybody living in one apartment house to be best friends?

All the office parties I've ever attended were either so proper they were stifling or so unleashed they were indecent. At the unleashed parties little accountants, who during working hours never unpursed their lips and called fellow employees of twenty years' standing, "Mister" and "Miss," invariably turned into the most rapacious of fanny pinchers; the primmest and most unyielding of all the office females immediately got disheveled and hysterical; the boss, who had always appeared gentlemanly and above average, turned out to have a wife who told dirty stories and insisted on fixing everybody "jusht one more lil drinkie"; and a silvery-haired woman from the bookkeeping department told me that the switchboard operator was sleeping with the vice president, and the traffic manager's wife's uterus had turned to stone.

For weeks, even months, after a real bang-up office party the involvees would go shamefacedly around apologizing and being tiresomely humble or else nursing little hurts and slights.

For a long time I worked in offices too small for any office get-togethers, but I was not spared, because my friends, Mary's friends, Mary, even my sister Dede, worked in bigger places where they had lots of parties. I was dragged to bank picnics, insurance dances, oil company masquerades, construction company country club debauches, canned salmon swimming parties, department store dinners, radio station free-for-alls, electrical sales roller-skating, even ferry boat christenings. These were all distinguished, as far as I was concerned, by either an anaesthetic dullness or a great deal of hysterical activity. Whether or not you enjoyed yourself depended on your idea of fun.

I remember the auto parts Christmas party that the try-to-be-grand wife of the office manager had insisted be formal (which meant merely tuxedos and a dress any length below the calf) and at her "home." Both guarantees of misery. How choked and stuffed the men looked. How overcurled and unsure the women.

There was a large blue Christmas tree in one corner of the crowded living room and as each couple was herded past it to be introduced, the uncomfortable wives remarked, "Oh, what a beautiful Christmas tree. My, I just love blue Christmas trees. They look so frosty," and the husbands said, "I like a plain green tree myself," which elicited a dirty look from the manager's wife and a nudge or kick from his own.

There were little dishes of nuts and olives and a very few tiny crystal ash trays placed here and there. The nuts and olives brought forth, "Would you wish for some err-derves?" "No, thanks, I wouldn't care for some," or "Oh, thanks, don't mind if I do," and "My, it certainly is a lovely party. There's nothing like seeing folks all dressed up." "I'll just take one almond—I'm on a diet. I told Charlie, 'You can't wear overhalls all your life.'" "Oh, heavens, no more for me. I'm full up. But they're lovely err-derves."

As the room filled so did the tiny ash trays. The hostess apparently didn't notice this but several of the guests did and carrying them carefully, made self-conscious trips to the neat swept empty fireplace, lost their nerve and carried them back again. A husband spilled ashes on the rug, his wife scrubbed at them with her best handkerchief, looked embarrassed and said, "Men!" As was inevitable after a while there was the unmistakable smell of burning wool and a frantic search which revealed the overflowing ash trays, some marks on the tables and one cigarette stub smoldering on the rug under the edge of the davenport. Immediately the host and hostess were down on all fours rubbing at the burn, checking the burn, measuring the burn and making everyone in the room as miserable as possible. I fully expected them to dust for fingerprints. After a great deal of discussion but no confessions they let the case rest but I noticed nobody smoked after that.

About midnight some very small glasses of a very raw sherry and several plates of a dry bready fruitcake were passed. Most of the men downed the sherry quickly like straight shots, but they were not given refills. The wives sipped at theirs, remarking, "My, what lovely sherry. I think fruitcake and sherry go lovely in the evening."

After the sherry, gifts were exchanged and the little chambers and mustard pots shaped like toilets that had seemed so killing in the trick store and such a sure bet for a big laugh when they were being wrapped, now produced nothing but averted eyes and red faces.

At once everybody started for the upstairs and their wraps and as each couple said goodnight I heard the host and hostess say, "Now don't you worry about that rug—accidents are bound to happen—and a Merry Christmas to you too." I had a feeling that the minute the door closed on the last guest they were going to have a big fight about office parties and that burn on the rug and I was glad.

The other extreme was a construction company party at a country club outside of town. We were a little late and when we drove under the porte-cochère it sounded as if we were entering an amusement park. "Help, somebody help me!"

"Ohhhhhhhhhhhhh!" "Wheeeeeeeeee!" "Ouch! Georgie!" "Stop!" "Don't you dare, Hank!" "Oops, try again," sprang at us like "The News of the World" at movie theatres. "This is going to be quite a party," my escort said.

It was a come-as-you-please party, and suits and plain blacks mingled with beige laces and orchid taffetas as did pin stripes and plain browns with the two dinner jackets. There were two or three bottles of whisky on every table and several under them. Everybody danced every dance and deliberately bumped into each other on the crowded floor. "Hey, watch where you're going!" our partners yelled at each other, laughing as they clashed us womenfolk together like cymbals just for the hell of it. It was certainly lively. One man fell into and broke the drum—another punched the orchestra leader in the nose because he wouldn't let him lead the orchestra—another went around filling the men's pockets with seltzer water.

By the time supper was served everyone was at the wrong table, everyone was drunk, the poor waiters were almost in tears, and I seemed to be alone. My waiter, a small sadlooking man, said, "What are they celebrating?" and waved his arm around to include all the staggering, milling, yelling crowd. "Being alive and having a job, I guess," I said.

A small girl with a thick white skin and half-closed eyes came over to the table, leaned down on her elbows and said, "Boo!" I said, "Who are you?" She said, "I'm the wife of blue prints over there but it doesn't make any differenshe honey, I jusht came over to tell you that your nose is shiny. Here," she reached down her neck, drew out a large gray powder puff and slapped it briskly around on my face, covering my nice shiny makeup with a thick white powder. "Thash better," she said, putting her powder puff away and swaying as she tried to focus her eyes on me.

I went into the ladies' room to take off the powder and found it crowded and terrible. The first vice-president's wife had thrown up in her purse and was sobbing, "I've been poishoned." A small drab girl in a plum-colored suit was sitting in a corner twisting her handkerchief, looking very green and saying nothing. Several girls were repairing their makeup and exchanging notes. "'So what if you're married?' I says to him. 'Who isn't?' And he says, 'Honey, I've had my eye on you for a year,' and I says, 'So has your wife and here she comes now.'—God, is he an old wolf!" One older woman was sniffing smelling salts. The colored attendant who carried a sheaf of one dollar bills in her hand like a bridge hand said, "Anything I can do for you, honey?" I said no, wiped off the powder and left. When I got back to our table my escort had returned and we went home.

I remember a picnic held on the cool green banks of a river which might have been a perfect office party, the exception, if one of the older secretaries hadn't suddenly jumped into the bonfire after her weenie that had dropped from its stick, which bold action and subsequent drunken ravings as she was being bandaged, revealed that the sick old mother she had been staying home from work to care for over the years, was named Three Star Hennessy.

I resolved never to go to another office party.

Then just after Christmas and the closing of the NRA, Dede announced that her office was giving a skiing party and would I go with her. I enjoyed the mountains in winter, the stillness, the deep blue shadows, the untouchedness, the thin tingling air, the creak of shoes on snow, the funny little marks made by the feet of birds and animals, the round pregnant contours of anything snowcovered, the starlike beauty of a lighted window against the night, but unlike thousands of other Seattleites I was not at all enthusiastic about skiing.

Even as a child I had never cared for outdoor activities. "Little Houso," Daddy had called me as he unclamped my hands from a book and shoved me out into the fresh air. I liked fresh air but I didn't see why people had to be out in it all the time. Anyway, as I'm not good at sports and not very well coordinated, I didn't see any point in forcing the issue.

"No," I told Dede. "I don't know how to ski, I don't want to learn, and I loathe office parties."

Mary, who had by this time married a Danish doctor and spent all her weekends skiing, said, "Skiing is a wonderful sport. It is the closest you'll ever come to flying. You must go. It is very healthful, stirs up the blood, especially when you ram into a tree, and I think everybody in the family should learn."

I said, "But I'm no good at sports and I'll probably break my leg."

"Nonsense," Mary said. "Skiing is all a matter of relaxing and balance. Anybody that can bend their knees can ski."

I said, "How did Claire do last weekend?"

Mary said, "Oh, she broke her leg but it was only a simple fracture of the tibia-astragalus so she'll be back on skis in no time."

I said, "How did Margaret make out?"

Mary said, "Well she was going up a steep hill and she had forgotten her climbers or slipped or something—anyway she landed sitting down wedged in a hollow tree stump and she wasn't hurt at all but she was terribly mad."

"Why?" I asked.

"Because," said Mary, "we thought she'd gone back to the practice hill and so we didn't look for her for about four hours."

"I can hardly wait," I said. "Imagine looking forward to spending next weekend breaking my tibia-astragalus and being wedged in an old stump for four hours. Are you crazy?"

Mary said, "Betty, skiing is the coming sport. Everybody is learning, there are excellent instructors at the mountains and the air is wonderful."

I said, "No."

Then Alison, who loved skiing, was very fearless and at her first lesson had shot down the mountainsides like a bullet, said, "Betty, you should go. Everybody's skiing and it's so much fun, just like flying."

Dede said, "Oh, come on Betty. We haven't anything else to do and it might be fun."

So I asked Mary if I could borrow her skiing clothes and she said, "Of course you can. Oh, I know you'll love skiing. There isn't anything as exhilarating as flying down the mountains in the early morning, your skis hissing through the powdery snow, your blood singing, your skin tingling. Now remember, the most important thing to do is to learn to fall, then remember to keep all your weight on the balls of your feet and your knees bent."

I said, "Just lend me your pants and your boots and keep the address of a good bone man handy."

Mary said, "Where are you going?"

"I don't know," I said. "Just up until we reach snow."

So we went. All forty of us to a lodge in the Cascade Mountains. The car Dede and I were in had no chains and after we passed the snowline the back end veered from one side of the road to the other so that one minute we were peering down over the edge of a thousand-foot precipice and the next were crouched against the bosom of a thousand foot mountain. Everyone else in the car laughed loudly at these antics but Dede and I looked at each other grimly.

Finally, about dusk, the car stopped, we unloaded our luggage and skis and started through the knee-deep snow toward the lodge, which was leering down at us from a pinnacle in the distance. "Just like flying," Dede said bitterly as she ploughed along, her skis over her shoulder, her suitcase dragging in the snow. It had begun to rain and enormous globs of wet snow slid off branches and plopped on to our heads. Every once in a while when we stepped down into the deep snow we'd find ourselves wading in a stream, the icy water well over the tops of our ski boots, the footing as uncertain as walking on billiard balls.

Finally, after about an hour, it stopped raining, we reached the inn, had a few coffee royals in front of a big fire and skiing began to seem like a pretty nice old sport after all.

After dinner the moon came out and skiing and tobogganing parties were organized. Everyone was very eager and excited and soon the mountain stillness was threaded with a bright pattern of shouts, screams, laughter, and singing. It seemed to make little difference to these true sports enthusiasts that the organizer of the tobogganing party had neglected to notice that the toboggan slide he had marked off crossed the ski run so that sometimes the skiers would have to jump the toboggan, sometimes they landed on the toboggan, their ski poles digging deep into the backs of the tobogganers, and sometimes the toboggans banged into the skiers, knocking them down if they were lucky.

After the first collision, Dede and I went back to the lodge and to bed. But from the screams and yells that persisted until almost morning, the danger of a collision was only the extra thrill that made these already dangerous sports even more irresistible to the other thirty-eight. The bed was hard, narrow, and damp but at least it was stationary.

In the morning it was raining again and the little red flags that marked the slalom course hung down wetly and sadly against the gray slushy snow. Occasional large icicles let go and silently disappeared in the drifts against the lodge.

The floor of the ski room was awash with mud and as each wet foolish skier came in to dry off, the fire hissed and spat and the air was filled with the smell of hot wool. "Oh, you must come out," the people who had been out said to the ones in front of the fire. "You don't notice the rain and it's so much fun."

Finally, uneagerly, Dede and I put on our jackets, caps, and mittens, left the nice comfortable fire, and went out. It was wet and slushy but the rain had relented to spitty gusts. I put on my skis, adjusted the clamps, gave myself a push, and went sailing down a little hill and into a snowbank. "Hey, Dede," I called excitedly, scooping the snow out of my mouth as I brought my left leg over my right shoulder, "Come on, it's fun."

Dede slid down the little hill and didn't fall down until she hit the bottom. She said, "It's the farthest thing from flying I can think of but it is kind of fun. Let's follow the path outlined by those little flags." So we did. We fell down hundreds of times but the snow was soft and it didn't hurt.

When we came out after lunch we found that the temperature had dropped noticeably and turned the wet surface of the snow to a glare of ice. Now that *was* fun. We couldn't steer our skis at all and slid rapidly even on the level. We had built up a large stockpile of confidence by this time, so yelling excitedly we pushed ourselves over banks, down ravines, through the trees, anywhere. "This is one sport I'm going to like and be good at," I thought exultantly as I slid off a boulder, swerved around a tree, and waited for Dede.

When she caught up with me she said, "There's a hamburger stand over on the highway and it's within skiing distance if we can make it down that steep icy hill over there."

"That little thing," I said confidently skiing over. "Why that's nothing," and shouting, "Track!" I gave myself a big push, but only one ski took off. The other stayed on the top of the hill and the next thing I knew there was a tearing pain and I found myself suffocating inside my waterproof parka, which had suddenly encased me like a tight cellophane wrapper. "Help, help," I yelled, tugging wildly at the parka. Everyone was laughing and pointing at me but no one offered to help.

"Help, I'm hurt," I yelled louder and a girl said, "Track!" and skied right over my arm. Finally a man in a white jacket, seeing me spread over the face of the hill and sensing trouble, brought my leg down to me, undid my ski, helped me out of the parka, and said, "Now, you've just turned your ankle. Get up and walk on it right away and you'll be skiing again in no time."

He helped me to my feet and everything went black. I came to to find him rubbing my face with snow and saying, "Just a little sprain and the best cure for it is walking."

So I scrambled to my feet and slowly and very painfully started up the hill to the lodge. The first few steps felt as though my ankle were being crushed in a giant vise. "I simply can't stand this," I said sitting down and starting to unlace my ski boot. Immediately several people rushed over and said, "Oh, don't do that. Never take off your ski boot, it supports the sprain and anyway you'll never get it on again. Just get up and walk on it."

"I can't," I said. "It feels like my ankle is crushed."

"Nonsense," said a tall man with a mustache, grabbing my foot with his big strong hands and pinching my ski boot to test for broken bones.

I screamed, "You're hurting! Don't touch my ankle."

He dropped my foot, it clunked down, I moaned in agony and he went away mumbling things about poor sports and only trying to help.

Fortunately, just before it was time to leave, someone who didn't belong to our hardy group, and who knew something about skiing, told me I should not walk on my foot and produced a toboggan to take me to the car.

When I got home Mother cut off my ski boot and sock, put my foot in a bucket of boiling water and called Mary's husband. He came right over, examined my foot, gave me some codeine and said my ankle was broken.

"And I was relaxed and my knees were bent," I told Mary bitterly.

She said, "Nobody but a fool would ski in the rain. Terribly dangerous."

Mary's husband said, "Nobody but a fool would ski. Mary has the right idea. She doesn't risk her limbs in the snow. She stays in the lodge drinking whisky and playing the slot machines."

That was my last office party.

16

"Hand Me That Straitjacket, Joe—the Government"

ONE OF THE FIRST THINGS I LEARNED AND LOVED ABOUT THE Government was that I wasn't the only bonehead working for it. There were thousands of us who didn't know what we were doing but were all doing it in ten copies.

I got my first Government job by falling down a flight of stairs. Mary and I had gone to a dinner party at the apartment of friends of ours. I can remember that I didn't want to go. "I should be going to nightschool," I told Mary. She said, "Betty, you only live once. There will be some very charming people at this dinner party and we're going to a concert afterwards. Now for God's sake let's forget nightschool."

So we went to the party and the people were so charming that I didn't look where I was going and fell down my host's small winding stair and ripped the knee out of my stocking.

"Oh," I moaned as they all hurried to help me. "No job and my only pair of stockings."

"Don't you have a job?" said a very shy man with a French wife.

"No," I said. "Not since yesterday."

"I'd like you to work for me," he said. "The Government. National Recovery Administration. It'll only be temporary for a while but then there should be some good permanent jobs."

"You see," said Mary later. "People like Mr. Sheffield don't hang around nightschools. He's terribly brilliant, an Oxford graduate, and speaks French."

"Not in the office, I hope," I said, remembering my struggles with the Serbo-Croat.

"For heaven's sake, Betty," said Mary. "You haven't even started to work and you don't even know what the job is but you're already worrying about not being able to do it. This is your chance! You're in on the ground floor and you can get to be an executive."

I'll always remember my first day with the Government. At eight forty-five, Monday morning, Cleve and his Cord convertible deposited me in front of the Federal Office Building. It was a cool bright July morning but the irritable croaking of foghorns from the Sound two blocks away, indicated low, heavy morning mists and gave promise of a hot afternoon.

The Federal Office Building, occupying a whole block on the west side of the street, bathed placidly in the summer morning's warmth and brightness and radiated respectability and solid worth from every one of its neat red bricks.

I looked across at the occupants of the other side of the street, a burlesque theatre, pawnshop, cigar store, pool hall, and old hotel, huddled in the shadows in a pitiful attempt to protect their aging faces from the searching rays of the sun, and thought, "How un-fair—it is like putting some poor, old, unshaven, shabby Alaskan prospectors in competition with a fat, pink, smooth-shaven, pomp-ous young business man."

Then I flicked a speck of dust from my skirt, straightened my seams, adjusted my clean white gloves, and went skipping up the marble steps. I was on the right side of the tracks, at last. The Government. Working for the Government! What a firm ring it had. How pleasantly it would slide off my tongue when I applied for credit. I waved to Cleve, who, in spite of a gas tank that had registered empty all the way to town, was easing sleekly away from the curb accompanied by many envious glances, and pushed open the swinging door.

The inside of the building was as cool as a springhouse. The tiled foyer, crowded with people going to work and waiting for elevators, had a nice, gay, relaxed atmosphere and afforded a complete contrast to mornings in other office buildings where I had worked. Mornings marred by worried grumpy business men, shuffling their feet, glancing irritably at their watches, hunching their shoulders, twitching, blinking, rattling things in their pockets, and jerking at their collars as they awaited their chance to push into the elevator and be whisked up to where they could hurry and get started doing something obviously distasteful to them.

Government people had a delightful "It'll keep until I get there" attitude. "What a day!" they said to each other. "Look at those mountains rising out of the fog! This is beautiful country." "When are you taking your leave, Joe? Looks like vacation weather." They exchanged morning pleasantries with the elevator starter and the operators and laughed and kidded a small colored man called Bill who loaded his car as though it were a train—"All aboahd for Evrett!" he shouted. "This cah's goin' to Evrett! Shake a leg, Colonel, youh julep's gettin' wahm waitin' foh you."

Several people looked at me, recognized me as a stranger and smiled. I smiled back and felt welcome.

I asked Bill where Mr. Sheffield's office was and he grinned and said, "Eighth flooh. You startin' to work theah?" I said I thought so and he said, "Well, now, I'm real glad. We don't have any red haih in this building at all. It look mighty nice on cold mornings."

I said, "Maybe I won't last until winter."

He said, "You'll last all right. Don't worry about that. Evybody last with the Govment." As I got in, he winked and whispered for me to look behind me. A woman in a coonskin cap and sheepskin coat was leaning on the window sill eating doughnuts out of a greasy bag. "She lasted," Bill said. "She left over from Daniel Boone's time, he, he, he!"

Mr. Sheffield's office, on the top floor, was labeled Bureau of Foreign and Domestic Commerce but taped below the black lettering was a white cardboard bearing a large blue eagle and the letters NRA. I opened the door and walked into what might have been a receiving room at a terminal post office. Everywhere were bulging gray canvas mail bags and new confused employees.

I waited uncertainly by the door. The room was large and light with huge windows that framed a magnificent view of mountains and islands, all up to their knees in mist which made them appear detached and like mirages. Some of the windows were open and let in the croaking foghorns, the shouts of warehousemen and truckers on produce row just below us, and a pungent odor of burning coffee and vanilla beans.

At the far end of the room, against the windows, seated facing each other at mahogany desks, were two young women. They were opening mail, exchanging occasional remarks, and exuding an air of stability and leisure that seemed to cut them off from the hurrying and confusion of the rest of the room as completely as though they were glassenclosed. I knew instinctively that they were Civil Service—and had nothing to do with the new regime.

I was watching them enviously when a tall, dark girl, who introduced herself as Miss Mellor, told me to hang my hat up and follow her. She led me into what had been Mr. Sheffield's private office, and to a chair by his desk which had been pushed against the wall.

Mr. Sheffield, a slender, nervous man, was talking on the phone, running his hands through his hair and staring wildly at a stack of telegrams, airmail, and airmail special delivery letters that the office boy added to continually, in spite of its already overflowing the desk and spilling onto the floor.

This room was also very attractive. The large windows along its west wall had the same wonderful view of mountains, islands, and mist; against the other walls were bookcases and files; the mahogany furniture was large, simple, and comfortable and there was a thick rug on the floor. It had obviously been a quiet, delightful place in which to write leisurely letters and reports and to contemplate the price of grain in Algeria. Now it was like a subway station. At long mahogany tables in the center of the room were seated about fifteen assorted people, old, young, male, and female, all armed with letter openers and canvas bags of mail. As they grabbed out letters, slit them open, and unfolded the contents, they laughed and talked.

I asked Miss Mellor what was in the mail sacks. She said, "PRA's—President's Re-employment Agreements. Everybody in business is supposed to sign one and promise that he'll pay his office employees at least fourteen dollars a week and cut their hours to forty a week and pay his factory workers at least forty cents an hour and cut their hours to thirty-five a week. When he signs he gets a sticker like this to put in his window." She pulled from under the confusion on Mr. Sheffield's desk a sticker about five by eight inches with the letters NRA in bright red across the top, then small letters in blue stating MEMBER, then a fierce-looking blue eagle with one foot on some sort of gear, the words WE DO OUR PART across the bottom. Miss Mellor said, "According to the National Industrial Recovery Act that was passed June thirteenth, you can't have Government contracts unless you have a blue eagle in your window. This is the district office for four states."

Just then Mr. Sheffield hung up the phone, jumped to his feet, and looked at me dazedly for a minute without the slightest sign of recognition.

I said, "Remember me, I fell down the stairs Friday night and you offered me a job."

He said, "Oh, yes. Betty Bard." The telephone rang again. He picked up the receiver and began talking.

Miss Mellor, who drawled and appeared to be as unruffiable as slate, laughed and said, "That's enough. He recognized you. Come on, I'll put you to work."

She led me to the table, introduced me, gave me a paper knife and a stack of mail and I set to work at the first job I had ever had that really fitted my capabilities. Lift, slit, take out, unfold, lift, slit, take out, unfold, lift, slit . . . By eleven o'clock my shoulders ached and my slitting hand was cramped, so I got up and went down the hall to the restroom for a cigarette.

The restroom, clean and light, with large windows facing the Sound, was deserted except for a slender girl with tinselly blond hair and gray eyes, who was smoking and staring pensively at the jagged pale blue mountains in the fog. We looked shyly at each other and then she said, "Are you working for Mr. Sheffield?" I said I was and she said so was she, she typed.

I said, "I thought I would like a monotonous job but I'm already bored and tired."

She said, "This is my third day and by five o'clock I'm so tired I could die but I keep saying, 'Four dollars a day.' 'Four dollars a day,' and going out for a cigarette whenever I can."

I said, "Is four dollars a day all we get?"

She said, "All? I think that's dandy. My last job paid eight dollars a week and I ran the whole company. Anyway, as soon as we're put on a permanent basis, we'll get either a hundred and five or a hundred and twenty dollars a month. Can you type?"

"Sure," I said, adding bravely, "shorthand too."

"Better tell the office boy," she said. "He assigns the work and he needs typists. Are you going to eat lunch with anybody?"

"No," I said.

She said, "I brought my sandwiches but we can eat at a grocery store in the next block. They have little tables upstairs and if you buy coffee and dessert they let you take your sandwiches up there. My name's Anne Marie Offenbach and my mother's a friend of the Sheffields."

I said, "My name's Betty Bard and my sister Mary is a friend of the Sheffields."

We walked back to the office together and on the office boy's next trip I told him that I could type and take shorthand, so he moved me to another room, sat me at a wiggly little table back of Anne Marie and started me typing alphabetical lists of the PRA signers.

At twelve o'clock, Anne Marie and I went over to the grocery store which catered to charge customers and carried things like cherimoyas, canned tangerines, and rattlesnake meat and had a wonderful over-all smell of cinnamon, roasting coffee, and ripe cheese.

The restaurant, a small balcony around the store, had the regulation faded parsley-colored tearoom tables and chairs, very inexpensive, very delicious food, and terrible service, owing no doubt to the crowds and a dumbwaiter that never seemed to work except when a harassed waitress leaned down the shaft and yelled to someone below.

For twenty cents I had shrimp salad, fresh brown bread, and butter and coffee. Anne Marie had a Mocha éclair with her coffee and as we ate she told me that she hated being poor, hated bringing her lunch, and already hated most of the people working with us. She said, "A woman came over to me yesterday, gripped my arm and hissed, 'Don't work so fast. Make it last.'"

I said, "That's the trouble with big offices, if you're slow you get fired, and if you're fast everybody hates you."

She said, "Already there's a strained feeling in the office—everybody listening and watching to see who you know. Don't tell anybody you know Mr. Sheffield."

I said, "How can I? Nobody speaks to me."

She said, "That's because you came to work in that big cream-colored car. Somebody saw you and the word has already gone around the office that you're rich and don't need to work."

I laughed, told her that we were on our sixty-third straight Sunday of meatloaf and I didn't see how we could be any poorer and that anyway Cleve had acquired the car by a series of trades dating back to his tenth birthday and a saddle Mother had had made in Mexico. Anne Marie said, "Well, if I were you, I'd have your brother let you off a block from the office, a lot of those people seem kind of desperate."

When we got back to work at one o'clock, I asked the office boy if he'd heard I was rich and he said, "Sure, that's why I like you," and winked. A woman sitting across the room nudged her neighbor, whispered something to her and they both glared at me. I typed my lists and tried to ignore them but I could feel their hostility smoldering across the room, its acrid smoke growing thicker and more noticeable as the hours passed.

The afternoon was very hot, the minutes crept by, and there sprang into being that oldest and most bitterly fought of all office feuds. No air versus fresh air. Anne Marie and I both sat by windows which we had opened wide. When we came back from lunch we found them shut and locked, the office thick with heat and acrid with the smell of perspiration. We opened our windows wide again and immediately remarks, like little darts, went flitting through the air. "Brrr, it's so cold I can hardly type," or "Pardon me a minute while I get my sweater. Some people seem to have been raised in the North Pole." "Would you mind if I put your coat around my knees. It's so draughty."

At three o'clock, Anne Marie signaled to me and we went over to the grocery store for coffee. When we got back the windows were shut and locked again and there was a note on my typewriter: "Listen, you, type slower—you're working us out of a job."

I crumpled the note up and threw it in the wastebasket and opened the window again. There wasn't any air either inside or outside now, and my fingers splashed on the typewriter keys. As soon as I would get to the last of a large stack of the PRA's another appeared in its place. I had to stop and think whether C came after or before E and there were sharp shooting pains between my shoulderblades.

Noticing that several of the typists were hunt-and-peckers, I tried to tell myself, "Look, that's their problem. They should have gone to nightschool." But I knew that these people were desperate for work and there wasn't going to be enough to go around. One of the hunt-and-peck typists was as old as my mother and had a gentle, most unbusinesslike face. I smiled at her and she smiled back and just before we went home she gave me a recipe for a one-egg cake. On the streetcar I prayed that there would be some sort of a permanent filing job for her.

That night we had supper with our neighbors in their backyard. Everyone was eager to hear about my new job and I was eager to tell everything. When I reached the part about the woman gripping Anne Marie's arm and the note on my desk, Mary said, "Communists undoubtedly. They are everywhere. We're tottering right on the edge of a revolution."

Rhodsie, our dear little neighbor, said, "I thought that revolution was averted when Roosevelt closed the banks." Mary said, "Just held up temporarily. Frankly, I think we should put cots in the basement and lay in groceries."

"Why should we lay in groceries when we've got cots?" Dede asked and Mary gave her a cold look.

Mother said, "I think everything is going to be all right from now on."

I said, "Well, there's certainly room for improvement. Why Anne Marie Offenbach, a girl who sits in front of me, ran a whole office for a year for only eight dollars a week."

Mary said, "And I hate her because she did. It's the Anne Maries of this world who cause depressions. People are just so constituted that if they can get some little Kick-Me-Charlie to run their whole offices for them for eight dollars a week they are not going to hire you or me and pay us twenty-five dollars a week."

"Now they are," I said. "They've all signed pledges saying they will. Anyway, Anne Marie isn't a Kick-Me-Charlie. She's smart, pretty, and very independent. She just couldn't get another job."

Mary said, "Nonsense. Anybody can find a job."

I said, "They can not. You know very well if it hadn't been for you we would have stayed home and starved to death."

"Which," said Dede, "would have been a welcome change from some of the jobs Mary got *me*."

Alison said, "Lorene, a girl in my room at school, says her mother and father are Communists. She says they go to meetings all the time and they say that the bricks on the Federal Office Building where you work, Betty, are only stuck together with chalk and the whole building's going to crumble any day and the relief shoes are made of cardboard and the commissaries give people horsemeat."

Mary said, "You tell Lorene that if she really wants to taste awful food she should go to Russia and if her mother and father are so sure about the chalk instead of mortar in the Federal Office Building they must have put it there."

Dede said, "Let's not get an X put on our gate or whatever Communists do to mark their enemies. Alison, you tell Lorene that every cloud has a silver lining and hard work never hurt anybody."

Alison said, "Lorene says her father doesn't ever work. He just makes beer and hits her mother."

Cleve said, "Sounds like a natural executive to me. Surely you could fit him into your program somewhere, Mary."

Alison said, "Lorene says that when the Communists take over everything she is going to have an ice skating costume with white fur on the skirt and white figure skates that cost twenty-three dollars."

Mary said, "You tell Lorene that when the Communists take over all she'll get will be a job in a factory, cabbage soup, and a book on birth control."

Mother said, "Do you really think the NRA can do any good?"

I said, "Well, of course I've only worked there seven hours."

Cleve said, "Plenty long enough for a Bard to become an expert."

I said, "Well right now it seems to be mostly a matter of everybody signing the President's Re-employment Agreement and singing 'America the Beautiful' but later on there will be wage and hour and fair trade practice laws."

Mary said, "A man who sat next to me at the Ad Club luncheon yesterday, said that it is too late for the NRA and we might as well give up, because Standard Oil owns everything. He said they own Standard Brands, which in turn own Safeway Stores, which in turn own Pacific Fruit and Produce, which in turn has mortgages on all the farms. He says they are responsible for all the wars and that we are all just slaves being allowed to exist until the time comes when we can go into the trenches to protect Standard Oil."

Dede said, "Eeny, meeny, miney, mo, Standard Oil or the

Communists—what do you want: a soldier's uniform or white fur on your skating costume?"

Mother said, "In Butte people used to say there was no use going on because the IWW's controlled everything."

Cleve said, "There was an old fellow in Alaska who stayed drunk for three years because the German Jews owned everything. He said he'd invented a cure for cancer and the American Medical Association wouldn't accept it. He said it was a mixture of ground beets and whale blubber and all you had to do was rub it on the cancer and pouff, it disappeared. I asked him how he knew it would cure cancer and he said he'd used it on his mother. I asked him where his mother was and he said she was dead and began to sob. 'She was killed by them German Jews. The Jews own everything. They even own the American Medical Association lock, stock, and barrel.'"

"What did his mother die of?" we asked.

Cleve said, "Some say she died of cancer, but I think she died in self-defense because you see she had cancer of the stomach and the only way Sonny could get his magic formula on her cancer was to make her eat the ground-up beets mixed with whale blubber."

Rhodsie said, "Let's heat up the coffee and have one more cup before we go in. We'll drink to the New Deal for America and Betty's new job."

Mother said, "That's a fine idea. Alison, you and Anne and Joan start carrying in the dishes."

While we waited for the coffee we sat at the cluttered picnic table and watched a thin little moon come up over the fir trees at the end of the alley. Shrill cries of "Alle, alle outs in free" came winging over from the children playing in the next street and overhead the leaves of Rhodsie's cherry tree rubbed against each other with soft rustling noises like old tissue paper. The air, fragrant with new-cut grass, rose up from the ground thick and warm like steam from the dishpan.

Suddenly from three houses down the street a radio ripped

apart the soft summer evening with the strident cheerful strains of "The Star-Spangled Banner." The children sang as they carried in the dishes.

"Oh, say can you see
Any red bugs on me
If you do, take them off
They make very good broth"

Rhodsie said, "Well, you've got the world by the tail now. You're all healthy and Betty's got a job with the Government. Government jobs are awful good for women. You get sick leave and annual leave and you can cash your checks anywhere."

Dede said, "The only flaw I can find is that I'll have to take Betty's place with Mary. I can hear her now. 'Dede, dear, stop whatever you are doing and come right downtown immediately. I have a marvellous job for you. It's working for a perfectly darling man in a diamond mine in South Africa and the cattle boat leaves Sunday morning.'"

Mary said, "A job like that would be too good to give away, I'd take it myself."

Everybody laughed but I felt sad. As sad as a poor but carefree girl who has married a big, dull, rich man and knows that security can never take the place of romance.

I stayed with the NRA until the office closed on December 31, 1935, and true to Mary's predictions I rose from a four-dollar a day typist to a one-hundred-and-twenty dollar a month secretary, to a clerk at $135 a month, and finally to a labor adjuster at $1,800 per annum.

Those were vital, exciting times, my work was intensely interesting, I could bask in the warmth and security of accumulative annual and sick leave and old age retirement, and best of all, better than anything, I was at last on the other end of the gun. Somebody else was now worrying about getting my thoughts down in her notebook. That to me was success.

I could tell the day I started to work there that the Treasury Department and I were worlds apart. In the first place they had people working for them *who had never made a mistake;* in the second place they chose to ignore all previous experience not gleaned in the department and started everyone, no matter who they were or what they had done, even brilliant former labor adjusters who had their own secretaries, at the very bottom, and in the third place they thought that all Treasury Department employees, even those crawling around on the bottom, owed loyalty and should be at attention ready for a call twenty-four hours a day.

But it was the Government with sick and annual leave and they seemed to have no objection to employees with broken legs, so I filled out, in triplicate, all the forms accounting for every minute of my time since birth, took my oath of office, and set to work abstracting bids at $100 a month.

"We do not allow mistakes," I was told and so my hands shook and I made lots of mistakes. All mistakes were immediately noticeable because the wrong person got the bid and the angry low bidder pounded on the counter in the outer office and wanted to know what in hell was going on around there.

This was the Procurement Division of the Treasury Department and we were buying supplies and letting contracts for the WPA, which was a very large order.

Every day for weeks and weeks from eight-thirty to four thirty or seven-thirty or ten-thirty I entered names and prices on big sheets of paper and tried to find a comfortable position for my broken leg.

From the Award Section I progressed very slowly to the Contract Section where the atmosphere was much freer but there was ten million times more work and no more money.

Even though we worked a great deal of overtime, we were always behind in our work and got many little penciled letters on lined paper, addressed to the Treasurer of the United States and pleading for the money long overdue for rental of a team. "I can't buy no more oats and I need new harness. Please send me my money," Charlie Simpson would write and I would get tears in my eyes as I took out his file and found that we were returning his invoice for the fourth time because he had only sent one copy, or had not put on the certification, or hadn't signed it.

For months I worked overtime and almost gave myself ulcers trying to make our contractors do things the Treasury way and trying to make the Treasury do things in a way not quite as frenziedly hurried as glacial movement but not quite as slow as the decomposition of ferns into coal.

Then finally I became resigned and became a regular but happier Treasury employee. When a pitiful letter came in pleading for long overdue payment, instead of getting choked up and running from department to department, I would callously toss it into the enormous ready-for-payment stack, say, "Old X-3458962 is screaming for his money again," and go out for coffee.

I found that I had to have an entirely different sense of values in the Treasury Department. There, the big issues were not that we were spending millions of dollars in an effort to rehabilitate Americans; not the fact that Charlie Jones hadn't been paid for months and was in danger of losing his truck; not that the money we were spending was actually our own and it was up to us to see that it was put to the best possible use; but, whether the files should be kept by purchase order number, by requisition number, or by voucher number; whether invoices should be in six or three copies; whether being late should be knocked off our annual leave; or whether we should turn in the stubs of our old pencils when we got new ones.

I had been working for the Treasury Department a little less than a year when it came time to make my Christmas cards. I drew a nice little design, bought an enormous stack of paper that would take water color, obtained permission from the office boy to use the office mimeoscope and stylii, one stencil, and the office mimeograph, and one night my friend Katherine and I stayed on after work and ran off my Christmas cards. The paper I had bought was too thick and had to be fed through the machine by hand so by the time I had run off my usual four or five hundred cards, which I wouldn't have time to paint and didn't have enough friends to send to, it was after midnight and all the janitors and watchmen had gone home.

The next morning when I arrived at the office, flushed with accomplishment and bearing a painted sample of my art work, I was greeted by furtive looks and whispered conferences. "What in the world's going on?" I asked, thinking they had at last uncovered some enormous bribe or misappropriation of funds.

"Someone broke into the building and used the mimeograph last night," a frightened co-worker whispered. "They're holding a conference about it downstairs now."

"Well I used the mimeograph," I said. "I got permission from the office boy. I'd better go tell them."

"I wouldn't if I were you," she said. "It's a pretty serious offense and everybody's very upset."

"Nonsense," I said. "I'm going right down."

Just then the office boy came tearing into the office. He was pale and frightened. "Don't tell them I gave you permission," he gasped. "Please don't."

"Okay," I said. "But why?"

"There's a big meeting going on downstairs," he said. "They're going to send for you in a minute."

They did and I went down and was confronted with the evidence—a spoiled Christmas card saying "Merry Christmas and a Happy New Year—Betty Bard."

"What do you know about this?" the officer in charge of mimeographing said.

I said, "It's my Christmas card. I stayed down here after work last night and ran them off on the mimeograph."

He said, "Betty, that mimeograph is Government property—it is against the law to use Government property for private use."

I said, "I asked permission to use the mimeograph—anyway I always used the mimeograph at the NRA to make my Christmas cards."

ANYBODY CAN DO ANYTHING

He said, "*That* was the National Recovery Administration. *This* is the Treasury Department."

I said, "Well, I'm sorry, I didn't know I wasn't supposed to."

He said, "Being sorry isn't enough."

I said, "Well, I'll pay for the stencil and the ink, then."

He said, "I can't accept payment because there is no proper requisition or purchase order authorizing you to purchase them from the Government."

I said, "Well, what do you want me to do?"

He was so solemn about it all that I thought for a moment he was going to hand me a pistol and tell me that he would leave the room while I took the only way out. He didn't though. He looked out the window. Stared straight ahead. Leaned back in his chair and jingled coins in his pocket and finally said to me, "Well, I'm going to forget the whole thing. I'm just going to pretend it never happened. But don't . . . ever . . . let . . . such . . . a . . . thing . . . happen . . . again . . . while . . . you . . . are . . . in . . . the . . . employ . . . of . . . the . . . Treasury . . . Department."

I took great pleasure in sending one of the Christmas cards to every single person in the entire Treasury Department, many of whom I didn't know. I could just see them burning them in ash trays and burying the tell-tale ashes in old flower pots.

I finally collapsed with tuberculosis and was wheeled away from the Treasury Department. When I got well again I went to work for the National Youth Administration.

The NYA and Mary would have seen eye to eye about a lot of things. Executives for instance. Mary believed that everybody but our collie was a potential executive and the NYA proved it.

Never have there been so many directors directing directors, supervisors supervising supervisors, or ping-pong games. To this day the click of ping-pong balls brings to my mind a nostalgic picture of a big bundle of executives back from coffee and ready to go to work.

Another thing the NYA and Mary had in common was a belief that if you had to you could. I was originally hired as a secretary to one of the executives, a man who believed strongly in the proprieties of his rank and was wont to buzz for me to put out his cigarette or listen to a poem he had written on a field trip, but who had a delightful sense of humor, a degree in history, and didn't care how long I took for lunch.

However, during my three years with the NYA, except for the memorable time I was asked to take but fortunately never to transcribe verbatim testimony at an enormous hearing, my secretarial ability was the least of my worries.

My worries, to name a few, were: looking up all historical data and writing brochures for the State Highway Department about a floating bridge which floated and a suspension bridge which collapsed; writing publicity releases on NYA for the papers; teaching youth workers the arts of silkscreen reproduction; thinking up designs for posters, book covers, murals, and pictures; supervising the writing, editing, illustrating, mimeographing, and assembling of numerous house organs and bulletins for non-profit organizations such as the Government, YWCA, and Boy Scouts; helping organize the Youth Orchestra tryouts; buying groceries and cooking Leopold Stokowski's lunch; teaching spastics to typewrite and run the mimeograph; producing artists to paint murals for schools; designing programs for various government-sponsored activities such as an Indian Reservation Totem Pole Carving Project celebration and a smelter employees' recreation hall; planning and maintaining booths at the state fairs; supervising the typing of statistical reports for the Juvenile court; reading manuscripts and giving encouragement to young writers; giving prenatal advice to pregnant youth workers; furnishing vocational guidance and trying to find jobs for the others; while filling out in tentuplicate millions of forms for the "older youths" who headed the organization.

To accomplish these little missions I was given anywhere from forty to ninety-five youth workers who presented a problem in supervision, but were for the most part university, art school, trade school, and business college students who knew much more about what I was trying to teach them than I did.

My memories of the three years I spent with the National Youth Administration are fragmentary but vivid.

The smell of coffee percolating in the requisition office.

A pale young artist wearing a large Jesus Saves button, running the silkscreen and trying futilely to fend off the amorous advances of Thelma, his well-developed assistant.

A small Negro sleeping behind a stack of Army signs, his body in its faded jeans and frayed dirty shirt as thin and relaxed as a cat, his hand still clutching a half-eaten banana. His report at the end of the day, "Four hours spent guardin' them Army signs."

A very intense eccentric young artist given to wearing purple stockings, and chopsticks in her bright red hair, trying to explain her mural design to a group of hesitant graduate social service workers. The mural design, which was enormous and gruesomely realistic, bore in its four corners large leering likenesses of Death, Disease, Famine, and War, each standing knee-deep in white skeletons, eyeballs, and blood. All this the social service workers understood and approved of. What baffled them and what the artist was unable to explain to their satisfaction, even though in exasperation she finally kicked off her shoes, danced around in her purple stocking feet, hummed Stravinsky, and swore, was the big red satin valentine filled with red roses which she had placed dead center from Famine, Death, Disease, and War.

"I, uh, er, uh, don't get the significance of this, uh, er, uh, red, uh, heart," said one of the glibber of the graduate social service school members.

"Oh, my God," said the young artist, jerking one of the chopsticks out of her hair and gesturing with it. "It is the most obvious thing in the world. I simply cannot understand how you people can be so deliberately obtuse. This dark gray background represents the depravity of civilization. Here is Warr, here is Fameen, here is Deeseese, here is Death, and here, in the center, the only bright spot, is epitomized Social Service."

"We don't like it and we don't understand it," was the verdict, however, so I gave the problem to another artist. The other artist produced a sketch showing a lot of cripples on cots, in wheelchairs, and on crutches working their way toward a big ginger-colored building labeled Social Service and from whose wide front door and down whose wide front steps bubbled nurses, doctors, and kind-faced people with their arms outstretched to the approaching cripples.

"Now, uh, er, uh, that uh, is what uh, we uh, had in mind," said the delighted graduate school of social service.

"Oh, my God in Heaven," said the purple-stockinged artist. "It looks like an advertisement for the Blue Cross."

A smart, most efficient youth secretary, who, after an unexplained absence of several weeks, came swishing into my office, dressed in black satin and monkey fur and resigned. "I wish to resign as I have obtained private employment," she said smiling happily.

"How nice for you, Muriel," I said. "What kind of work are you doing?"

"Helping a lady," she said.

"Housework?" I asked.

"No, not exactly," she said. "But I take care of my own room."

On her card I wrote "Reason for leaving—private employment—mother's helper." Two days later I was informed by a police matron that my youth worker was on record as a regular prostitute and had reported for a medical checkup. I changed the notation on her card but I harbored no ill will toward her. I didn't like shorthand either.

A small, pearl-skinned girl fresh from a convent who shattered into a million little delighted giggles every time a boy looked at her. "Oh, Miss Bard," she told me breathlessly at the end of the first week, "I love the NYA. I'm never going to try to get a job."

A spastic girl, so timid and convulsed by embarrassment that she couldn't fill out her employment card or tell us her name for several weeks, but who finally valiantly learned to cut stencils and run mimeograph.

An arrogant young director who inspected us as though he were poking through a dustpan with the toe of his shoe.

A lone young colored office worker whose loud footsteps and slamming doors always made me think of a little boy whistling to keep up his courage.

The smell of baking bread from the nursery school kitchens in the basement.

A small gray official who threatened to report my friend Katherine and me to President Roosevelt because we put a padlock on our restroom door and wouldn't give him a key. "Wherever I have worked I've always used the women's restroom," he told us, adding almost tearfully, "I've never before been refused a key."

The old red brick school building, one of Seattle's oldest, where the NYA had its first projects. The stair treads, rounded and scooped out by thousands of shuffling feet, creaked and groaned menacingly even under the slight weight of the nursery school children. The draughty halls always dark even on sunny days. The towers at each end of the top floor reminding me of the olden days, especially during storms when the wind screamed in the eaves, the rain lashed at the windows, the building shifted its weight from one foot to the other, and the tower seemed suspended on its hill above the misty city like a castle in a fairy book.

A woman with long greasy curls, sagging purple cheeks, and a tarnished gold turban, who demanded that I give her a job teaching charm to youth. "I've been on the stage for yeahs and yeahs," she said. "I've met all the big names-know all the famous people. I could give them kids some tips they'd never get anywheres else."

A young artist who rode a motorcycle, belonged to a motorcycle club whose insignia was in silver nailheads on the back of her wide black belt, and often reported to work with heavy casts on one or more of her limbs.

A handsome boy who talked like a dead-end kid, had three brothers in reform schools, wore a black satin shirt, and was gentle and good and worshipped his mother. "De old lady wants I should be an artist, see?" he told me the first day he reported for work. "I ain't never done much but I can copy anything." He wasn't much of an artist but he was a fine craftsman and became an expert silkscreen operator. "I seen one of them artists snitching a sable brush," he told me one day rolling down his black satin sleeves. "I had to bloody his nose a little but I got the brush back."

A young Japanese girl giggling with a girl friend while the mimeograph ran off five thousand extra copies of page three.

The mother of a young artist who "just had to come down and tell you how artistic we all are. There's one of us layin' around on the floor colorin' or cuttin' out any time of the day or night you come around."

It was very fortunate for me that at the time of the Leopold Stokowski Youth Orchestra tryouts, the executive in charge of me (also the originator of the Publicity Project) was a Mr. Morrison, a man who knew a bassoon from an English horn as he had for several years, before coming to NYA, handled the publicity for Seattle's largest school of music and art and for most important local impresarios.

Immediately after the first announcements of the Youth Orchestra tryouts, we were besieged by music teachers in flowing capes and foreign accents and by eager mothers who insisted on trying to force their little geniuses and their harps into our small office. The tryouts were to be held at the Cornish School, we announced in the papers, over the telephone, and on the radio, but still mothers came and unleashed Mervin and his cornet solo right in the midst of our project.

I kept fervently thanking somebody for setting the age limits at fourteen to twenty-four—because at least I was spared all the seven-year-old Darleens with their white diamond-studded accordions and the nine-year-old Rudys in their dress suits and violin solos a quarter-tone off.

The first thing that was accomplished at the preliminary Youth Orchestra tryouts was the elimination of anyone who played the "Flight of the Bumblebee" on anything. Then we weeded out the *Caprice Viennois* violinists, the gasping wind-instrument players, and the mothers.

After that came the semi-finals, which were held in the Cornish School auditorium and were judged by some of the faculty at the University, a local violin teacher, a symphony conductor, a composer, and some members of the Seattle Symphony Orchestra. I listened and kept the tally, even though the judges' reasons were as far above my head as Mother's hocks and withers talk when she got with horsey people.

I loved the tryouts because I enjoy any amateur contest and in addition I learned the names, shape, and sound of many instruments such as the timpani, and I had the pleasure of hearing the oboe, my favorite instrument, played for hours at a time.

I was very impressed with the importance of the work I was doing for Mr. Stokowski and I grew weak with excitement at the prospect of meeting him. Everywhere I went I talked Stokowski and orchestra, trying to give the impression that I was Leopold's personal representative here on the Coast. At home I turned the symphonies up to full volume on the radio and tried to force the family to evince more of an interest in great orchestra music. I even toyed with the idea of starting Anne and Joan on flute and oboe lessons.

Nobody was at all cooperative. They all liked orchestra music all right but only certain orchestras. Dede liked Glenn Miller,

Alison liked Artie Shaw, and Anne and Joan wanted to be members of a horrible orchestra run by some music institute in which huge groups of untalented little children all played together on little tiny violins.

One Maudie, a little girl in our neighborhood, who had been taking tap dancing lessons since she was nine months old, belonged to this institute and insisted on bringing her tiny little violin over to the house and sawing out "Home on the Range" on it. Anne and Joan thought she was wonderful. When I refused to let them join the institute they were furious, wouldn't listen to any more of my orchestra talk, and fought loudly when the symphony was on.

I longed for the days when Mary was in charge of our house and would have had every single one of us plucking, blowing, or beating on something while the Youth Orchestra was still foundering around as an embryonic idea.

Finally one day a friend of mine loaned me her violin and I threatened Alison into taking lessons. Mother stood it for one week and then said, "I have put up with a great deal from all of my children including mallard ducks and guinea pigs but I am now too old and too tired to listen to anybody practising on the violin." That was that.

Because he was famous, was on a very grueling trip, and didn't want to cope with crowds, Stokowski elected to get off his train in Tacoma and be driven to Seattle by Mr. Morrison and me. I was so excited I thought I'd die. Imagine driving Leopold Stokowski the thirty miles from Tacoma to Seattle, talking intimately and laughing over amusing things that had happened at the tryouts. I even went so far as to imagine him saying at the end of the delightful drive, "You know, Miss Bard, I could use a secretary on this trip. Do you think that the NYA could spare you for a while?"

When the night finally came and it was determined that Stokowski's train was due to arrive in Tacoma about eight-thirty, Morrison had the NYA Garage Project boys prepare one of the best Government cars, a 1923 Reo or reasonable facsimile thereof, and we set off. It was cold and rainy, and the car had no heater but the NYA boys had thoughtfully provided two rather musty army blankets left over from the C.C.C. camps to tuck around the august presence.

The station in Tacoma, which is below the street, was not only dark and wet, but apparently deserted. We were joined there by the State Director, a gentle, learned man, and for three-quarters of an hour we smoked cigarettes, stamped our cold feet, wandered around peering into boxcars and detached pullmans, and wondered what had happened to Leopold Stokowski and if we would be held responsible.

Finally, however, the train, which was late, came in. Mr. Stokowski, appearing very waxy and distant, debarked with the conductor of the Florida Symphony, there were introductions and we set off. Morrison, an exceedingly glib and very witty man, made several small overtures toward conversation. He was answered by the Florida Symphony man.

On the way back to Seattle, I tried and tried to think of something to say to Mr. Stokowski, something short so that he would listen, but outstanding enough to stamp me on his memory. I couldn't think of a thing but it didn't matter because all during that thirty-mile drive Mr. Stokowski either talked exclusively to the Florida Symphony man or kept his eyes closed.

When we got back to Seattle the news leaked out that Mr. Morrison, the State Director, Mr. Stokowski, and the Floridan were going to a cocktail party and I was to stop off at the office and type a certain kind of list of contestants desired by Mr. Stokowski. It was then ten-thirty and as I climbed the stairs of the deserted school building and let myself in to its cold, dark interior, I had many bitter thoughts about woman's place in the business world.

It took me until twelve-thirty to finish the lists and though I ran for three blocks, I missed the last streetcar home and had to take one that turned down through the park and left me to walk across a bridge and up two blocks to our house. The park by our house, well known as a nesting place for exhibitionists, was not a location I would have chosen to be in at one forty-five on a dark windy night.

I stepped onto the bridge and shivered as branches whipped across the lights and made reaching menacing shadows. The noisy playful wind picked up papers and leaves and pushed them along in front of me, rubbed branches together until they squeaked in protest, tapped on the bridge with bare twigs, and jumped out at me suddenly from behind trees. There wasn't a soul in sight—not one lighted house.

Then suddenly above the racket of the wind I thought I heard footsteps. I looked over my shoulder and a tall man stepped from the trees and started across the bridge. I hurried my steps and it seemed to me he hurried his steps. I began to run and from the hollow echo of his footsteps on the bridge I knew he was running too. I was terror-stricken. I ran so fast my feet didn't touch the sidewalk but I could hear his footsteps ringing out behind me in the lonely darkness, above the wind, getting closer and closer. He was only about twenty feet behind me when I got to our house. I took the steps in one leap and threw myself through the front door which Mother was holding open for me.

When I finally caught my breath, I asked her how she happened to be up. She said that she was in bed but was awakened by the sound of my running clear down by the bridge. We called the police and they spent the rest of the night cruising up and down the streets flashing their strongest spotlights in our bedroom windows and knocking on the door periodically to report that they weren't finding the man.

My enthusiasm for Leopold Stokowski and his Youth Orchestra was at a very low ebb the next morning when I reported to the music school for the final tryouts. These tryouts, held in a parlor on the main floor, were witnessed by the conductor of the Florida Symphony, the NYA Director's secretary, Mr. Morrison, and me.

Mr. Stokowski wore a lavender shirt and a pink tie, but was very gentle and kind to the contestants as he asked them to sight-read a very difficult manuscript. Invariably, as each contestant adjusted his neck or pursed his lips for his first note, the Florida Symphony conductor would signal violently at me to go out and stifle some little noise that was filtering in from some other part of the building. Out I would dash to tell a surprised piano student in a third-floor practice room, "My God, don't do that now—don't you know who is downstairs?"

About eleven o'clock Morrison took me outside and told me to go down to the waterfront and get some seafood and whatever else I would need to fix a nice lunch for Mr. Stokowski. I spent $27.18 and came staggering back with jumbo Dungeness crabs, Olympia oysters, little neck clams, lettuce, celery, French bread, butter, coffee, cream, and French pastries. I fixed the lunch and some of the contestants served it to Mr. Stokowski, the Florida man, and the judges.

After lunch while I washed the dishes, Mr. Stokowski decided that the only young musician in Seattle really worthy of his orchestra was a viola player from the Seattle Symphony, a girl who was undoubtedly a fine musician but was not between the ages of fourteen and twenty-four.

After Leopold had left town I asked our head office for the $27.18 I had spent. They turned the matter over to the Treasury Department who said, "We can't authorize payment for a thing like Leopold Stokowski's lunch. There is no regular requisition, no purchase order, not even a proper appropriation symbol to cover such an unorthodox situation."

I'll always feel that Leopold Stokowski owes me at least an oboe solo.

17

"Anybody Can Write Books"

AT THE TIME MARY DECIDED THAT ANYBODY CAN WRITE BOOKS, I was married, living on Vashon Island, and working for a contractor with cost-plus Government contracts, making a very good salary.

Then an old friend of Mary's arrived in town and announced that he was a talent scout for a publishing firm and did she know any Northwest authors. Mary didn't so she said, "Of course I do, my sister Betty. Betty writes brilliantly but I'm not sure how much she has done on her book." (I had so little done on it I hadn't even thought of writing one.) The publisher's representative said that the amount I had done was not the important thing. The important thing was, had I talent? "Had I talent?" Why, Mary said, I had so much talent I could hardly walk. She'd call and make an appointment for him to just talk to me and see. She did too. That very afternoon at five and she called me at a quarter to five.

"Betsy," she said. "Forrest's in town and he is a publisher's representative and needs some Northwest authors so I've told him you were one. You're to meet him at the Olympic Hotel at five o'clock to discuss your new book."

"My what?" I yelled.

"Your new book," said Mary, perfectly calmly. "You know that you have always wanted to be a writer and Betsy, dear, you've got great talent."

"I have not," I said. "You know perfectly well that the only things I've ever written in my life were a couple of punk short stories, some children's stories, 'Sandra Surrenders,' and that diary I kept when I had t.b."

Mary said, "Betty, this is your big opportunity. Don't waste time arguing with me."

I said, "Mary, you told me the same thing when you got me to run a Brownie Scout troop, work as an expert accountant, illustrate a book for Standard Oil, pick peaches, and millions of other things."

Mary said, "The trouble with you, Betty, is that you have absolutely [she said "ab . . . so . . . lute . . . ly"] no sense of proportion. Instead of using your great brain to write a book and make fifty thousand dollars, you in . . . sist on getting a mediocre job with a mediocre firm and working yourself to the bone for a mediocre salary. When are you going to wake up? When?"

"I don't know," I said, wondering if the switchboard operator had heard all that mediocre stuff and if it would do any good to point out to Mary that if my present salary was mediocre, then most of the jobs she had gotten me were so far down the scale as to be subterranean.

Mary said, "I told Forrest you'd meet him at the Olympic Hotel at five to discuss your book."

I said, "But I can't write a book."

Mary said, "Of course you can, particularly when you stop to think that every publisher in the United States is simply dying for material about the Northwest."

"I never noticed it," I said sullenly.

Mary said, "Betty, listen to me. We are living in the last frontier in the United States. The land of the great salmon runs, giant firs, uncharted waters, and unsealed mountains and almost nothing has been written about it. If you told the people in New York that salmon leaped in our front doors and snapped at our ankles they'd believe it. Most of the people in the United States either think we're frozen over all the time like the Antarctic or that we're still wearing buckskin and fighting Indians. Now personally I think it's about time somebody out here wrote the truth."

"If I wrote the truth about my experience in the mountains," I said, "I would only be proving that salmon snap at our heels and that there are still Indians."

Mary said, "What difference does it make? At least you'd be writing and using your great talent."

All that talk about my great talent was beginning to hit home. Up to that moment I had never shown any particular talent in anything except making Christmas cards and picking and cleaning chickens, and it was a nice feeling to sit there at my golden oak desk littered with unchecked purchase orders and think that every publisher in the United States was foaming at the mouth with impatience waiting for me to write about the Northwest.

"What time is the appointment?" I asked.

"Five o'clock," Mary said. "You've only got five minutes so hurry."

As I put on lipstick and combed my hair, I told one of the girls in the office that I had to hurry as I was going to meet a publisher's representative at the Olympic Hotel to discuss my book. She said, "Gosh! Betty, are you writing a book?"

"Sure," I said with the casualness of great talent, "and this publisher's representative has come all the way from New York to talk to me about it."

"What's your book about?" she asked.

"About my experiences on a chicken ranch," I said.

"Oh," she said, with obvious disappointment and changed the subject.

Walking up to the hotel in the February rain, I decided that I would tell Forrest that I was going to write a sort of rebuttal to all the recent successful I-love-life books by female good sports whose husbands had forced them to live in the country without lights and running water. I would give the other side of it. I would give a bad sport's account of life in the wilderness without lights, water, or friends and with chickens, Indians, and moonshine.

The publisher's representative, who was very friendly anyway, liked my idea and told me to go home and write a five-thousand-word outline and bring it to Mary's dinner party the next night.

Having never written either an outline or a book, I was a little slow and found it necessary to stay home from work the next day to finish it. I called the construction office and told my best friend there that I had to stay home and write an outline for a book but would she please tell the boss I was sick. She said sure she would, wished me luck, hung up the phone, and skidded in and told the boss that I was staying home to write a book and so I was fired and in one day transferred my great talent from construction to writing.

When I told my husband and daughters that I was going to write a book they were peculiarly unenthusiastic. "Why?" they asked. And I couldn't think of any reason except that Mary thought I had great talent, so I said, "Because every single publisher in New York wants me to, that's all." A likely story they told each other, as they tapped their foreheads and suggested that I take a nice long rest.

During that long, long year between the conception and birth of *The Egg and I,* I sometimes got so depressed I put the book away in disgust and went into town and applied for and got dreary little part-time jobs that seemed much more in keeping with my ability than writing. Then after a month or so, Mary would hear about it and call me up and demand that I quit and again unleash my great talent.

One Monday morning during the summer, I was hanging out the last of a huge washing when Mary called and demanded over the long distance phone, "Betty Bard MacDonald are you going to spend the rest of your life washing your sheets by hand or are you going to make fifty thousand dollars a year writing?" It didn't leave much of a choice so I got out the manuscript and got started writing again.

Toward the end of the summer, when the book was almost finished, Mary called and told me to write to Brandt and Brandt, literary agents whose name she had gotten from the former editor of the Seattle *Times.* All successful writers have agents, she told me, and Brandt and Brandt are the very best. I thought, "Well, if they are the very best at least I'll be starting at the top and after they turn me down I'll go to the Public Library and learn the names of some others."

Mary said, "Be sure and tell them about the short stories, the children's stories, and the t.b. book. Remember, Betty, nobody likes a one-book author."

From that day on until I wrote my second book, Mary waved that "Nobody likes a one-book author" slogan around like an old Excelsior banner. When I finished my second book she changed it to "Nobody likes a two-book author." Then three. But now the tables are turned because she has written her first book and I'm on my fifth.

Feeling exactly as though I were trying to join an exclusive club on forged credentials, I wrote to Brandt and Brandt and sent them the five-thousand-word outline I had shown the publisher's representative. In my eagerness to prove that I wasn't a stinking old one-book author I made it sound a little as though we had to wade through old manuscripts to go from room to room in our log house, and that I was a veritable artesian well of the written word. Much to my amazement and chagrin, Brandt and Brandt, immediately on receipt of my letter, wired me that they were delighted with the outline and to send every manuscript I had, which certainly wouldn't take long.

I called Mary and told her about the telegram and she said, "Now, bonehead, are you convinced that you're a writer or do you still want to work in some musty little office?"

We both laughed and then Mary, speaking with clenched teeth I could tell even over long distance, said, "Of course, your book will be a best seller and they'll want you to go to New York and then to Hollywood."

"What's the matter with Europe?" I asked.

Mary said, "Just wait and see."

Before I could answer Brandt and Brandt's telegram, I got an airmail letter from them telling me that J. B. Lippincott Company, publishers, wanted to buy the book on the strength of the outline and would I accept a $500 advance? Would I accept a $500 advance? Huh, would I accept a fifty-cent advance was more like it.

I was on my way to town and had stopped at the mailbox on the way to the ferry and there nestled among a pile of bills, was this long white important-looking envelope. My first thought, of course, when I saw the Brandt and Brandt on the back, was that it was a letter taking back the telegram. I didn't have time to open it on the dock so I waited until I was installed in the Ladies' Cabin of the ferry before ripping open the flap and removing with trembling fingers the letter that rocked my world.

I read it over and over and with each reading it became more wonderful. My book, that nebulous product of Mary's faith in me, had suddenly materialized into an actual thing. I was a writer and I had to tell somebody. I hurried all over the upper deck of the ferry but the cabins were empty. I went down to the car deck but there were only trucks.

When we docked at the other side, I scanned the waiting cars for a familiar face and finally in desperation rushed over to a man and his wife whom I knew very slightly and told them that my book had been accepted and I was to get $500. I couldn't have picked nicer people. They were as enthusiastic as though it had happened to them and I left them feeling very successful and terribly talented.

The next dandy thing that happened was the next spring when I was learning that the darkest, lowest period in a writer's life is that awful interval between acceptance and publication. I knew I was a failure, I knew the book was no good, I was sure I was going to get the manuscript back, and I had spent all the advance.

I decided to go to town and look for a job. Preferably one involving the filing of the same card over and over and over day after day. I had found a reasonable facsimile of the job I had in mind and was making my weary way home along our trail, when Anne came running to meet me calling, "There's a telegram for you and you're to call Seattle operator twenty-eight right away." It's come, I thought. They have decided not to publish the book and they're demanding their money back. "Hurry, Betty," Anne said. "Find out what the telegram is." "No," I said. "I'm going to wait until after dinner. I'd rather get bad news on a full stomach."

After dinner I called the operator and Whispering Sam, who was at that time relaying all messages to Vashon before burning the only copy, read me a very long wire of which I got about ten words. Three of these were "Atlantic Monthly" and "serialization," which I knew must be wrong, as the *Atlantic Monthly* represented to me the ultimate in literary achievement and I was certain they couldn't be interested in anything I had written.

I called Mary and she immediately changed her tune from best sellers, and trips to New York, to awfully important books, not very good sellers, and trips to Boston. She said she'd call Western Union for me and call me right back. She did in a matter of minutes and told me that I was to call Boston the next morning at eight o'clock and she thought I'd better get the next ferry and pick up a copy of the telegram which Western Union was reluctantly holding at the edge of their telegram burner. The next ferry left in sixteen minutes so I sent Anne and Joan up to stay with my sister Alison and I ran the mile and a half to the dock.

The main office of the telegraph company is located on a dark side street in the financial district in Seattle and as I got off the bus and walked in the rain across the deserted streets, I kept thinking, "This is the most important moment of my life. I must remember everything." I felt enchanted and as though I should be leaving a trail of light behind me. My steps made no sound and I was as light as a petal when I entered the telegraph office and asked for my telegram. I read it standing by the counter and then, stuffing it in the pocket of my raincoat, I floated out to my sister Mary's.

I told Mary about my strange enchanted feeling and she said, "You just feel successful, but imagine how I feel. All of a sudden my big lies have started coming true!"

THE END

ABOUT THE AUTHOR

Betty MacDonald was born Anne Elizabeth Campbell Bard in Boulder, Colorado, on March 26, 1907. She married Robert Heskett in 1927 and settled on a forty-acre chicken farm near Chimacum, Washington. Her experiences there became the subject of her first book, *The Egg and I* (1945), which sold over a million copies in the year following publication, was made into a film starring Claudette Colbert and Fred MacMurray, and spawned the successful series of "Ma and Pa Kettle" films. She continued to weave her life into books with, *The Plague and I* (1948), *Anybody Can Do Anything* (1950), and *Onions in the Stew* (1955), taking breaks to write books for children, including the Mrs. Piggle-Wiggle series. She died in Seattle on February 7, 1958.